MW01253338

The Language of Sexual Crime

Also by Janet Cotterill

LANGUAGE AND POWER IN COURT: A Linguistic Analysis of the O. J. Simpson Trial

LANGUAGE IN THE LEGAL PROCESS (*editor*)

The Language of Sexual Crime

Edited by

Janet Cotterill
Cardiff University

/6/00/

First published 2007 by
PALGRAVE MACMILLAN
Houndmills, Basingstoke, Hampshire RG21 6XS and
175 Fifth Avenue, New York, N.Y. 10010
Companies and representatives throughout the world

PALGRAVE MACMILLAN is the global academic imprint of the Palgrave
Macmillan division of St. Martin's Press, LLC and of Palgrave Macmillan Ltd.
Macmillan® is a registered trademark in the United States, United Kingdom
and other countries. Palgrave is a registered trademark in the European
Union and other countries.

ISBN-13: 978–0–230–00170–1 hardback
ISBN-10: 0–230–00170–X hardback

This book is printed on paper suitable for recycling and made from fully
managed and sustained forest sources. Logging, pulping and manufacturing
processes are expected to conform to the environmental regulations of the
country of origin.

A catalogue record for this book is available from the British Library.

A catalog record for this book is available from the Library of Congress.

10   9   8   7   6   5   4   3   2   1
16   15   14   13   12   11   10   09   08   07

Printed and bound in Great Britain by
Antony Rowe Ltd, Chippenham and Eastbourne

Contents

List of Tables

List of Figures

Acknowledgements

Any book, particularly an edited collection, is necessarily the sum of many parts, but this book more than any other I have overseen so far, has required the patience and forbearance of all of its contributors, during the most challenging year and a half of my life. My thanks must go to Palgrave Macmillan, especially Jill Lake, for keeping the faith, and to all of the talented contributors, for withstanding with good humour the various delays and hairpin turns that life has thrown at me recently. Outside of the academic arena, I must pay tribute to the small army of family, friends and medics who have managed to keep me afloat and latterly, working. Love and thanks, both woefully inadequate words, go in particular to Jean and Doug, who went the extra mile and then further still, in seeing me through serious illness, (chemo)therapy and rehabilitation, helping me reach a point where life and work was possible again. The support of the forensic linguistics community, in their many cards, letters, emails and hospital visits, was invaluable in keeping up morale and faith that this is a field worth returning to. And my special thanks are due to the remarkably talented people at the Walton Centre, Liverpool, who brought me back from the brink with their skill and dedication. Particular thanks are due to specialist nurse Kerry Mutch, for caring enough to care, even in incredibly difficult circumstances, Dr Anita Rose, for her patience and understanding, and especially my consultant Dr Mike Boggild. Without the serendipity and incredible good fortune that brought me to his clinic, and into his remarkable treatment programme, things would have been very different. This book is dedicated to him, with gratitude for poisoning me so regularly and so expertly with the blue stuff.

Notes on the Contributors

Michelle Aldridge received her Ph.D from the University of Wales, Bangor in 1989 and remained there as a lecturer and then Senior Lecturer until 2002 when she joined Cardiff University. Her research interests include child language acquisition, communication disorders and forensic linguistics. Her particular expertise is in the linguistic experiences of vulnerable witnesses in the initial police interview and subsequent court appearance; as well as in the training of police officers working with vulnerable witnesses.

Kelly Benneworth is a Postdoctoral Research Fellow in the Department of Sociology at the University of York. Kelly arrived at York in 2005 after completing her Ph.D. 'A discursive analysis of police interviews with suspected paedophiles: the implications of "open" and "closed" interviewing for admission and denial' conducted at Loughborough University and funded by the Economic and Social Research Council. The next stage of her research will involve developing her analysis of paedophile talk by obtaining data from therapeutic interventions with convicted offenders and establishing a consultancy role within local police constabularies. Her research interests include the social psychology of crime, police interviewing, discourse analysis, conversation analysis and the study of language interactions in forensic contexts.

Susan Berk-Seligson is Associate Director for Graduate Studies of the Centre for Latin American and Iberian Studies at Vanderbilt University, and Associate Professor in the Department of Spanish and Portuguese of that university. One of her primary areas of research interest is forensic linguistics, particularly issues concerning the linguistic rights of immigrants and ethnic minorities in the judicial system. In this context she has focused on the experience of Hispanics in the USA, especially from the standpoint of rights to interpreting services. This research has dealt with pragmatic aspects of interpreting in both the courtroom proper as well as in pretrial phases of the judicial process, such as police interrogations.

Bryna Bogoch is a Senior Lecturer at the Departments of Political Studies and Interdisciplinary Social Sciences at Bar Ilan University. She has also been a visiting scholar at the Centre for Socio-Legal Studies at Oxford University, and at the Center for the Study of Law and Society at the University of California at Berkeley. Her main areas of research have been in the fields of language and communications, the sociology of law, and gender studies. She has published studies analysing interaction in law offices and in the courtroom, as well as the language of wills and judicial decisions Her most recent projects have investigated gender and power in mediated and lawyer-negotiated divorce proceedings, and the press coverage of Israeli Supreme Court decisions.

Michael J. Breen is Head of Department, Media and Communication Studies and Joint Director, Centre for Culture, Technology and Values at Mary Immaculate College, University of Limerick. His primary research has been in the area of media effects, analysis of media content, the role of media content in public opinion formation and the nature of media representation of marginalised groups. He is particularly interested in the influence of communications media on individual beliefs, attitudes and values, and on the formation of public attitudes and values.

Susan Ehrlich is Professor of Linguistics in the Department of Languages, Literatures and Linguistics, York University, Toronto. She has published in the areas of language and gender, language and the law, and discourse analysis in journals such as *Discourse & Society, Language in Society*, and *Forensic Linguistics*. Her most recent book is *Representing Rape: Language and Sexual Consent*.

John Gibbons retired recently from Hong Kong Baptist University, and is now an Adjunct Professor at the University of New South Wales. He has varied experience of language and law issues, including working with the New South Wales Police on their language procedures, and as an expert witness in more than 30 cases. He has published widely in the field of language in the law, including *Language and the Law, Forensic Linguistics: an Introduction to Language in the Justice System*, and (chief editor with H. Nagarajan, V. Prakasam and K. V. Thirumalesh) *Language in the Law*. His most recent book (with E. Ramirez) is *Maintaining a Minority Language: a Case Study of Hispanic Teenagers*.

Tim Grant has worked across the disciplines of forensic linguistics and forensic psychology for the last ten years. His Ph.D. was in forensic authorship analysis and he is a lecturer in the Forensic Section of the School of Psychology at the University of Leicester in England. He has worked as a linguistic expert in both criminal and civil cases. In the criminal field he has provided expert evidence in cases involving terrorist conspiracy, murder and stalking, working for both police and defence. He has also assisted in civil cases of literary and student plagiarism and intellectual property theft.

Ester S. M. Leung had extensive experience interpreting in different legal settings in England before she returned to teach in Hong Kong in 1997. She has translated the entire Bankruptcy Law of the Ch'ing Dynasty Penal Code; the Bankruptcy Law of PRC (Draft) and has published in *Babel*, the *Translation Quarterly* and also book chapters for the publishers Palgrave Macmillan and Sweet and Maxwell (Asia). She has also constructed a corpus: 'From legislation to translation, from translation to interpretation: the narrative of sexual offences' which includes recordings from courtroom proceedings and legislation about sexual offences.

Clare MacMartin is an Associate Professor and Associate Chair in the Department of Family Relations and Applied Nutrition at the University of Guelph. She has published discourse analyses of trial judgments in cases of sexual abuse in *Discourse & Society*, the *Canadian Journal of Behavioural Science*, and with Linda A. Wood in the *Journal of Language and Social Psychology*. Her work with Curtis D. LeBaron on sex offender therapy talk appears in *Research on Language and Social Interaction* and in *Discursive Research in Practice* edited by Alexa Hepburn and Sally Wiggins. Current research includes conversation analysis of psychotherapy talk. These projects, including this chapter, were funded by the Social Sciences and Humanities Research Council of Canada.

Annabelle Mooney is a Senior Lecturer at Roehampton University on the English Language and Linguistics programme. Her research interests include marginal religious movements, globalisation, gender and the semiotics of law. She is author of *The Rhetoric of Religious 'Cults': Terms of Use and Abuse*.

Anne O'Keeffe is a Lecturer in Applied Linguistics, Department of English Language and Literature, Mary Immaculate College, University of Limerick, Ireland. She has published widely in the area of media discourse, including the recent title *Investigating Media Discourse*. She has extensive expertise in the areas of corpus linguistics, research methods, language and power, language teaching and pragmatics. She is lead author in the forthcoming *From Corpus to Classroom: Language Use and Language Teaching* (with M. J. McCarthy and R. A. Carter).

Diane Ponterotto is Professor of English Language and Linguistics at the University of L'Aquila, Italy. Her research interests reside primarily in the area of cognitive linguistics and discourse analysis with attention also to questions of ideology and gender.

Peter M. Tiersma is Professor of Law and Joseph Scott Fellow at Loyola Law School in Los Angeles. Following graduation from Stanford University, he received a Ph.D. in linguistics from the University of California, San Diego. Subsequently, he obtained a Juris Doctor degree from Boalt Hall School of Law at the University of California in Berkeley. He has been teaching at Loyola Law School, Los Angeles, since 1990. Tiersma is the author of the books *Frisian Reference Grammar*, *Legal Language*, and *Speaking of Crime: the Language of Criminal Justice* (co-authored with Lawrence Solan). Further information is available at www.Tiersma.com.

Linda A. Wood is a Professor in the Department of Psychology at the University of Guelph. She has published articles on social identity, methodology in social psychology, rape, forms of address, verbal abuse, aging, politeness and facework (a number of these with Rolf O. Kroger). With Kroger she also published *Doing Discourse Analysis: Methods for Studying Action in Talk and Text*. Her current research involves discourse analyses of the treatment of remorse and the guilty plea in trial judgments in cases of child sexual assault (with Clare MacMartin), of police talk (with Alyssa Taylor), of person-referencing practices (with a particular focus on gender), and of issues in home palliative care (with Lorraine E. Wood).

Jessica Woodhams is a Lecturer in Forensic Psychology at the University of Leicester. Prior to commencing this post in 2002, she worked as a crime analyst for the London Metropolitan Police, specialising in the analysis of stranger sexual crime. Her research topics reflect her previous employment. She has conducted and continues to conduct applied research into investigative techniques for sexual and non-sexual crimes, the behaviours of offenders and victims during sexual offences, and the identification of false allegations. She has advised police forces on the development of systems for linking crimes and local Youth Offending Teams working with juvenile sexual offenders.

1

Rape as Social Activity: an Application of Investigative Linguistics

Tim Grant and Jessica Woodhams

Introduction

Investigative linguistics, that branch of forensic linguistics which assists investigation, has tended to concentrate on authorship analysis of written texts (see Grant and Baker, 2001; McMenamin, 2002), speaker identification (Rose, 2002; Yarney, 2001) and disputes of meaning and use (Shuy, 1993, 1998). The first two of these presume that there are features of linguistic output which are sufficiently invariable across time and situation to allow a degree of person identification. In the case of phonetic analysis this presumption can be supported by the constant physiology of the speaker over time, for authorship attribution work the presumption may be supported by the notion of an idiolect which could in turn rest on psycholinguistic or socio-linguistic theory (Coulthard, 2004). The wider notion of behavioural consistency is similarly explored and exploited in forensic psychology, in particular in the work of crime analysts who attempt to determine whether a collection of apparently unrelated offences can be linked behaviourally, so indicating a common offender (see Bennell and Canter, 2002; Grubin, Kelly and Brunsdon, 2001; Hazelwood and Warren, 2003). This practice of linking offences into series can be a useful tool in the wider investigative process, providing information to enhance police decision-making and allowing the concentration of police resources into the detection of serious serial offenders. This chapter describes a project which is attempting to improve the use of linguistic information in case linkage work in rape cases.

The aim of this chapter is to set out some of the theoretical assumptions in the current project, namely that rape can be considered as a social activity type which can be usefully analysed into phases with different pragmatic-linguistic patterns. This analysis allows informative contrasts to be made to other related activity types and these are illustrated with reference to one-night stranger sexual encounters. This background discussion leads to a categorisation of the rape utterances in terms of their pragmatic force with subscales measuring more detailed interpersonal variables. Finally applications of the categorisation system are considered and early results from a number of projects indicated.

Data considerations

A significant constraint in linguistic analysis in this work is the nature of the data. The language of the crime scene is available to the analyst only as a report by the victim (or another witness) and may be significantly degraded both through the normal processes of verbatim memory, which effectively involve the reconstruction and the recall of gist (Reyna and Kiernan, 1994), through the additional factors of stress (Christianson, 1992) and the potential interference effects of less than ideal, or non-expert, interviewing (Sternberg, Lamb, Davies and Westcott, 2001). The reconstruction of rape (and other) conversations from memory must be treated cautiously and detailed lexical and grammatical analysis in particular might be considered suspect. Accepting the reported direct and indirect speech as remembered gist, and analysing this gist as the recognition of the pragmatic force of an utterance is one way forward suggested by the literature (Dale, Davies and Wei, 1997; Kendall, McElroy and Dale, 1999) and is adopted and extended in the present study.

With regard to the data a further point is necessary. The current research was carried out on a database of rape cases held by the Serious Crime Analysis Section (SCAS) of the UK, National Crime and Operations Faculty. The initial categorisation system was based on 188 utterances collected from 16 accounts over a two month period. Since then more than 200 further accounts have been analysed containing many hundreds of utterances. The SCAS database contains information on solved and unsolved rapes all of which is highly sensitive. Because of the ethical issues involved, direct quotation from the witness statements is not always possible. In the course of this chapter where example references to rapists' speech are given, only the most generic examples are used so avoiding possible identification of either victim or offender.

The nature of rape

Rape as legally defined might be seen to include a variety of quite different social interactions. Prior to 2003 in the UK, rape was restricted to non-consensual penetration by the penis of the vagina, with other types of penetrative offence falling into the category of sexual assault. In the UK Sexual Offences Act (2003), rape is defined as non-consensual penetration of the vagina, mouth or anus by the penis. Under this act there is also an offence of 'assault by penetration' which criminalises sexual, non-penile penetration.

Within the literature on rape there are recognised distinctions across a variety of parameters. Considered as a social activity, perhaps the primary distinction to be made concerns any prior relationship with the victim. Typically contrasts are made between stranger attacks and those where there is some form of prior relationship, and within this latter category further distinctions can be drawn between acquaintance, date and familial attacks (see Dale, Davies and Wei, 1997; Groth, 1979). Whilst often left under-defined and applied intuitively these distinctions prove to be fairly robust in providing a useful taxonomy in research and operational work (Hazelwood and Warren, 2003). Linguistically of course we might expect considerable variation according to the degree and nature of the prior relationship between offender and victim. With rapes involving acquaintances and family the policing challenge is clearly not the identification of the offender and whilst stranger rapes are relatively rarer, comprising 17% of rapes reported in the 2001 British Crime Survey [BCS] (Walby and Allen, 2004), the identification issue is likely to be central and crime analysts are more likely to be involved in assisting the investigation. Full analysis is yet to be produced for the 2005/2006 BCS but figures show an 3% increase in rape of females (Walker, Kershaw and Nicholas, 2006). The current project therefore concentrates on this class of rape as a starting point.

The rape activity itself has been commonly broken down into phases and each of these might in turn be considered a different type of social activity. Holmström and Burgess (1979) make a distinction between the phases as 'opening', 'raping' and 'escape'. Other terms used for the first phase include 'initiation', 'approach' or 'acquisition'; for the second phase, 'offence' or 'maintenance'; and for the third phase, 'closure' (Dale et al., 1997; Davies, 1992). Kendall et al. (1999) notes that there can occur a cyclical pattern in longer offences where after the initial acquisition and offence an 'interval phase' may occur with further offence and interval phases following before final closure. As with the distinctions between stranger and acquaintance rapes, the distinction between phases often remains unclear but the essential structure is useful in capturing different aspects of a rape attack.

Finally within the approach stage there is a further common distinction which can be made. This is the distinction between blitz attacks, con and surprise attacks developed by Burgess and Holmström, 1974; Hazelwood and Warren, 1990; Silverman, Kalich, Bowie and Edbiel, 1988, and is related by Dale et al. (1997) to the foot-in-the-door versus door-in-the-face strategies for achieving compliance (Stahelski and Patch, 1993). Paradigmatically the distinction is that a blitz attack will be sudden and involve violence early in an attack, a surprise attack might be similarly sudden but involve less violence, whereas a con attack might have a more prolonged (and thus linguistic) opening through which the offender lures the victim into a situation in which they are powerless.

Analysis of rape as a social activity

Each of the stages of rape might be considered distinct social activities and thus give rise to distinct patterns of social interaction. For the question of identification, the analysis of these patterns is crucial in determining whether some specific aspect of a rape conversation is constrained more by the situational factors on the one hand, or, on the other hand, by the individual or idiolectal differences between offenders. Further to this there is interest in how the different stages of rape are realised by the rapists and reported by the victim. It might be hypothesised, for example, that rape stereotypes have little to say about the closure stages of the rape activity and so this might be a revealing stage to study in terms of the rapists' individual variation and in terms of victim variation in recall and description.

In considering analysis of rape as a social or linguistic interaction one objection which could be raised is that rape should not be considered a social activity in the normal sense. It might be argued that it is such a transgressive act, so literally anti-social, that it is not amenable to analysis using social activity models. Answers to such an objection could appeal to both the true prevalence of rape and sexual assault reported in for example BCS and to the power of media representations (see Ehrlich, 2001). The issue of prevalence might be supported by evidence from victimisation surveys such as the BCS which reports that nearly 25% of women had suffered sexual victimisation since the age of 16 whilst nearly 5% had been raped (Walby and Allen, 2004). These figures suggest that non-consenting sexual activity is a social norm of which rape is an extreme extension. In addition to this both the rapists and the victim will have been exposed to fictional and news media representations of sexual assault and this may lead them to interactional expectations. The rapist certainly may bring to the interaction desires and expectations and can be seen as acting to have these expectations fulfilled. One interesting issue in this regard which applies primarily to the victim perspective is that until the victim recognises that the interaction constitutes a rape such expectations may not be elicited. In some cases, particularly of familial or date rape, the power imbalance is reinforced through the fact that the rapist prevents the victim arriving at the realisation until late in the interaction, or sometimes, until long after it has finished.

The practical application of the current project in police intelligence work has driven the initial focus onto the language of the rapist. This obviously cannot be examined in isolation to victim responses in a rape discourse but the intent is to analyse the rapists' language in such a way as to lead to their identification. As will become apparent this applied focus leads to a concentration on the rapists' speech acts but these have to be considered in the wider context of the interaction. Hymes' (1962) theory of speech events and theories of genre (Askehave and Swales, 2001; Swales, 1990) were rejected as useful models of this interaction. Essentially these theories have been found to apply usefully to more formal and social sanctioned situations, such as, classroom or patient–doctor discourse, but less well to more fluid informal situations of purely interpersonal interaction (Thomas, 1995). Instead Dale et al.'s (1997) suggestion that rape might be considered an activity type (Levinson, 1979) was taken and developed. The weakness of more systemic or genre approaches in this applied context might be considered their strength in other work. However, even if one considers just the specific example of the approach phase of a con rape attack, where there is no prior relationship between the offender and victim, the room for genre variation is enormous. This class of rapes for example might range from bogus callers to bar-room chat-ups. Prostitute rapes, where post-intercourse a client refuses to pay, were excluded from the current study but might also be included in such a classification. Although the psychological expectation is for a degree of behavioural consistency (Shoda, 1999), the aim is to identify a common offender across potentially different situations and so a degree of abstraction to a higher level than genre is necessary. Levinson (1979) provides a framework which has proved to provide a practically useful level of abstraction. Arguing that our language is systematically constrained by the context of the activity type in which we are engaged, Levinson allows for individual variation in the observance and breaking of these constraints and one further advantage of Levinson's approach is it allows for the comparison of related activity types. Within the context of the approach phase in con rape attacks an interesting contrast can be made with stranger, consensual sexual encounters. To provide parallel data to the rape reports, a series of interview studies is currently being undertaken in this area. In these studies women participants have been interviewed about recent, single-night, sexual encounters with men who were previously strangers (one-night stands). Using cognitive interview techniques the conversations are reconstructed and analysed to provide contrasts with the speech data from rape reports. This research is ongoing but we have a small amount of data drawn based around an initial set of interviews (Maddox, 2004) to which more data is currently being added and this allows engagement in some early comparisons.

Activity type analysis

In terms of activity type theory Levinson suggests six headings which drive the analysis. These are the goals of the participants, allowable contributions, Gricean maxims, interpersonal maxims, turn-taking and topic control and the manipulation of pragmatic parameters.

The first of Levinson's categories is the goals of the participants. Thomas (1995) notes that different participants may have diametrically opposed goals and this might be expected to be more the case in the approach to a rape interaction than in a consensual encounter. This is supported to some degree in the rape data where an analyst with the luxury of an external viewpoint on a conversation can discern the goal directed nature of a rapists' speech contrasting with the initially more interpersonal motivation of the prospective victim. Similar patterns can however be discerned in some of the data for consensual encounters. Within this data the man can frequently be observed to adopt an assertive goal directed posture and with the woman fulfilling a more responsive role and often offering what has been called a ritualised 'token resistance' (Edgar and Fitzpatrick, 1990; Muehlenhard and Hollabaugh, 1988). Thus one woman reported '*I wasn't that interested at first, but he was kind of persistent and grew on me. . . . Eventually I kind of gave in. . . . [Laughs] Enjoyed it though!*' One, potentially surprising finding, was how little difference there was between the 1980s/1990s studies of American college students and the interview data collected from twenty-first century UK students fifteen years later. Muehlenhard and Hollabaugh (1988) warn of potentially negative consequences of this social convention and one analysis of the rapists' behaviour might suggest that the con rapist is deliberately using ritualised, patriarchal social patterns, to disguise their anti-social intent. The commonplace structure of the social activity enables the rapists' con.

One turning point in both interactions is where the female respondent to an approach recognises (or is forced to recognise) the goal of the man. In an offence this is the point which can mark the transition from the acquisition to the offence phase. In those non-sinister encounters where the man was the instigator of the encounter the recognition of his sexual intent by the woman led variously to resistance to the intent, consensual compliance with the intent and the enthusiastic acceptance of the intent. Examples of resistance included direct '*No*' responses and less direct examples such as '*I'm staying with a friend tonight*'. Consensual compliance was indicated sometimes by silence, '*I didn't say anything but I wasn't that keen*', but also by verbal acquiescence, '*I'll not get a taxi.*'

The second of Levinson's categories for describing an activity type is that of allowable contributions. In a rape conversation the allowable contributions of the victim can be seen to be increasingly restricted in the approach phase, resulting in a strong constraint being placed upon the victim as the move is made to the maintenance phase. This can ultimately be seen in the process of scripting where an offender tells the victim what to say; for example, that she is enjoying the experience. Scripting marks the linguistic end point of the assertion of power. In the consensual encounters it might be expected, as with other interpersonal activities, that allowable contributions are not closely constrained. One interesting observation was that an apparently unconstrained, abrupt topic shift was interpreted as a typical move in this activity type and was intended to indicate resistance. This occurred in several of the interviews, for example, one interviewee commented '*I wasn't keen so when he suggested we return to his room I started talking about the football.*'

The third of Levinson's categories refers to how far Gricean maxims are observed or suspended (Grice, 1975). The rapist in initially hiding their goals is clearly not adhering to the maxims of quality (truth) or relation, in general however a successful approach requires that the maxims are generally observed. The breaking of Gricean maxims is likely to lead to a socially uncomfortable conversation and so less likely to engender trust in the victim. A similar observation can be seen with the interpersonal maxims which form Levinson's fourth category. These maxims refer to qualities such as modesty and politeness. Politeness is particularly well studied in the literature (Brown and Levinson 1978/1987) and perhaps surprisingly can be seen to apply in a large number of rape interactions. As with the Gricean maxims the purpose of the rapist may be to assert a feeling of normality and this requires the maxim's observance. Thus one rape victim recalled '*He was telling me he liked me . . . he kept saying it.*' Where impoliteness does occur through the expression of insults for example, this can mark a necessary explicit assertion of power, and one explanation of this is that where the rapist is secure in his power over his victim, he can afford to be polite. Politeness in rape communication can therefore been seen as having both expressive and instrumental function. In the consensual encounters these maxims appear to be more flexible. Some of the interviews reveal impolite approaches to consensual sexual encounters. Startling examples include the woman who recalled that, '*He said I was a crap kisser. He said he expected me to be better as I clearly put it about.*' Theorists have noted that politeness is related to both power and formality, as well as gender (Mills, 2000), and this seems to be recognised and used, at least in some cultures, in conversations where there is a growing but uncertain intimacy. In these cases a certain degree of occasionally rude and crude 'play insults' and teasing appear to be used to both recognise and achieve greater intimacy.

The fifth of Levinson's categories is turn-taking and topic control and can be seen in relation to the rapist's escalation in his assertion of power, for example in telling the victim to '*shut up*'. The occurrence of scripting has already been noted and this marks complete control of topic and turn-taking. In the consensual encounters topic control moved more freely between the conversationalists and as has been noted abrupt topic change was occasionally used to indicate a degree of resistance.

The last of Levinson's categories is the manipulation of pragmatic parameters. What is meant here is the formality of the situation and the control of social distance between partners in a conversational activity. In rape, as the approach phase moves into the offence phase there is conflict between the sexual intimacy of the rapists' actions and the distance created by the power imbalance and possible violence. This conflict may explain some of the individual variation observed with some rapists attempting normalisation (Holmström and Burgess, 1979) by adopting more intimate forms of address whilst others maintain powerful distance through abuse and insult. Examples of normalisation are represented in the data where offenders use terms of endearment or ask their victims to do the same. In contrast, distancing is used to avoid intimacy recognising that the offender is acting upon the victim without pretence of mutuality. In the consensual situation the trajectory is towards informality and intimacy and this as has been noted can similarly be facilitated through the use of insults. This paradoxical use of insults contrasting in the rape and consensual situation requires more study but the different experiential meaning of the insult must relate to the security of the interpersonal relationship.

This brief analysis suggests the usefulness in comparing and contrasting activity types using Levinson's schema. More work is being undertaken using consensual encounters which result in sexual activity and contrasting these with encounters where a sexual invitation is successfully turned down and further work to this is being planned on exchanges in Internet chat which may constitute sexual grooming. Within the rape activity, the activity type model is being used to compare and contrast the three rape phases and also types of attack. However, the initial motivation in considering rape as a communicative activity was to provide a theoretical context for categorising the utterances of rapists in case-linkage work. In this aspect the analysis suggests that the language used by the rapist must be constrained by changing linguistic expectations as the attack develops. These constraints will limit the possible linguistic variation in some aspects of the activity and perhaps promote individual variation in other aspects. For example it can be seen that variations in politeness may be more constrained early in the approach phase and more optional in the maintenance phase of an attack. Similarly exhibitions of linguistic power may be unnecessary in a maintenance phase and so be more indicative of the choices of the individual rapist.

Categorising rapists' utterances

For the activity type hypotheses to be tested the categorisation scheme itself requires development and as has been suggested this classification was undertaken at the level of pragmatic force. This decision was based largely on the fragility of the data. Full systemic analysis requires a greater examination of lexis and grammar than is possible with these remembered conversations, whereas the gist which is better remembered, is reasonably interpreted as the pragmatic force. Choosing to code the pragmatic force of the utterances also follows the previous work in the area; Davies (1992), Dale, Davies and Wei (1997) and later Kendall et al. (1999) base their system on a database of the victim statements of about 250 stranger rape offences, situate their coding within this theoretical context and using a data driven approach create up to 23 categories based loosely around the pragmatics driven approach (Table 1.1).

A literature search revealed a number of typologies of speech acts. Allan (1998) usefully discusses the difference in perspective taken by four of the leading attempts to provide a universal taxonomy for speech acts. He notes

Table 1.1: Linguistic strategies

Directive/Regulatory speech
Threats
Limitation Reassurance/Diminution of Threat
Lying*
Bargaining*
Implied Threats*
Negotiation
Contract
Concessions
Sexual Questions
Non-sexual Questions
Reply to Content of Questions
Reply to Act of Questioning
Replies Which Form Questions
Self-disclosure
Scripting
Announcement
Compliments
Apologies
Excuses
Justifications

Source: taken from Dale, Davies and Wei (1997) and
Kendall, McElroy and Dale (1999).
Note: Strategies marked by an * are not present in the
Kendall et al. (1999) system.

for example that Austin (1962) and Vendler's (1972) taxonomies are created from lexical distinctions whereas the competing taxonomies of Searle (1969) and Bach and Harnish (1979) both have a greater interest in the speaker's act or attitude. Allan himself prefers to concentrate on the hearer's evaluation or understanding of what was said. As the data in this case is the report of the rapist's speech by the victim, this hearer's perspective seems most appropriate to provide a categorisation system in the current study. Allan's taxonomy was however adapted by borrowing from the alternative taxonomies. This adaptation was largely driven by the intended application rather than theoretical considerations.

Each of the alternative taxonomies Allan (1998) considers suggests five or six related top level speech acts. Allan suggests just four, *statements, expressives, invitationals* and *authoritatives*.

Allan argues that from a hearer's perspective the distinction made in the other taxonomies between *assertives* and *commissives* is inappropriate. The hearer perceives statements which may differ in content between matters of fact and matters of intention but the pragmatic effect is the same. In the rape conversation it was felt important to reinstate this distinction. Considering three possible rapist's statements:

(i) *I'm called John.*
(ii) *I've got a knife.*
(iii) *I'm going to kill you.*

The degree of difference in heard commissive force can be seen to be important; *Statement (i)* contains no commissive force, *Statement (ii)* contains a degree of threat and thus has implicit, or indirect, commissive force and in *Statement (iii)* this threat is made explicit. Under the current system *Statement (i)* is coded as containing assertive force, *Statement (ii)* as containing assertive and commissive force and *Statement (iii)* as containing commissive force alone. This approach captures important aspects of this data set for the purpose for which the coding is being used.

The coding of *Statement (ii)* as containing more than one element of pragmatic force is a departure from Dale et al.'s (1997) stipulation that each utterance be coded only once. It seems a reasonable position that when doing things with words we are able to do more than one thing at a time and this is in part supported theoretically by discussions of indirect speech acts (Thomas, 1995). One effect of this approach, however, is that it emphasises the subjective decisions of the coder and raises the necessity that such coding be demonstrated to be reliable.

Allan's (1998) identification of *expressives* is adopted but a further departure from his system is made in consideration of his categories of *invitationals* and *authoritatives*. This distinction is essentially suggested by the power differential evident in an utterance. The traditional distinction Austin (1962) makes between *verdictives* and *exercertives* (interpreted by Searle's (1969) intention based taxonomy as a distinction between *authoritatives* and *directives*) rests on the difference between culturally supported commands and requests and those which, in contrast, rely on lower level interpersonal factors for their force. The classic example of the former is the jury whose verdict directs a defendant to be guilty. Allan suggests that from the hearer's perspective the source of the authority is irrelevant, there are simply authoritative directives and those which are perceived to give more power of choice to the hearer. As rape however is not socially sanctioned to the extent that makes verdictives possible this distinction loses its force. The rapist is unable to utter verdictives and so does not appear in the categorisation system.

Within the remaining directives Vendler (1972) suggests a useful distinction which is carried forward into the current system. This is the distinction between directives which request or demand action and those which request or demand information. This distinction between *directives* and *interrogatives* is again considered to be important to the current context and so is taken forward into the current system.

The final list of speech acts adopted for categorising the rapist's utterances is therefore *assertives, commissives, expressives, directives* and *interrogatives* as shown in Table 1.2.

The second part of the categorisation system involves qualitative measurement of the interaction by the use of a number of subscales. These subscales are drawn from three main theoretical sources; the pragmatics literature (measuring degrees of politeness (Brown and Levinson, 1978, 1987)), the literature on rape typologies (measuring degrees of threat and control (Davies, 1992)) and the clinical literature on offenders (measuring degrees of perceived empathy to the victim (Marshall, Barbaree, and Fernandez, 1995)).

Table 1.2: Classification of the rapist's utterances

1. **Commissives**
   a. How polite was the offender?
   b. How much implied control did the victim have?
   c. How much commitment did the offender make to carry out the action?
   d. Does the utterance imply a positive or negative outcome for the victim?

2. **Constatives/assertives**
   a. How identifying was the information disclosed?
   b. How threatening was the utterance?
   c. How intimate was the information stated?
   d. How much was the utterance intended to build rapport?
   e. How much was the utterance in response to the victim's speech or behaviour?

3. **Directives**
   a. How polite was the offender?
   b. How threatening was the utterance?
   c. Does the utterance imply the offender or the victim has more control? (6 point scale)

4. **Expressives**
   a. How much does the offender recognise the victim's feelings?
   b. How much reference was made to the victim?
   c. How much responsibility did the offender appear to take?
   d. How far was the attitude expressed positive or negative?
   e. How specific was the utterance?

5. **Interrogatives**
   a. How polite was the offender?
   b. How much practical relevance did the query have for the offender?
   c. How much emotional relevance did the query have for the offender?
   d. How much was the utterance intended to build rapport?
   e. How specific was the utterance?
   f. How much was the utterance in response to the victim?
   g. How intimate was the information sought?

Note: All subscales were measured on a 7 point scale unless otherwise indicated.

The reliability of the system was tested in two linked studies (reported in Woodhams and Grant, 2006). First the coding of speech acts was tested through the coding of 188 separate utterances collected, with a little context, from 16 statements. These utterances were coded and reliability scores were calculated. Speech acts were coded with a 78% agreement and these scores compared favourably with a similar exercise carried out on Dale et al.'s (1997) coding system which was used with 73% agreement. Qualitatively the top level coding was reported as being relatively straightforward with the most difficult decisions surrounding issues of whether a secondary or even tertiary coding was appropriate.

Subsequent to this testing a pool of potential subscales was devised and tested for reliability and discrimination. For this testing a pool of ten examples of each of assertives, commissives, directives, expressives and interrogatives were created. The subscales were then tested, rejected and amended until reliability levels of at least 70% could be reported for all subscales. The final result is as reported in Table 1.2. This testing has proved an important step in the preparation of the coding system and has led to considerable confidence in its further extension and use.

Applications of the method

The application of the categorisation system and the analysis on which it is based is ongoing but has already given up some interesting results. The first truly applied project has been a comparison of rape statements which have been withdrawn-as-false with a set of statements which continue to be maintained-as-true (Woodhams and Grant, 2004). This study shows differences between the types of reports at the level of the activity type, the speech act and the subscale. For example, analysis of the overall activity show that the withdrawn-as-false allegations contained significantly less closure stage conversation and where such conversations did occur they showed proportionally fewer assertives and directives than expected when compared with maintained-as-true accounts. Amongst other findings of difference the qualitative subscales revealed that utterances in the maintained-as-true statements were less polite, more specific and more threatening. There are numerous possible interpretations of these findings but they do provide some empirical evidence which it is hoped might be used in court to counter defence assertions that an allegation was fabricated.

The main purpose of the categorisation system is to improve case linkage and a further study is underway to explore whether there is sufficient linguistic consistency to support this. This study requires the development of the coding of the victims' side of the conversation. This coding may not need to be to the same level of detail as for the coding of the rapist's utterance as the issue is not the identification of the victim but rather the effect the victims' utterances have on the offenders. One possibility drawn from the psychological consideration of victims is to use a small number of codes such as 'compliant' and 'resistant' for victim utterances which may then allow conditional statements to be made about the rapist. In personality psychology recent work has concentrated on developing conditional statements such as *in situation X this person is likely to respond by doing Y* (Shoda, 1999). Applying this to the rape conversation one might say that a particular rapist is consistent when confronted by a particular type of victim response.

Finally there are a set of possible avenues of exploration which might contribute to the investigative process but which are less related to case-linkage work. For example Kendall et al. (1999) looks for demographic correlates with different linguistic strategies and this could be done with the current system. Also the analysis of rape as a communicative activity gives rise to hypotheses, the testing of which may have investigative uses. For example, analysis of a very small data set suggests that rapists vary more in their degree of politeness in the maintenance phase of an attack than in the approach phase ($t_{(7)} = 2.49$; $p = 0.041$). If this were to be confirmed by further study it might suggest that this would be an area of greater individual variation between rapists.

Conclusions

In conclusion, what has been achieved by this project so far is a reliable system for categorising rapists' utterances. The situation of the categorisation system in speech act theory has contributed to its success in being able to classify data which at first sight might be considered so poor as to resist linguistic analysis. The application of this system to a variety of research projects is underway. Findings so far strongly suggest that the categorisation system can be a useful forensic tool for the crime analyst; the most important test of its usefulness in this context will be in the forthcoming consistency and case-linkage study. Investigative linguistics has rarely been promoted as a useful tool to the police and other investigators and where this has occurred it has been limited to a small number of fields mostly associated with authorship analysis. The development of the current system has shown that practical results derived from rigorous research can be a persuasive argument in interesting investigators in what linguists may have to offer. Irrespective, however, of whether the system can be demonstrated to be practically useful, advances in understanding have been made through consideration of rape as a communicative interaction. The theoretical analyses presented in this chapter have not only helped derive a reliable and complete system for the classification of rapists' utterances, but have also shed light on the nature of rape and its context within the wider society and this analysis suggests that certain types of rape can be enabled by stereotypical roles adopted in consensual sexual social activity.

References

Allan, K. (1998, 2003) *Meaning and Speech Acts*. Retrieved 28 June 2004, from the World Wide Web: http://www.arts.monash.edu.au/ling/staff/allan/speech_acts_allan.html

Askehave, I. and Swales, J. M. (2001) Genre identification and communicative purpose: A problem and a possible solution. *Applied Linguistics*, 22(2): 195–212.

Austin, J. L. (1962) *How to do Things with Words*. Oxford: Oxford University Press.

Bach, K. and Harnish, R. (1979) *Linguistic Communication and Speech Acts*. Cambridge, Mass.: MIT Press.

Bennell, C. and Canter, D. V. (2002) Linking commercial burglaries by modus operandi: Tests using regression and ROC analysis. *Science and Justice*, 42: 1–12.

Brown, P. and Levinson, S. C. (1978, 1987) *Politeness. Some Universals in Language Usage*. Cambridge: Cambridge University Press.

Burgess, A. W. and Holmström, L. L. (1974) *Rape: Victims of Crisis*. Bowie, USA: R. J. Brady.

Christianson, S.-Å. (1992) Emotional stress and eyewitness memory: A critical review. *Psychological Bulletin*, 112(2): 284–309.

Coulthard, M. (2004). Author identification, idiolect and linguistic uniqueness. *Applied Linguistics*, 25(4): 431–47.

Dale, A. Davies, A. and Wei, L. (1997) Developing a typology of rapists' speech. *Journal of Pragmatics*, 27(5), 653–69.

Davies, A. (1992). Rapists' behaviour: a three aspect model as a basis for analysis and the identification of serial crime. *Forensic Science International*, 55(2): 173–94.

Edgar, T. and Fitzpatrick, M. A. (1990) Communicating sexual desire: Message tactics for having and avoiding intercourse. In J. P. Dillard (ed.), *Seeking Compliance: the Production of Interpersonal Messages*. Scottsdale, Ariz.: Gorsuch Scarisbrick, pp. 107–23.

Ehrlich, S. (2001) *Representing Rape: Language and Sexual Consent*. London: Routledge.

Grant, T. D. and Baker, K. L. (2001) Identifying reliable, valid markers of authorship: a response to Chaski. *Forensic Linguistics: The International Journal of Speech Language and the Law*, 8(1): 66–79.

Grice, H. P. (1975) Logic and conversation. In P. Cole and J. L. Morgan (eds), *Syntax and Semantics III: Speech Acts*. New York: Academic Press. pp. 41–59.

Groth, A. N. (1979) *Men Who Rape*. New York: Plenum Press.

Grubin, D., Kelly, P. and Brunsdon, C. (2001) *Linking Serious Sexual Assaults through Behaviour* (HORS 215). London: Home Office Research Development and Statistics Directorate.

Hazelwood, R. R. and Warren, J. (1990) The criminal behaviour of the serial rapist. *FBI Law Enforcement Bulletin*, February 1990(1): 1–16.

Hazelwood, R. R. and Warren, J. I. (2003) Linkage analysis: Modus operandi, ritual and signature in serial sexual crime. *Aggression and Violent Behavior*, 8(6): 587–98.

Holmström, L. L. and Burgess, A. W. (1979) Rapists' talk: Linguistic strategies to control the victim. *Deviant Behaviour*, 1(2): 101–25.

Hymes, D. (1962) The ethnography of speaking. In T. Gladwin and W. C. Sturtevant (eds), *Anthropology and Human Behavior*. Washington DC: Anthropological Society of Washington. pp. 13–53.

Kendall, D., McElroy, H. and Dale, A. (1999) Developments in offender profiling: The analysis of rapists' speech. *Police Research and Management*, 3(3): 1–24.

Levinson, S. C. (1979) Activity types and language. *Linguistics*, 17(5/6): 365–99.

Maddox, S. (2004) Interactions between rapist's and victim's speech. Unpublished M. Sc., University of Leicester, Leicester.

Marshall, W. L., Barbaree, H. E. and Fernandez, Y. M. (1995) Some aspects of social competence in sexual offenders. *Sexual Abuse: A Journal of Research and Treatment*, 7: 113–27.

McMenamin, G. R. (2002) *Forensic Linguistics: Advances in Forensic Stylistics*. Boca Raton, Fla., USA: CRC Press.

Mills, S. (2000) *Rethinking politeness, impoliteness and gender identity*. Retrieved 10 December 2004, from the World Wide Web: http://www.linguisticpoliteness. eclipse.co.uk/GenderandPoliteness.htm

Muehlenhard, C. L. and Hollabaugh, L. C. (1988) Do women sometimes say no when they mean yes? The prevalence and correlates of women's token resistance to sex. *Journal of Personality and Social Psychology*, 54(5): 872–79.

Reyna, V. F. and Kiernan, B. (1994) Development of gist versus verbatim memory in sentence recognition: Effects of lexical familiarity, semantic content, encoding instructions and retention interval. *Developmental Psychology*, 30(2): 178–91.

Rose, P. (2002) *Forensic Speaker Identification*. London: Taylor and Francis.

Searle, J. R. (1969) *Speech Acts*. Cambridge: Cambridge University Press.

Shoda, Y. (1999) A unified framework for the study of behavioral consistency: Bridging person–situation interaction and the consistency paradox. *European Journal of Personality*, 133(5): 361–87.

Shuy, R. (1993) *Language Crimes: The Use and Abuse of Language Evidence in the Courtroom*. Oxford: Blackwell Publishers.

Shuy, R. (1998) *The Language of Confession, Interrogation and Deception*. London: Sage.

Silverman, D. C., Kalich, S. M., Bowie, S. I. and Edbiel, S. E. (1988) Blitz rape and confidence rape: a typology applied to 1000 consecutive cases. *American Journal of Psychiatry*, 145(11): 1438–41.

Stahelski, A. and Patch, M. E. (1993) The effect of compliance strategy choice upon perception of power. *Journal of Social Psychology*, 133(5): 693–8.

Sternberg, K. J., Lamb, M. E., Davies, G. M. and Westcott, H. W. (2001) The 'Memorandum of Good Practice': theory versus practice. *Child Abuse and Neglect*, 25(5): 669–81.

Swales, J. M. (1990) *Genre Analysis: English in an Academic Research Setting*. Cambridge: Cambridge University Press.

Thomas, J. (1995) *Meaning in Interaction*. London: Longman.

Vendler, Z. (1972) *Res cogitans*. Ithaca: Cornell University Press.

Walby, S. and Allen, J. (2004) *Domestic Violence, Sexual Assault and Stalking: Findings from the British Crime Survey* (Home Office Research Study 276). London: Home Office Research, Development and Statistics Directorate.

Walker, A., Kershaw, C. and Nicholas, S. (2006) *Crime in England and Wales 2005/2006*. London: Home Office.

Woodhams, J. and Grant, T. D. (2004) Statements of truth and deception: Using rapists' language to contrast maintained-as-true and withdrawn-as false rape allegations: Serious Crime Analysis Section – National Crime and Operations Faculty.

Woodhams, J. and Grant, T. D. (2006) Using speech to link crimes: Developing a categorisation system for rapists' speech. *Psychology, Crime and Law*, 12(3): 245–60.

Yarney, A. D. (2001) Ear-witness descriptions and speaker identification. *Forensic Linguistics: The International Journal of Speech Language and the Law*, 8(1): 113–22.

Legislation

Sexual Offences Act 2003 (United Kingdom) Retrieved 10 December 2004, from the World Wide Web: http://www.opsi.gov.uk/acts/acts2003/ 20030042.htm

2
The Elicitation of a Confession: Admitting Murder but Resisting an Accusation of Attempted Rape

Susan Berk-Seligson

Introduction

Within the field of Language and the Law, a recurring issue is how power is enacted linguistically in the day-to-day interactions between institutional authorities and those who deal with them. This study focuses on the power of the interrogator – specifically the police officer – to extract information from the interrogated, and the power held by the interrogated, namely the ability to withhold information being sought. In short, this analysis focuses on the phenomenon of resistance to linguistic coercion.

The study uncovers the mechanisms by which police interrogators achieve the linguistic construction of sexual violence. In a criminal case analysed here, dealing primarily with murder and secondarily with attempted rape, the interrogation tactics are shown to gradually, over a lengthy series of question/answer sequences, present the detainee as a would-be rapist, and portray his failed rape attempt as the principal motive for the murder.

The enigma facing the analyst is why the police were successful in eliciting a confession to murder, a crime that carried with it the threat of either life imprisonment or the death penalty, but failed in their attempt to obtain a confession to a less serious crime, attempted rape. An inadequate understanding of the detainee's sociocultural background is posited as one of the principal explanations for this paradoxical finding. Whereas it could be argued that the police interrogators were able to elicit a confession to murder but not to rape because the suspect was guilty of the former offence but not the latter, this is highly unlikely, given the state in which the victim's body was found. The fact that the young woman's bra was pulled up leaving her breasts exposed and her underpants were found down at the ankles, is circumstantial evidence indicating that the perpetrator intended to force himself on her sexually. Whether he succeeded or not is another question, and in fact the court found him guilty of 'attempted rape' rather than rape itself.

The linguistic construction of sexual violence through interrogation

A number of studies of language in legal settings have shown that sexually violent behaviour, including rape, can be constructed by interrogators through a variety of linguistic means. Matoesian (1995) and Conley and O'Barr (1998) make the point that while the ordinary tactics used by attorneys for cross-examining witnesses typically result in the domination of examinees, in rape trials such strategies will go even further, producing a 'revictimisation of the victim'. Whether it is through lexical choice, such as a repeated reference to the victim's 'having *pantyhose* on' (Conley and O'Barr 1998: 36), or syntactic form, such as the use of statements rather than questions, or aspects of conversational structure, such as the management of sequence type and the restriction of topics through the manipulation of question/answer sequences (Matoesian 1993: 100), lawyers have been shown to dominate women on the witness stand who make accusations of rape. Atkinson and Drew (1979: 258), using a conversational analytic methodology as does Matoesian (1993; 1995; 2001), demonstrate how a lawyer can convey his scepticism of the testimony of the victim of an alleged rape by repeating her statements and by prefacing those repetitions with the phrase 'You say'. Drew (1992: 472), in analysing the speech of lawyer and alleged victim in another rape trial, discovers the devices that a lawyer will use to discredit the witness, among them being offering 'alternative and competing descriptions or versions of events'. Atkinson and Drew (1979), Matoesian (1993), and Conley and O'Barr (1998) all point out that rape victims on the witness stand at times try to defend themselves against the unflattering characterisations of them insinuated by lawyers, but that their efforts at countering such insinuations more often than not fail. The net result is that alleged rape victims often are made to appear partly responsible for the unwanted sexual advances of the accused, or, alternatively they are accused of having engaged in consensual sex.

Alleged rape victims are not the only ones who defend themselves against the insinuations of lawyers. Those who are accused of rape also have been found to marshall their linguistic forces against interrogators who try to cast them in a blameworthy light. Ehrlich's (2001) analysis of acquaintance rape hearings and trial proceedings involving a college student accused of sexual assault demonstrates that the accused used a constellation of syntactic features which together comprise a 'grammar of non-agency', and that he used this grammar to divest himself of responsibility for any actions that could be construed as constituting sexual violence. Matoesian (1999), too, examines the ways in which a man accused of sexual violence defends himself under interrogation. Analysing the testimony of William Kennedy Smith at his high-profile rape trial, Matoesian shows how the defendant deflected the insinuations of the prosecutor by taking on the footing of 'expert witness', namely physician, and as such countered the prior testimony of an authorised medical expert.

The case being analysed here deals with the linguistic construction of sexual assault, but not at the trial court stage. Rather, the context is that of a police interrogation in the investigation of a crime. The study focuses on the construction of an accusation by the police shortly after they have arrested a young man whom they suspect of murder and attempted rape, and the resistance of the suspect to the accusation.

Background of the case

The case of *The People* v. *Alvarez*[1] involves the arrest of an eighteen-year old undocumented[2] Mexican man living in the San Francisco Bay area of California. The man, Carlos Rivera Alvarez, was charged with first-degree murder and attempted rape and subsequently was convicted of both crimes and sentenced to life imprisonment without possibility of parole. Four years after the trial, a California appeals court reversed the conviction of first-degree murder (not freeing the defendant, but decreasing the time he was to spend in prison), yet it upheld the attempted rape conviction. The basis for the reversal of Alvarez's conviction, argued the appeals court, was the use of coercive interrogation tactics by the police in extracting a confession from him. A detailed analysis of the interrogation that produced the murder confession is found in Berk-Seligson (2002).

According to the appellate court, Alvarez had been caught running away from the scene of the crime, a row of hedges dividing a parking lot adjacent to a metro station. In the words of the appellate judge who wrote the opinion, 'the semi-nude body of a young woman was found' behind the hedge, the place where the defendant was believed to have begun 'a stabbing frenzy' (Court of Appeal p. 2). The wording used by the appellate judge who wrote the opinion hints strongly at a sexually motivated type of murder: the fact that the victim was semi-nude and young. It also depicts the perpetrator as having been out-of-control, in that he had stabbed her repeatedly. The judge also points out that the defendant had not eaten anything on the evening of the murder, but had drunk eight or nine beers. From this commentary the reader is meant to infer that Alvarez must have been inebriated on the night of the murder, a factor assumed to partially account for his violent behaviour.

The appellate court refers to Alvarez's having undergone two interrogations, both conducted by a monolingual English-speaking police detective, Officer Calhoun, with the aid of a non-Hispanic Spanish/English-speaking bilingual detective, Officer Larson. The first interrogation began at 4:03 in the morning and the second – initiated at the request of Alvarez – started at noon of the same day. In short, both interrogations were carried out within twenty-four hours of the murder, when the sequence of events surrounding it were still fresh in the detainee's mind.

It is the thesis of this chapter that the defendant's verbal behaviour in reaction to police coercion during the first interrogation superficially appears to be different from that which he displayed during the second one, namely, that at the first interrogation he simply refused to provide factual information related to the murder by repeatedly saying that he felt bad and did not wish to talk about his 'problem'. Clearly he was doing his utmost to resist the efforts of the police to induce him to confess to the murder. By the end of that interrogation, however, he implicated himself sufficiently to be considered to have confessed.

The second interrogation, which he himself requested at the urging of the police, focused on the accusation of attempted rape. In contrast to his refusal to be forthcoming at the first questioning, at the second one Alvarez ostensibly seemed to be answering the detectives' questions. However the manner in which he did so represents a different form of resistance. It is the nature of this resistance that will be addressed in this chapter.

The construction of an accusation and resistance to it

One of the many tactics used by police interrogators to obtain a confession from a suspect is providing him or her with a justification for having committed the crime. In the case of Carlos Alvarez, the accusation of attempted rape begins with the police suggesting to the suspect a motive for his attack on the victim. The suggestion occurs two-thirds of the way into the first interrogation, and is mentioned in passing, *a propos* of nothing that had been said thus far, from a discourse point of view totally disconnected from what had been said immediately prior to it. After talking about 'the problem' that Alvarez had had earlier that evening – never once specifying the nature of the problem he was alluding to – Calhoun suddenly asks him some pointed questions about the behaviour of the young woman he had met in the parking lot of the BART[3] station. The significance of the line of questioning is that it suggests to the detainee a justification for actions that he has not yet admitted to, but which he can foresee could be upcoming in nearby question turns. Thus far in the interrogation, no mention has been made of the topic of murder, rape, or even of anyone having been injured in any way.

Extract 1

Calhoun: Okay. Ah, would you tell him that, ah (pause) we . . . we pretty much know what happened?

Larson: *Okay. Francisco, generalmente nosotros sabemos qué pasó.*[4]
          [Okay. Francisco, generally we know what happened.][5]
Alvarez: Um hum.
Calhoun: I would ... I need to fill in just a couple of areas.
Larson: *Necesitamos saber qué pasó en unos áreas que todavía no están muy (inaudible).*
          [We need to know what happened in some areas that are not yet very (inaudible).]
Calhoun: Okay. Did she attack you in any way? Did she hurt you in any way?
Larson: *¿Este muchacha, le atacó a usted o le, le hizo daño a usted?*
          [This girl, did she attack you or did she hurt you?]
Alvarez: *No recuerdo.*
          [I don't remember.]
Larson: He doesn't remember.
Calhoun: Okay, did you want to hurt her just a little bit? Did you just want to scare her?
Larson: *¿La quiso ...?*
          [Did you want ...?]
          (inaudible)
Calhoun: Did you just want to try to scare her a little bit?
Larson: *¿La muchacha esta noche ... La quiso asustarla, nada más ... esta noche?*
          [The girl tonight ... did you want to scare her, nothing more ... tonight?]
Alvarez: *No recuerdo, no quisiera hablar de esto más.*
          [I don't remember, I should not like to talk more about this.]
Larson: He doesn't remember, and he doesn't want to talk about this anymore.

The interrogation sequence presented in Extract 1 is important both from a discourse perspective and from the standpoint of doing policework in interrogation contexts. By proposing a rationale for the suspect's having stabbed the victim (lines 11, 18 and 26), the police are giving him a way out, a plausible and psychologically excusable reason for the acts they believe he committed. By shifting the responsibility for his actions onto the victim (in other words, if she had not provoked him, he would not have killed her), the detectives are empathising with him, and conveying the impression that they can understand what might have led him to take such an action against a young woman. The strategy is highly successful, because once the detainee really starts to talk, in the second interrogation, he uses the justification provided him by the police, sometimes using their very phrases, over and over again.

Noteworthy is the use of the active voice with agent-naming when Calhoun asks if the girl had attacked Alvarez. Clearly it is to make the girl look blameworthy, and to make Alvarez's violence appear to be a reaction to being attacked. Similarly, in accounting for Alvarez's behaviour toward the young woman, by asking him if he 'wanted to hurt her just a little bit', 'just wanted to scare her', Calhoun is making Alvarez's actions appear to be less weighty, of less consequence, and easier to comprehend. In short, the detective is mitigating the gravity of the crime[6]. Affirmative answers by Alvarez to his questions would imply that if he did attempt to rape her and then murdered her in the botched attempt, then his actions could be considered to be not premeditated.

Only at one other point during the first interrogation does the topic of whether the young woman had hurt Alvarez arise, and this is when Detective Larson is left alone with him. Calhoun had left the room purportedly to find out the results of laboratory tests performed on the bloodstains found on Alvarez's clothing.

Extract 2

Larson: *José, okay. El o . . . Dick ya le dijo que nosotros podemos hacer, okay, en cuanto a las huellas, um, sangre y todo eso . . .*
[José, okay. The oth . . . Dick already told you what we can do as far as the prints, um blood and all that is concerned . . .]

Alvarez: *Sí.*
[Yes.]

Larson: *. . . ¿okay? Quisiéramos saber qué pasó antes que podemos ver el sangre y todo, ¿okay? Es (pause) quisiera saber . . . quisiéramos saber si, si había un problema donde este muchacha hizo algo a usted o dijo algo a usted . . .*
[. . . okay? We would like to know what happened before we can see the blood and all, okay? It's (pause), I would like . . . we would like to know if there was a problem where this girl did something to you or said something to you . . .]

Alvarez: *No.*

Larson: *. . . ¿que le provocó, okay? Porque no . . . usted tiene dieciocho años. Es . . . está joven todavía, ¿okay? Nun . . . nunca ha hecho nada malo en su vida. Okay. Nunca ha estado en un cárcel. Nunca ha . . .*
[. . . that provoked you, okay? Because . . . you are eighteen years old. You are still young, okay? You have never done anything bad in your life. Okay. You have never been in a jail. You have never . . .]

Alvarez: *No.*

In Extract 2 (lines 11–14), which also comes from the first interrogation, Larson brings up the topic of whether there was something in the behaviour of the young woman that had provoked Alvarez, either by word or by deed. At this point in the questioning, Alvarez denies any such provocation. Subsequently, in the second interrogation, he will pick up on this notion, and will use it in his defence. Five turns later Larson asks Alvarez to do him the favour of telling him whenever he remembers something of the incident, even if he does not want to talk about it, rather than to keep repeating, 'I don't remember.' Larson's topic-initiation is followed up by a pointed question regarding whether what happened that night was sexual in nature (Extract 3, lines 1–2).

Extract 3

Larson: *Okay. Voy a estar un poquito franco a ... aquí ahora, ¿okay? ¿Um, algo sexual pasó esta noche?*
          [I am going to be a little frank h ... here now, okay? Did something sexual happen tonight?]

Alvarez: *¿Conmigo?*
          [With me?]

Larson: Um hum.

Alvarez: *No.*

Larson: *¿Nada sexual?*
          [Nothing sexual?]

Alvarez: *Nada sexual esta noche.*
          [Nothing sexual tonight.]

Larson: *Okay. ¿Qué ... quiso que, que algo así pasa?*
          [Okay. What ... did you wish that, that something like that would happen?]

Alvarez: *No.*

Larson: *Esta mujer, est ... esta muchacha, mujer, invquest quiso conocerla?*
          [This woman, thi ... this girl, woman, did you want to know her?]

Alvarez: *No quisiera hablar más.*
          [I shouldn't like to talk more.]

No further reference is made in the first interrogation to the possibly sexual nature of the encounter between suspect and victim, and the lexical stem 'sex-' and its derived forms, 'sexual', and 'sexy', are not mentioned again. Neither is the word 'rape' ever uttered. Nevertheless, Larson has made his point, and with the cat out of the bag about what the detectives suspect, Alvarez is now aware that the line of questioning may turn in this direction once again. In fact, it becomes the exclusive focus of the second interrogation.

Questioning strategies and forms of resistance

Overt questions regarding sexual assault come only in the last quarter of the three-hour long interrogation session, and they are made not by Calhoun, but by Larson, who officially is there to serve as interpreter. The questioning strategy used by Calhoun is to get the suspect to relate chronologically his actions on the evening of the murder, including the hours before the encounter between Alvarez and the victim took place. A number of questions relate to information required for the police intake sheet (for example, correct name, height, weight, nationality, occupation, place of work, names of closest relations living nearby). While most of these questions do not pose problems for the average US resident or citizen, for undocumented persons living in the US answering questions even as mundane as these is problematic. In the case of Carlos Alvarez, he had already lied once to the police, giving a false name at the initial interrogation. When asked for his social security number – in the US one of the most basic, multi-purpose forms of identification – he has to admit to not having one. When asked the seemingly innocuous question, 'What occupation do you have? What do you do for work?' his response is the expression of a desire not to reveal this (in his words, '*Quisiera, si es posible, que no se supiera nada de, de mi trabajo*' [I would wish, if it is possible, that nothing be known about, about my work]). It is clear from subsequent questions that he is trying to protect his brother and cousin, with whom he shares an apartment, through whom he has found employment, and who most likely are also undocumented workers. He might even be attempting to protect the identity of his employer, who may have broken the law in hiring him. Calhoun does not press the point regarding his occupation. Following a routine strategy recommended by police interrogation manuals (Aubry and Caputo 1980; Van Meter 1973), he works at establishing an amicable, empathetic relationship with the suspect.

Resistance to invitations to narrate: preference for fragmented answers

One of the most salient characteristics of Alvarez's answers to police questions is the use of fragmented style. Fragmented answering style, characterised by brief, non-elaborated answers to questions, stands in contrast to narrative style. The research of O'Barr (1982) and his colleagues (Conley, O'Barr and Lind 1978) first brought to light the impact of such styles on listeners, specifically when they are used by witnesses on the stand and the listeners are jurors. They found that witnesses who answer attorneys' questions in the lengthier, more elaborated, narrative style give the impression of being more competent and socially dynamic than are witnesses who answer in a fragmented style. Alvarez's style of answering the questions of Calhoun and Larson is consistently fragmented, and in those rare instances when he does provide a narrative answer, it is merely to repeat information he has given in previous answers, without adding anything to what is already

known. My interpretation of his unwillingness to speak in narrative style
is that this way of speaking represents a strategy of self-defence, a continuation of the stance taken in the earlier interrogation, namely, not to say any
more than absolutely necessary. Since the police are trying to elicit narrative
types of answers, and the interrogation process is slow-going, the fragmented
answers represent a case of the violation of Grice's maxim of quantity, that
is, they do not say enough, and therefore do not satisfy the conversational
needs of the interlocutors. Extract 4, below, vividly demonstrates the pattern
of fragmented answers that Alvarez gives.

Extract 4

Calhoun: Did you, ahh ... when you were coming back to Concord, did
you see a girl?

Larson: *Al regresar a Concord, ¿conoció o vió una muchacha?*
[Upon returning to Concord, did you meet of did you see a
girl?]

Alvarez: In BART?

Larson: Uh huh.

Alvarez: No.

Calhoun: Okay. When you got back to Concord, you got off BART, and
where did you go then?

Larson: *Okay. Al regresar a Concord, salió, bajó del BART, ?dónde se fue de
allá?*
[Okay. Upon returning to Concord, you went out, got off BART,
where did you go from there?]

Alvarez: *Allí conocí a una muchacha.*
[There I met a girl.]

Larson: Okay, he said that there he met a girl.

Calhoun: At the BART station?

Larson: *A la estación de BART ... ¿conoció a la muchacha?*
[To the BART station ... you met a girl?]

Alvarez: *Afuera de la de Concord, de la estación de BART de Concord.*
[Outside of the Concord one, the Concord BART station.]

Larson: *¿Fuera de la estación, en el lote de estacionar?*
[Outside of the station, in the parking lot?]

Alvarez: Uh huh.

Larson: Okay. He said in the parking lot of the BART station.

Calhoun: Did you talk to her?

Larson: *¿La habló?*
[Did you talk to her?]

Alvarez: *Sí.*
[Yes.]

Calhoun:	Ah, that was yes?
Larson:	Yes.
Calhoun:	He did talk with the girl?
Larson:	Yes.
Calhoun:	Ah, did you walk with her?
Larson:	*¿Andó con ella?*
	[Did you walk with her?]
Alvarez:	*Sí.*
	[Yes.]
Larson:	Yes.
Calhoun:	Where did you walk to?
Larson:	*Adónde andó?*
	[To where did you walk?]
Alvarez:	*No sé, caminé con ella como dos blocs, tres blocs.*
	[I don't know, I walked with her about two blocks, three blocks.]
Larson:	He says that he walked with her for two or three blocks.
Calhoun:	Were you still talking with her?
Larson:	*Estaba hablando o charlando con ella?*
	[Were you talking or chatting with her?]
Alvarez:	*Sí.*
	[Yes.]
Larson:	Yes.
Alvarez:	*O sea, sea, an . . . cuando, cuando anduve con ella, anduve, pos cuando platiqué con ella, anduve platicando con ella (inaudible) un bloc conmigo.*
	[Or that is, that is, I wa . . . when I walked with her, well when I chatted with her, when I walked and chatted with her (inaudible) one block with me.]
Larson:	Uh huh. He says he was walking and talking with her for about a block.
Calhoun:	And then what happened?
Larson:	*Okay. ¿Y qué pasó de allí?*
	[Okay. And what happened from there?]
Alvarez:	*(Pause) Pues, pasó, pasó eso.*
	[(Pause) Well, it happened, that happened.]
Larson:	Okay, he said this, this passed, that happened.
Calhoun:	Were you arguing when you were talking with her?
Larson:	*¿Había una lucha de palabras?*
	[Was there a fight of words?]
Alvarez:	*No.*
Larson:	No?
Calhoun:	Tell me what she looked like.

Larson: *¿Puede describir la, la muchacha?*
   [Can you describe the, the girl?]
Alvarez: *Bueno, alta ....*
   [Well, tall ....]
Larson: Tall.
Alvarez: *Bueno, de pelo corto.*
   [Well, short hair.]
Larson: Short hair.
Calhoun: Dark? Dark hair?
Alvarez: *No, como, como castaño.*
   [No, like, like chestnut.]
Larson: *¿Castaño? Es un poquito más oscuro que, que café, no?*
   [Chestnut? Is it a little darker than coffee-coloured, no?]
Alvarez: *Sí.*
   [Yes.]
Larson: Okay.

The police need a description of the victim from a suspect to make sure that they have the right suspect. In other words, they need to match the appearance of the crime victim with the description given of her by the suspected perpetrator of the crime. Physical descriptions naturally lend themselves to narrative types of characterisations. Most adults would provide details of height, weight or build, hair length and colour, colour of skin when relevant. When Calhoun says (line 73), 'Tell me what she looked like', he is requesting a physical description that includes some of these details. When the request for a description fails, he has to work harder at obtaining the information he wants, and resorts to asking a series of specific questions to elicit these characterisations. For example, in providing a description of someone's clothing, one would normally include colour in referring to particular items of apparel, but Alvarez does not. His minimal answers force Calhoun to generate additional questions about a given referent. Without such prompts, Alvarez's descriptions are inadequate for Calhoun's purposes. The suspect is not being completely cooperative conversationally.

Perhaps the most glaringly uninformative answer to a question that was intended to produce a narrative reply is the one in response to Calhoun's (line 62), 'And then what happened?' Calhoun's expectation is an account of the attack on the woman. Alvarez's answer, 'Well, it happened, that happened,' in its total lack of information, reveals nothing about what he did or she did after they had walked together for a block. In its substantive vacuousness it says a great deal, however: it indicates that the subject is a highly sensitive one for the suspect. Seeing that Alvarez is not willing at this point to describe the incident on his own accord, Calhoun changes gears and asks a specific question about the nature of their conversation during the one-block walk, namely, had Alvarez been arguing with her. He is successful in eliciting a 'Yes' response.

The linguistic construction of violence

The scenario that the police attempt to construct together with the suspect is that he tried to pick up a young woman a block away from the metro station, and that she rejected his advances. Calhoun repeatedly asks Alvarez if the girl pushed him or yelled at him, implying that such actions on her part could have provoked him to attack her. To the question as to whether she had pushed him, he replies, '*Un poco*' [A little]. Later in the interrogation, however, he reveals that she tried to push him away from her, jabbing him in the stomach with her elbow, only after he had grabbed her by the throat from behind and flashed a knife in front of her face. So, while in fact she had pushed him, the pushing was not what provoked him to violence, but rather what came in response to the violent act that he had initiated against her. Nevertheless, the suggestion of the detective that perhaps she had pushed him, and that this in turn might have made him 'a little furious' (which he denies, saying that he had not been angry, but simply depressed and feeling rejected because the girl had rebuffed him, telling him to get away from her) will be used by Alvarez in subsequent go-arounds. He begins to incorporate into his story the fact that she had hit him in the stomach with her arm, and repeats this detail in the numerous tellings that the police elicit from him.

The sexual innuendo is introduced gradually by the two detectives, with questions as to whether Alvarez wanted to go home with her, wanted to spend the night with her, whether he liked her, and whether he thought she was pretty. To most of these questions his initial answers are in the negative. Several times he denies forcefully that she was pretty, and to the question, 'Did you like her?' he answers: '*No, no mucho. Pues, pues, fue una mujer y . . . pero no, no me gustó a tal grado como para haberla asesinado*' [No, not much. Well, well, she was a woman and . . . but no, I didn't like her to such a degree as to have murdered her]. This is a very strange comment, particularly in light of the fact he had already confessed to the murder.

The police detectives try to find out what he had said to her during that one-block walk during which, according to Alvarez, they were 'chatting'. Alvarez is highly reticent about the content of that interchange. He eventually divulges, after several attempts by Calhoun to find out the nature of the conversation between them, that he had asked her about how to get to a certain street, and that she was helpful enough to give him directions. But immediately after that he began saying things to her which put her off, and which prompted her to tell him to leave her alone. He never does reveal what sorts of things he said to her that would have produced such a reaction. It is conjectured that he was using pick-up lines, in Spanish known as *piropos*. These range in content from relatively innocuous, flattering comments to highly offensive lascivious remarks, often about the woman's body (Fuentes, 2001).

Upon being told by her to go away, he reports, he grabbed her by the arm, then put his hand around her throat, and pulled out a knife – which he claims to have found somewhere in the street, earlier in the day – and held it in front of her face. His explanation for pulling out the knife is that he simply wanted to scare her, because she had made him feel depressed and rejected. According to Alvarez, once he had her in his grip and the knife close to her face, she struggled to free herself and in the process, 'threw herself to the ground', a strange reaction when one is trying to get away from an attacker. It is more likely that either he knocked her to the ground or else that she fell in the struggle. Nevertheless, in the numerous times that he was asked to describe his actions and those of the girl, Alvarez never wavered from this version of the story.

Alvarez several times describes sticking the knife into the girl. At first he admits to only one stab, but after repeated questioning carried out in cyclic fashion, he acknowledges two stabs, and after further challenges from Calhoun, entertains the possibility of having stabbed her three times, but no more than that. An examination of her body revealed multiple stab wounds.

Why did he stab her, Calhoun asks? Alvarez's answer is that she screamed, which frightened him. He stabbed her to stop the screaming. When Calhoun asks him if her screams were 'very loud', Alvarez responds with a highly mitigated characterisation of them, '*Más o menos*' [More or less]. He thereby is minimising the terror the girl must have been experiencing, and at the same time verbally reducing the amount of harm he was inflicting on her.

Whereas Alvarez is not answering the questions in any way that could be considered to be narrative style, he does provide enough information to confirm the admission he made at the first interrogation, that he had stabbed the young woman twice. And he has been told by Calhoun that she died, which comes as devastating news to him, since he realises the implications of this for him. Yet whenever either of the detectives alludes to a sexual motivation for his violent behavior, he denies the assertion. The section below presents evidence of the linguistic construction of attempted rape effectuated by the police, and the steadfast rejection by Alvarez of any such characterisations of his behaviour.

Constructing attempted rape: strategies of denial

Calhoun's strategy for eliciting a confession to attempted rape is to gather bits of incriminating facts from the suspect, facts which in and of themselves do not necessarily indicate sexual violence, but which when viewed in their totality would point to such a conclusion. Alvarez, despite his youth and inexperience with the US criminal justice system, can follow the drift of

Calhoun's questions, and makes every attempt to counter the implications. Even the supposition expressed by the detective that Alvarez must have been 'upset' by the girl's rejection of him is rejected by the suspect, partly because Larson incorrectly rendered the adjective 'upset' as *enojado* [angry], aggravating the illocutionary force of Calhoun's adjective. Alvarez, with a contrasting version (Drew, 1992: 516) of his emotional state, flatly denies having felt angry, replying with, '*No, estaba espantado, asustado*' [No, I was frightened, scared]. It is possible that the image of the girl being capable of getting with him angry does not sit well with him. It might be an affront to his male pride. In addition, by portraying himself as 'frightened' and 'scared', he is presenting himself not as the aggressor, but in a sense as a victim, and therefore not to be blamed. Something that she did frightened him. What he overlooks is that his feelings of fear come as a result of the girl's screams, and the girl began screaming only after he began the cycle of physical violence: grabbing her by the neck, and brandishing a knife in front of her face. Her screams were heightened by the stabbing itself, and this in turn frightened him even further, he told the detectives. Once he started stabbing her, and her body lost the strength to resist him, he was faced with what to do with her. At this point, according to his account, he began dragging her behind a nearby hedge, apparently to hide her body from the view of passersby.

Alvarez shows resistance to the questioning by continuing to refer to the crimes with vague, unspecific expressions. While helping Calhoun draw a map of the crime scene, he is asked to identify where the street is in relation to the parking lot, and to locate the bushes and trees that played a significant role in the events. Larson at one point asks Alvarez to identify a mark he has made on the map. Alvarez's answers to Larson's questions demonstrate an unwillingness to name his crimes, even though he is willing to provide a certain amount of information on one of them. Ironically, the suspect is merely capitalising on verbal mechanisms that the detective himself had provided for him. It was Larson who had first used the term 'problem' to refer to Alvarez's violent actions, and the suspect adopted this term and used it in subsequent questioning as a way of not incriminating himself.[7] Extract 5 shows that Larson continues to refer to the euphemism 'problem', this time coupling it with the murder weapon, 'knife'. The notion that Alvarez had had a problem with the knife conveys the impression that there was something problematic about the knife, that it was giving Alvarez trouble. Alvarez, therefore, is made to look like the inadvertent, unfortunate victim of knife troubles. Just as uninformative as the noun 'problem' is the neutral demonstrative pronoun *esto* [this]. Its lack of specificity allows Alvarez to protect himself, in that by using it he is able to avoid giving a name to his illegal acts. In its vagueness it encompasses both the stabbing itself and the interaction between assailant and victim immediately preceding it. Its use, therefore, is a form of resistance to a line of questioning that the detainee knows could be damaging to him.

Extract 5

Larson: *Y esto aquí?*
           [And this here?]
           What is this here?
Alvarez: *Esto, aquí fue donde, donde pasó esto.*
           [This, here was where, where this happened].
Larson: Okay, this 'x' you've marked on your drawing is, is where you
           had the problem with the knife, where you stuck her?
Alvarez: *Sí, aquí fue el problema.*
           [Yes, here was the problem.]

The pre-accusation

The episode within the overall interrogation speech event that can be clearly
demarcated as the overt beginning of the accusation of sexual assault comes
after the crime scene map is completed. A 'pre-accusation' (a type of 'pre-
sequence' [Atkinson and Drew, 1979; Maynard, 1992; Sacks, 1992; Schegloff,
1968], in this case a prefatory announcement that precedes the accusation)
is uttered by Calhoun (line 1), followed by a warning from him that Alvarez
had better tell the truth. And then suddenly, unexpectedly, a reference to
the victim's bra and its irregular placement on her body (line 10). The text
follows in Extract 6.

Extract 6

Calhoun: Okay. I have a tough question for you, tough question.
Larson: *Ah, tenemos una pregunta bien difícil.*
           [Ah, we have a very difficult question.]
Alvarez: Um hum.
Calhoun: But the truth is necessary.
Larson: *Pero es necesario que sabemos la ¿verdad.*
           [But it is necessary that we know the truth.]
Alvarez: *Sí.*
           [Yes.]
Calhoun: When you left her there, her bra was up. *Verdad?*
           [True?]
Alvarez: *Sí.*
           [Yes.]
Larson: *¿Al dejarla allí, la ropa de ella fue ... estaba bien levantada?*
           [Upon leaving her there, her clothing was ... was raised up a
           lot?]
Alvarez: Uh hum.

Larson: *¿Verdad?*
            [True?]
Alvarez: *Sí.*
            [Yes.]
Larson: Yes.
Calhoun: Ah, how did it get that way?
Larson: *¿Cómo llegó a ser eso?*
            [How did that come to be?]
Alvarez: *Es que, cuando ella estaba aquí, yo, yo la agarré del sueter de aquí y
            la agarré del brazo y entonces cuando yo la jalé se le alzó la ropa. Y,
            y la, la agarré del brazo y la agarré del sueter y la, la jalé así.*
            [It's that, when she was here, I, I grabbed her by the sweater
            from here and I grabbed her by the arm and then when I pulled
            her, her clothing came up. And, and I grabbed her, her by the
            arm and I grabbed her by the sweater, and I pulled her, her like
            that.]
Larson: He says when he was pulling her he was, he had grabbed her
            by the arm and by the sweater, and it came up while he was
            grabbing her . . . or pulling her.
Calhoun: Okay. Another tough question, Manuel.
Larson: *Okay. Otra pregunta muy difícil.*
            [Okay. Another very difficult question.]
Calhoun: Her dress and underwear were pulled down, almost all the way
            to her feet.
Larson: *Okay. Los pantalones y también los pantalones anteriores estaban
            bajadas hasta las, las tornillos?*[8]
            [Okay. The pants and the forward pants were lowered to the,
            the screws.]
Alvarez: Um hum.
Larson: *Okay. invquest Cómo llegó a ser eso?*
            [Okay. How did that come to be?]
Alvarez: *Cuando la moví a ella, la jalé de la ropa también . . .*
            [When I moved her, I also pulled her by the clothing . . .]
Larson: *¿Usted la, la jaló a la ropa?*
            [You pulled on the, the clothing?]
Alvarez: *Porque cuando ella, ella la, la llevé y la puse . . . y ella dijo que 'no'
            y la, la agarré de la ropa y la jalé, cuando le jalé, cuando la puse allí
            le jalé la ropa, y ella dijo que 'no' y, y sacó sangre por la boca.*
Alvarez: *Porque cuando ella, ella la, la llevé y la puse . . . y ella dijo que
            'no' y la, la agarré de la ropa y la jalé, cuando le jalé, cuando la
            puse allí le jalé la ropa, y ella dijo que 'no' y, y sacó sangre por la
            boca.*

[Because when she, she, I carried her, her and I put her... and she said 'no' and I grabbed her, her by the clothing and I pulled her, when I pulled on her, when I put her there I pulled on her clothing and she said 'no' and blood came out of her mouth.

The pre-accusation performed by Calhoun, which precedes the accusatory declarative utterance containing the critical lexical item 'bra', functions to orient Alvarez thematically to sexual activities. It does so because the word 'bra' is charged with sexual innuendo: not merely an item of apparel, it is a garment that covers women's breasts, which both in European-American and Latin American hegemonic cultures are associated primarily with sexuality, and possibly only secondarily with lactation. For this reason, Calhoun's statement that the victim's bra was pulled up carries with it the accusatory implication that Alvarez, who was struggling with the young woman, was in some way responsible for the bra's being out of place, the underlying reason being that Alvarez wanted to see her naked breasts.

Alvarez's minimal response can be interpreted either as a back channel, indicating that he was following what Calhoun was saying, or it can be understood to be agreement with the detective. In and of itself it remains ambiguous. For this reason, Larson (line 15) follows up Alvarez's minimal response with a request for agreement, and Alvarez cooperates, with a minimalist '*Sí*'. Since Alvarez is not forthcoming and does not volunteer any further information, Calhoun must press him (line 23), about how the bra got that way.

Alvarez's answer (lines 26–8) is basically a repetition of statements he had made earlier, adding one piece of new information, '*se le alzó la ropa*' [her clothing came up]. The grammatical construction of this phrase is similar to the sorts of 'unaccusative constructions' found in the testimony of the college student accused of sexual assault in Ehrlich (2001). This sort of syntactic construction has been shown to be used by Spanish speakers in Costa Rica (Berk-Seligson, 1983) as well as in the US (specifically in courtroom testimony) as a mechanism of blame-avoidance (Berk-Seligson, 1990). By using this sort of construction, and capitalising on the grammar of non-agency, Alvarez is resisting any possible interpretation of Calhoun's that he pulled her bra up deliberately.

Calhoun uses a pre-accusation a second time (line 37), with the same type of wording ('Another tough question'), which serves as a warning that the question may not be one that the suspect would wish to answer easily or willingly. Again, it is not a question, as Calhoun claims it to be, but a statement, about the victim's dress and underpants being pulled down, almost to her feet. Unfortunately, Larson mangles the rendition of this statement in Spanish, mistaking *ropa interior* [underwear] for *ropa anterior* [previous clothing] and rendering 'ankles' as *tornillos* [screws], because of its phonetic resemblance to *tobillos* [ankles]. It is amazing that Alvarez can understand the question. Apparently his first-hand knowledge of the context, that is, the situation involving the victim and himself, gives him sufficient background to piece together what Larson is getting at.

The two accusatory insinuations portray a women who is naked, from the breasts down to her feet. Yet this is not said explicitly at this point in the questioning, it is only implied. Much later, it will be enunciated quite bluntly.

Repetition as denial and resistance[9]

The most striking aspect of the detainee's approach to handling the questions of the detectives, besides answering them in fragmented fashion, is the use of repetition. He uses both 'self-repetition' and 'allo-repetition' (repetition of others), to use a distinction of Deborah Tannen's (1989: 54). He also uses exact repetition as well as paraphrase (both of his own words and those of others).

Of Alvarez's numerous self-repetitions, both isolated lexical items and phrases, some seem to be stalling devices and many function as strategies of persuasion. At the same time, however, they function to deny certain actions and to resist the efforts of the interrogators to implicate him in them. In short, most of Alvarez's repetitions are 'repetitions of denial and resistance'. Such repetitions should be seen as important because they can empower a detainee with a strategy for self-defence in the face of a situation of asymmetrical power relationships. As will be shown below, the use of nearly word-for-word repetitions by a detainee, with barely any new information added to an answer, is a way for a detainee to avoid talking about a particular topic. By repeating his or her answers, a detainee gives the illusion of behaving in a cooperative manner with the authorities: s/he is answering their questions. The detainee keeps on talking (Van Meter et al., 1973), which coincides perfectly with one of the strategies that police interrogators routinely utilise in obtaining information from detainees, namely, keep the talk going. However, when the talk consists almost entirely of repetitions – both exact and paraphrased – and the replies do not always meaningfully answer the questions, then it can be said that repetition is functioning as a tool of resistance. As a resistance mechanism, it can serve to deny an accusation.

One of the most frequently repeated themes in Alvarez's answers is that he grabbed the young woman and pulled out his knife, but only because he wanted to frighten her, not to hurt her. It should be noted that early in the interrogation, Calhoun had suggested to him this possibility (see Extract 1), and so the wording of the answers below should be seen as an allo-repetition of Calhoun's words. The following excerpts comprise question/answer sequences occurring at different points in the interrogation in which this theme is reiterated by Alvarez.

Extract 7

Larson (interpreting for Calhoun):

>*¿Le pegó a ella cuando ella le hizo sentir furioso?*
>[Did you hit her when she made you feel furious?]

Alvarez: *No, no le pegué, pero la agarré. La agarré, la abrazé con la mano, porque la quería espantar.*
[No, I didn't hit her, but I grabbed her. I embraced her arm with my hand, because I wanted to frighten her.]

Larson: *Espantar, ¿invquest qué quiere decir 'espantar'?*
[Frighten, what does 'frighten' mean?]

Alvarez: *Pues la, la agarré con la mano por el cuello.*
[Well I grabbed her, her by the neck with my hand.]

Larson: Um hum.

Alvarez: *Y, y, y le saqué el cuchillo. Le enseñé el cuchillo para que se espantara . . . para que (inaudible) para que se, se asustara.*
[And, and, and I drew the knife on her. I showed her the knife so that she would be frightened . . . so that (inaudible) so that she would be scared.]

Other themes that are expressed by Alvarez in nearly an identical fashion throughout the questioning are (1) the woman hit him in the stomach with her arm/elbow; (2) she then threw herself to the ground, screaming; (3) he knelt beside her on the ground, grabbed her by the throat to stop her screaming, and stabbed her because (a) she wouldn't stop screaming, and (b) this frightened, scared him; (4) he dragged her along the ground, by the waist, pulling her by her clothes and by her arm, over to a tree to hide her behind it; (5) he did this to her because she had rejected his advances and consequently made him feel bad and depressed. Each of these themes is probed by the police many times over in cyclic fashion during the three hours of questioning, in accordance with routine police interrogation procedure, and each time Alvarez uses almost identical phrasing to describe the events and the scene.

The statement that he felt frightened and scared recurs more frequently than perhaps any theme. Partly it is because the police repeatedly ask him if he felt angry at the girl, if that is why he stabbed her. Alvarez steadfastly holds to his 'contrasting version' (Drew, 1992) of his state of mind: he was not angry, he was merely frightened. These repudiations of the police allegations are carried out with consistency and firmness. He never hesitates (his are not delayed responses), and he generally begins his replies with the negative marker, 'No', followed by a description of how he felt: *mal* [bad], *asustado, espantado* [scared, frightened]. He is very clear about this, and does not want to be accused of acting out of anger. Thus, he remains resistant to the end about this point, and does so by using the very same words to create his 'competing version' (Drew, 1992) of the story.

Exposing one's hand: a final police tactic

Throughout most of the interrogation the two police detectives are gradual and indirect in their approach to building up an accusation of attempted sexual assault. However, there comes a point toward the end of the session when they lay their cards on the table, and quite explicitly tell Alvarez their alternative version of the story.

At a point midway through the interrogation Larson asks, as he had done once before, at the first interrogation, if Alvarez had wanted to 'know' the girl in the Biblical sense – in the sense of having sexual relations with her – and defines the word for him. Alvarez flatly denies that this had been his desire. He does not like the word 'sexual' to be used in describing his desires or his actions. Nevertheless, much later in the questioning he admits that when he tried to 'get to know her' it had crossed his mind that after 'chatting' on the street maybe she would be willing to spend the night with him, that he would have liked to make love to her once they had gotten to know each other. He makes the point of saying that he would never go to bed with someone he didn't know, and that he was not one to frequent *cabarets* (in Mexico, these are topless dance bars or strip-tease clubs), or to pay women to sleep with him. It is clear from his remarks, however, that he considered 'getting to know' a woman as something that could happen in the span of a short walk down a street late at night.

In the last segment of the interrogation Calhoun asks Larson to, 'Tell him that, ah, as a man, I think he wanted to have sex with her,' to which Alvarez replies, 'No, yo nunca (inaudible)' [No, I never (inaudible)]. Unfortunately, Larson renders 'wanted' as *quiso* [attempted to, tried to]. This is predictable for a non-native speaker of Spanish because 'wanted' is the past tense form of the English verb, and so Larson uses the Spanish equivalent – the preterite tense form of the verb *querer* [want]. However, the verb *querer* has a special meaning in the preterite: it means 'tried to' or 'attempted to'. To express the equivalent of 'wanted to' in Spanish would involve using the imperfect tense (*quería*). It is likely that Larson's rendition, *quiso* is understood by Alvarez as meaning 'you tried to' have sex with her, rather than 'you wanted to'. In the case of an attempted rape charge, this is a crucial difference. The preterite form *quiso* in the utterance in which it was placed constitutes a direct accusation of attempted rape. It is no wonder that Alvarez so flatly denies it.

In constructing the accusation of attempted rape, Calhoun points out the scratches on one of Alvarez's hands. He interprets their presence as signs that the victim had scratched him as she was struggling to fend him off. Alvarez flatly rejects this possibility, explaining that the scratches were there as a result of putting his hand in the pocket that held the knife (in other words, that he had cut himself with the knife). Calhoun rejects this theory, telling him that the marks left by a cut look very different from scrape marks.

After this out-and-out dispute, Calhoun pulls out yet another revelation: that they, the police, had found something else on Alvarez's hands, besides scrapes – something that smelled like vaginal fluid. When Larson explains that this substance comes from 'where we do pee-pee', Alvarez vehemently denies any wrongdoing of his of this nature, saying, *'No, nunca toqué allí'* [No, I never touched there]. Calhoun, by now, openly confronting Alvarez with supposedly known facts, points out that there were fingerprints of Alvarez's on the victim's legs. To this he replies that because he pulled on her pants, perhaps he accidentally brushed against her legs, but that he 'never, never touched the, that part of her body'.

Finally, Larson, no longer mincing his words and always the more aggressive interrogator, says to Alvarez: *'Okay. Bueno lo que estamos diciendo, Carlos, okay . . . es que nosotros creemos que lo que pasó es que usted quiso tener o hacer amor con ella'* [Okay. Well, what we are saying, Carlos, okay . . . is we believe that what happened is that you wanted to have or to make love with her]. Oddly, Alvarez acquiesces, responding with a minimal, *'Um hum,'* not denying Larson's assertion. This is followed by another challenging statement from Larson, that he and Calhoun believe that perhaps this happened because she didn't want to make love with Alvarez. When asked by Larson if this is true, Alvarez denies it, saying, *'No, porque yo nunca le hablé de hacer eso'* [No, because I never talked to her about doing that], that is, he continues, he never told her that he had any desire to make love to her. This is interesting because it implies that he believes that only by saying something explicit to the woman about wanting to make love to her would it count as an expression of his desire to do so. Apparently he believes that some sort of speech act is required (for example, a request for permission to have sex) for a man to be considered to have made a sexual advance. Actions without words would not be sufficient, from his standpoint.

Conclusions

The case of *The People* v. *Alvarez* demonstrates that detainees undergoing police interrogation, even when subjected to what appellate courts deem to be 'coercive' interrogation techniques, have within their power a certain degree of ability to resist such coercive questioning tactics. By limiting themselves to fragmented answers and avoiding an elaborated, narrative style, and by making ample use of self-repetition and allo-repetition, detainees suspected of felonies – such as attempted rape – to some degree can thwart the efforts of the police to force confessions from them. The implication of this finding is that even under coercion, suspects can be considered to hold a measure of power over their interrogators, and that is the power of resistance. This is an interesting finding in the light of research based on trial testimony, most of which shows that the power to control testimony is in the hands of the interrogator. The production of fragmented versus narrative style testimony is one aspect of interrogation that has been believed to be under the control of the questioner (O'Barr, 1982; Conley et al., 1978).

One especially interesting finding emerging from the present analysis is that those being interrogated use as their tools of resistance the very tactics provided them by their interrogators. The common tactic used by police detectives of not naming the crime about which they are questioning a detainee, and referring to it as 'the problem' or the 'situation' can be picked up by a detainee to avoid mentioning the act for which s/he is being held. Similarly, when police detectives suggest a motive for the purported act of a detainee (for example, anger at the victim), and behave sympathetically toward them, expressing an understanding of the situation that provoked them into committing a serious crime, the detainee can exploit the suggested motive and capitalise on it during subsequent questioning, using it as a defensive strategy. Thus, verbal tactics used by the interrogator can be seen as potentially capable of appropriation by the interrogated, serving the latter's own strategic interactional needs.

In the particular case of Carlos Alvarez, no matter how many times the police suggest that it was anger that motivated him to stab a young woman to death, the suggestion does not have the perlocutionary effect on the suspect that they intend it to have. He does not adopt it as a motive for his violent behaviour. To the very end he remains resistant to the notion that he was angry at the victim, admitting only to feelings of rejection and depression.

Since there was sufficient evidence of attempted rape to uphold a conviction on appeal, what then accounts for Carlos Alvarez's persistent resistance to the police detectives' accusation against him? And why would he confess to murder but resist the accusation of sexual wrongdoing? Several possibilities suggest themselves, all of them at the level of conjecture, but all of them reasonable. Perhaps it is a combination of them that accounts for the seemingly paradoxical behaviour of the suspect.

One reason why he may have resisted the accusation of sexual wrongdoing is that this was the crime that he felt most guilty about, and probably the one he had in mind when he began to behave in a menacing way towards the young woman. It is unlikely that he was planning to murder anyone that night, but it is very likely that, in his drunken state, he was looking for a woman to pick up. From his perspective, his crime was attempting to force himself sexually on the unfortunate woman who crossed his path. The murder was unintended; it happened to result from a sexual crime gone awry. In fact, in his drunken state, Alvarez was unaware that he had done so much damage to her that she had died. The shock and grief he expressed at the first interrogation when the police informed him that the victim had died are evidence that he was not thinking clearly or perceiving the situation accurately when he ran away and left the young woman hidden behind some bushes. When the police gave him a seemingly excusable reason for attacking her, namely, that perhaps she had done something to hurt him, he seized on this rationale, and used it throughout the remainder of the interrogation. The police, by appearing to diminish Alvarez's responsibility for the violence, gave him a false sense of security, that is, they gave him the impression that the attack on the girl was understandable in the light of her behaviour toward him, and that therefore what he did was not so terribly reprehensible. Thus, if stabbing the girl could be excused by the police as a justifiable action on his part, then what remained to be held accountable for was the attempted rape, which he may have felt was indeed a crime and which left him feeling very bad about himself.

Another possible reason for denying the attempted sexual assault is that a second charge, added on to the murder charge, would result in a longer prison sentence if he were convicted of both. Perhaps he was not aware of prison sentence norms in the US, and if not, he would not have known that he could get either the death penalty or life in prison without the possibility of parole for murder, but that for the crime of rape he could be sentenced to only three-to-eight years in prison by a California state court. The disparity in sentences for the two crimes is quite pronounced in California. In Mexico City, in contrast, the difference in sentences for simple intentional homicide and rape is not as striking: it is from eight-to-twenty years for homicide, and from eight-to-fourteen years for rape. This makes the crime of rape weightier in Mexico City than it is in California, both in relative and absolute terms, and since it is unlikely that in eight months of living in California Alvarez would have learned the details of that state's criminal justice system, he probably was still thinking along the line of the Mexican legal framework, if he had any knowledge of it at all. Therefore, from a sentencing perspective, the idea of going to prison for rape would have been daunting to him.

Finally, a contributing factor in his unwillingness to confess to attempted rape might be the element of *machismo*, that is, assertive or aggressive manliness, or the 'cult of virility' as one psychologist has defined it (Goldwert, 1985). Oral communication to me from college-educated Mexicans, the writings of Mexican feminist writers (Poniatowska, 2000; Torres, 1997), and the analysis of a US anthropologist studying 'the meanings of *macho*' in a working class *colonia* [housing development] in Mexico City (Gutmann, 1996), all consider machismo to be a contributing factor to the rape rates in

Mexico. The Mexican observers explain that rape denotes a lack of virility, because a 'real man' would not need to go so low as to force a woman to have sexual intercourse with him; he should be able to seduce her without forcing her. And so to rape a woman is a vilifying crime in Mexico and embarrassing to the man who resorts to it.

One might conclude that Carlos Alvarez's resistance to the accusation of attempted rape may have had to do with all of the factors mentioned above. Explanations of human behaviour are usually multi-faceted, and it would be difficult to conceive of the denial of an action as serious as rape to have been caused by a single motive. It is not surprising, therefore, that the police in this case questioned the suspect about the burn marks on his body and about whether he had a history of psychiatric problems or not.

Alvarez's strategy of not giving any more information than absolutely necessary, yet still managing to give the appearance of conversational cooperation with his interlocutors, proved to be a successful one. He never relented on the accusation of attempted rape. He was, nonetheless convicted of it, and even though his murder conviction was reversed, the sexual assault conviction was not.

What this analysis has tried to show is that power in social interaction does not lie exclusively with any one participant, not even in sociolegal contexts such as police interrogations. Thus, while one might easily assume that all the power in such speech events would be in the hands of the interrogator, the findings presented here demonstrate that this is far from true. A suspect undergoing police interrogation has the power to withhold narrative style discourse and the power to fill a conversational turn with what are merely repetitions of substance provided in previous turns. Thus, like soldiers who are trained to provide only their name, rank and serial number to their captors, suspects who wish to resist implications of criminal wrongdoing have some powerful verbal resources at their disposal. Why some suspects make use of these resources and others do not is a separate question, one in need of further study.

Notes

1. The names of the persons involved in the case have been intentionally changed for this chapter.
2. An 'undocumented' person is someone who is residing in the USA without the legal papers (such as a visa, residency card) permitting him or her to do so. An older term, but one that is still in use, is 'illegal alien'. I prefer not to use this expression since its connotations seem to me to be far more pejorative than those of the newer designation, 'undocumented person'.
3. BART is an acronym for San Francisco's 'Bay Area Rapid Transit' system, which in other US cities would be considered the equivalent of a 'subway system' or 'metro line'.
4. The quality of Larson's interpreting will not be analysed here. Suffice it to say that it is highly deficient, in numerous ways, particularly in the conversion of English

to Spanish. The most frequent interpreting errors are (1) the use of ungrammatical Spanish forms, (2) the use of Spanish lexical items that are either non-standard or simply creations, (3) English-accented pronunciation, and (4) additions to, subtractions from, or entire changes in the substance of what was said in the original utterance (from either language to the other).

It should be noted that throughout the first interrogation the detectives address the suspect as 'Francisco' because that name, together with the surname 'Alarcón', form the alias that Carlos Alvarez gave them at the outset. He reveals his true name during the second interrogation.

5. English translations found in brackets represent the official translation provided by the courts. They generally diverge sharply from those given by Larson, and while I might question some of the official renditions of Spanish to English (for example, the choice of a lexical item that represents a register which to me sounds more formal in English than does the Spanish source), some of my questions regarding the translation deal with truly difficult decisions to be made, for example, how to best represent hesitation forms which in Spanish are partial repetitions of a phrase, and where the repeated element is an indirect object pronoun whose syntactic placement in English does not lend itself to repetition by itself without the accompanying verb. These are minor points, however, because on the whole the rendition of the official translator is excellent and questionable translations are few and far-between.

6. For an excellent discussion of the pragmatics of 'just' see Lee, 1987.

7. Police interrogation training manuals, such as Van Meter (1973), teach the police to use the technique of referring to the crime in vague terms such as 'the problem' until such time as they are ready to make an explicit accusation.

8. Larson's Spanish rendition of Calhoun's statement is particularly erroneous. While Larson justifiably changed 'dress' to 'pants' (*pantalones*), since Calhoun misspoke himself, his terms for 'underwear' (*pantalones anteriores*) and 'ankles' (*tornillos*) are incorrect in different ways. The former term does not exist, and if it did it would mean 'forward pants' or 'previous pants', which makes no sense. Larson was groping for the term '*ropa interior*'. The word '*tornillo*' means 'screw'. Larson was trying to remember the word for ankle, '*tobillo*'.

9. Resistance strategies in the face of interrogation in American judicial proceedings are manifested in numerous ways. Philips (1998) demonstrates how defendants going through change of plea proceedings typically resist the efforts of judges to induce them to confess to the crimes with which they are being charged. Resistance to confessing is accomplished through denial, obscurity, and mitigation (Philips, 1998: 93–106).

References

Atkinson, M. and Drew, P. (1979) *Order in Court: the Organization of Verbal Behavior in Legal Settings*. London: Macmillan.

Aubry, A. S. Jr. and Caputo, R. R. (1980) *Criminal Interrogation*. Springfield, Ill.: Charles C. Thomas, Publisher.

Berk-Seligson, S. (1983) Sources of variation in Spanish verb construction usage: The active, dative, and the reflexive passive. *Journal of Pragmatics*, 7(2): 145–68.

Berk-Seligson, S. (1990) *The Bilingual Courtroom: Court Interpreters in the Judicial Process*. Chicago: University of Chicago Press.

Berk-Seligson, S. (2000) Interpreting for the police: Issues in pre-trial phases of the judicial process. *Forensic Linguistics*, 7(2): 212–37.

Berk-Seligson, S. (2002) The Miranda warnings and linguistic coercion: The role of footing in the interrogation of a limited-English speaking murder suspect, in Janet Cotterill (ed.), *Language in the Legal Process*, London: Palgrave (formerly St. Martin's Press/Macmillan), pp. 127–46.

Conley, J. M., O'Barr, W. M. and Lind, E. A. (1978) The power of language: presentational style in the courtroom. *Duke Law Journal*, 78/6: 1375–99.

Conley, J. M. and O'Barr, W. M. (1998) *Just Words: Law, Language, and Power*. Chicago and London: University of Chicago Press.

Drew, P. (1992) Contested evidence in courtroom cross-examination: the case of a trial for rape. In P. Drew and J. Heritage (eds), *Talk at Work: Interaction in Institutional Settings*. Cambridge and New York: Cambridge University Press, pp. 470–520.

Ehrlich, S. (2001) *Reproducing Rape: Language and Sexual Consent*. London: Routledge.

Fuentes, R. (2001) Complimenting in two languages: A cross-cultural study of stranger compliments and *piropos* in the Mexican and American cultures. Unpublished ms.

Goldwert, M. (1985) Mexican machismo: The flight from femininity. *Psychoanalytic Review*, 72(1): 161–9.

Gutmann, M. C. (1996) *The Meaning of Macho: Being a Man in Mexico City*. Berkeley: University of California Press.

Lee, D. (1987) The semantics of 'just', *Journal of Pragmatics*, 11(3): 377–98.

Matoesian, G. M. (1993) *Reproducing Rape: Domination through Talk in the Courtroom*. Chicago: University of Chicago Press.

Matoesian, G. M. (1995) Language, law and society: Policy implications of the Kennedy Smith rape trial. *Law and Society Review*, 29(4): 669–701.

Matoesian, G. M. (1999) The grammaticalization of participant roles in the constitution of expert identity. *Language in Society*, 28(4): 491–521.

Matoesian, G. M. (2001) *Law and the Language of Identity: Discourse in the William Kennedy Smith Rape Trial*. Oxford: Oxford University Press.

Maynard, D. (1992) On clinicians co-implicating recipients' perspective in the delivery of diagnostic news. In P. Drew and J. Heritage (eds), *Talk at Work: Social Interaction in Institutional Settings*. Cambridge: Cambridge University Press, pp. 331–58.

O'Barr, W. M. (1982) *Linguistic Evidence: Language, Power, and Strategy in the Courtroom*. New York: Academic Press.

Philips, S. U. (1998) *Ideology in the Language of Judges: How Judges Practice Law, Politics, and Courtroom Control*. New York and Oxford: Oxford University Press.

Poniatowska, E. (2000) *Las mil y una . . . (la herida de Paulina)*. Barcelona: Plaza and Janés Editores, S. A.

Sacks, H. (1992) *Lectures on Conversation* (Vol. I and II), edited by G. Jefferson. Oxford: Blackwell.

Schegloff, E. (1968) Sequencing in conversational openings. *American Anthropologist*, 70: 1075–95.

Tannen, D. (1989) *Talking Voices: Repetition, Dialogue, and Imagery in Conversational Discourse*. Cambridge and New York: Cambridge University Press.

Torres, Marta F. (1997) La violación: Un enfoque socio jurídico. *Cotidiano*, 84(July–August): 78–86.

Van Meter, C. H. and Bopp, W. J. (1973) *Principles of Police Interrogation*. Springfield, Ill.: Charles C. Thomas, Publisher.

3
'Just Good Friends': Managing the Clash of Discourses in Police Interviews with Paedophiles[1]

Kelly Benneworth

Introduction

Many individuals operate outside the acceptable parameters of sexual practice in society. However, few things provoke as much public outrage as sexual offences against children. There is considerable social interest in paedophile activity, demonstrated by the widespread media coverage of child pornography, child sex-murders and celebrity child molesters. In 2005, pop star Michael Jackson was acquitted following charges of molesting a thirteen-year-old boy and broadcaster Jonathan King was released from prison after serving three and a half years for sexually assaulting five boys. Incidents of gross indecency with a child are allegedly on the increase with 1,942 cases reported to the police in 2004 compared to 1,880 in 2003 (Recorded Crime Data: UK, Home Office Research Development Statistics, 2004).

In addition to representing a public issue, the offence of paedophilia[2] also creates difficulties for the police investigation. The evidence in child abuse cases is often limited to the conflicting testimonies of the abuser and the abused and claims of sexual abuse often suffer from a lack of independent witnesses. There are also difficulties involved in extracting comprehensive statements from young victims, as sexual abuse is often not recognised as such by children (Lamb et al., 1999). Therefore, paedophile investigations frequently rely on establishing the veracity of suspect testimony through the effective implementation of police interviewing. As paedophiles are often perceived as self-serving and mitigating speakers, it is vital that the police interviewer is capable of obtaining the precise details of a sexual offence if the offender is to be convicted.

Paedophile justifications for sexual activity with children

The paedophiles' distinctive ability to rationalise their offending behaviour has been attributed to distorted cognitive reasoning (Abel et al., 1984,

Marshall et al., 2001). The paedophile selectively attends to information which construes the child as holding similar sexual desires. This permits the paedophile to minimise the seriousness of the abuse and deny responsibility for their behaviour (Wright and Schneider, 1999). Underwager and Wakefield (1999) invited 94 convicted paedophiles to explain the circumstances surrounding their incarceration. Eleven per cent of the sample denied the allegations outright, 12% provided admissions from the onset and the remaining 77% admitted yet *minimised* the extent of their offending. DeYoung (1988, 1989) analysed the newsletters of US paedophile organisations such as the North American May-Boy Love Association (NAMBLA) and catalogued the rhetorical devices used to redefine adult sexual behaviour with children in positive terms. DeYoung observed that, by portraying children as 'willing' partners and emphasising the sexual rights of children, the publications were 'neutralising' paedophile behaviour 'so as to make it more palatable or even acceptable to the law-abiding public' (1988: 585).

Pollock and Hashmall (1991) examined the clinical records of 86 male paedophiles convicted of sexually assaulting children and observed that 79% of the sample justified their offending behaviour. Of the 86 paedophiles, 22% described the sexual contact as 'victim initiated', 35% claimed that the incident was 'nonsexual', 35% cited psychological mitigators, including depression and childhood abuse, as grounds for the offence, and 48% cited situational mitigators, such as intoxication and financial stress. Offenders have often attempted to redefine sexual abuse as something desired by the child, 'some little girls are very seductive and promiscuous' or affectionate, 'I'm not hurting the child, just showing love' (Jenkins-Hall, 1989: 209). This misperception in the way paedophiles perceive their activities creates an interpretive framework with which they can redefine child sexual abuse as something acceptable and consensual (Howitt, 1995), construe their victims as willing and ultimately justify their offending behaviour.

Previous research has identified a distinctive self-serving discourse characteristic of pro-paedophile propaganda and the accounts of incarcerated offenders. It is evident that paedophiles employ minimising devices and a language of emotion, mutuality and affection to describe sexual relationships between adults and children. However, given the preoccupation with quantifying and categorising the justifications of paedophiles in sex offender treatment programmes, rresearch has failed to explore *how* these perpetrators use descriptions of adult–child relationships to account for their activities. It is vital that the implications of such justificatory language are examined in context, particularly contexts which rely on the factual reporting of criminal events.

The evolution of the investigative interview in the UK

Interviewing is one of the most important fact-finding methods the police have at their disposal when investigating crime (Gudjonsson, 1992). In 1992, legislation governed by the Police and Criminal Evidence Act (PACE) of 1984 led to the standardising of a police interviewing training programme for use by all police forces in the UK, the PEACE investigative interview. Prior to this, British police frequently adopted accusatorial interviewing techniques more commonly associated with US-style interrogations (Irving, 1980; Softley, 1980). These techniques were perceived as oppressive and coercive, subsequently increasing the risk of wrongful conviction. The development of the PEACE interview, the rationale for which is outlined in 'A Practical Guide to Investigative Interviewing' (2000), represented a transformation from the traditional adversarial nature of police interrogations to a universal 'search for information' (Shepherd, 1991).

There is a wealth of research evaluating the role of the investigative interview as a tool for enhancing the testimonies of witnesses and victims of crime. This research has addressed the development of the cognitive interview (Geiselman et al., 1984; Fisher and Geiselman, 1992) and the effective interviewing of vulnerable witnesses (Ceci and Bruck, 1993; Lamb et al., 1999; Perlman et al., 1994). However, few studies have considered the effectiveness of investigative interviewing for increasing the reliability of suspect testimony. In fact, literature suggests that, not only is there limited transference of PEACE principles to the questioning of suspects, there remains a prevailing 'confession culture' in British police forces (Mortimer, 1994; Williamson, 1993).

There have been several tentative efforts to identify features of the police–suspect interaction associated with increased admission in guilty suspects. Both Shepherd (1991) and Mortimer (1994) claimed that effective interviewing should involve obtaining a prolonged, uninterrupted narrative from the suspect, then examining the account in further detail. In a Home Office evaluation of PEACE investigative interviewing, Clarke and Milne (2001) observed a correlation between interview duration and suspect admission. Interviews in which the suspects denied the allegations were an average of 16 minutes in length, compared to 23 minutes for interviews resulting in confession. It would be interesting to explore the discursive characteristics of the admission interviews to see *who* exactly is doing the talking and *what* is being said. There is an obvious need for detailed empirical research into the qualitative effects of different police interviewing techniques on suspect admission and denial.

The application of discourse analysis

Discursive psychology emerged in opposition to the cognitivist notion of language as an outward manifestation of internal psychological phenomena. Discursive psychologists seek to demonstrate how psychological processes such as emotions, knowledge, memories, attitudes and thoughts are 'constructed, managed and oriented to' in social activity (Potter, 2000: 35).

This premise is derived from the views of Wittgenstein, who argued that what is socially involved in making claims about feelings and emotions is to be understood in terms of their usage in observable interactions (1951, cited in Billig, 2001). In addition to being observable *in* the social interaction, the implications of discourse are also *governed by* the social context in which it is produced (Lea and Auburn, 2001), 'what people say and how they say it is generally affected by the context in which they are interacting' (Drew, 1990: 39).

If discursive psychology is a form of theoretical thinking, discourse analysis represents an accompanying methodology. Discourse analysis shares a concern with the performative nature of talk (Auburn and Lea, 2001) and opposes the empiricist preoccupation with abstracting individuals from social activity. Discourse analysts favour the analysis of naturally occurring interactions and are interested in the ways that individuals use language functionally, to achieve certain ends (Wooffitt, 1992). Discourse analysis research involves the detailed, interpretative analysis of discursive actions, such as how descriptions are selected in preference to potential alternatives to perform actions (Edwards, 1997), how speakers formulate accounts as factual (Potter, 1996), how blame and accountability are managed (Drew, 1990), how speakers employ rhetorical devices (Billig, 1997) and how other speakers orient to what has been said (Auburn and Lea, 2001). The central tenet of discourse analysis is that talk is always *doing* something.

Discursive formulations of criminal behaviour

There has been considerable interest in the discourse analysis of courtroom talk, particularly, how competing versions of events are formulated by the prosecution and the defence (Atkinson and Drew, 1979; Drew and Heritage, 1992). Studies have examined constructions of sexual assault by magistrates in Canadian trial judgments (Coates et al., 1994), mitigated accountability in the discourse of guilty defendants in Dutch courtrooms (Komter, 1994) and the negotiation of economic and traffic offences between courtroom participants in Sweden (Linell et al., 1993). Drew (1990) described opposing formulations of rape in US criminal trials as a contest between the defence attorney and the alleged victim as to who can produce a more convincing story about *whether* and *how* a violation of law occurred. There have also been recent developments in the discourse analysis of sex offender treatment talk, for example, the mitigating devices used by convicted rapists undergoing therapeutic interventions (Lea and Auburn, 2001).

The discourse analysis of managing 'what actually happened' in the police–suspect interview is a relatively neglected field of research. However, research has demonstrated that discursive devices evident in everyday conversation are also characteristic of police interviews. Watson (1990) examined the language of US murder interrogations and found that police interviewers asserted their influence on emerging suspect narratives. Through the use of knowledge claims, for example, 'we also *know* about the gun in the Morris homicide . . . ' (p. 266), officers bolster the facticity of an accusation and ensure that a simple denial is insufficient to override the allegations. Whilst examining Swedish police interrogations with individuals suspected of minor economic offences, Linell and Jönsson (1991) observed a 'clash' between the 'everyday life' perspective of the suspect and the legal, 'professional' perspective of the police officer. In the analysis of UK police interviews with individuals suspected of violent assault, Auburn et al. (1995) also noted that officers sought an institutionally 'preferred' version of events (PO = Police Officer, I = Interviewee):

> PO: She's got knife wounds to both hands consistent with what she's
>   describing one of which required seven stitches where she says you
>   pulled the knife away from her when she was holding the blade and
>   you can imagine the knife cutting down along there, which is where
>   she's got the wound
>   Do you really expect us to believe that you can't recall an incident
>   like this.
> I: I'm telling–
> PO: It's not an everyday incident is it?
> (Extract from Auburn et al., 1995: 366)

Auburn et al. observed a 'discourse of disorderly violence' which positioned the suspect as the perpetrator of an uncontrolled and irrational offence, 'knife wounds to both hands . . . seven stitches . . . pulled the knife away from her when she was holding the blade . . . you can imagine the knife cutting . . . she's got the wound'. The act is also depicted as breaching normal codes of behaviour, 'It's not an everyday incident is it.' Auburn et al. concluded that, by upgrading the violence and constructing the offence as distinctly aggressive, the officer attributes responsibility to the suspect.

To summarise, there is a distinctive paedophile discourse of minimisation and denial, which strives to reformulate relationships between adults and children as romantic unions devoid of sexual contact. However, the investigative interview requires that police officers avoid normalising, emotional talk and encourage suspects to discuss their offences in explicit detail. These two conflicting approaches to describing child sexual abuse have significant implications for eliciting information in the police interview. Previous discourse research has identified rhetorical devices employed by police officers to upgrade accountability and formulate a 'preferred' version of events. Studies have also demonstrated the discursive resources employed by suspects to mitigate liability and redefine criminal acts as justified. However, research has failed to determine whether these resources are used to formulate sexual activity between an adult and a child as rational and acceptable.

There is an obvious need for a detailed qualitative understanding of the language interaction between the police officer and the paedophile. Are the two conflicting approaches to describing paedophilia suggested in the literature evident in the police interview? If so, how do speakers negotiate an account of a paedophilic offence whilst managing accountability, blame and denial?

Method

Materials

The interview examined in this chapter was extracted from a corpus of eleven police interviews with perpetrators of sexual offences against children, the analysis of which formed the basis of a more wide-ranging study (Benneworth, 2004). The interview was conducted at a Police Constabulary Child Protection Unit in 2001 and was tape-recorded as part of the requirements of the Police and Criminal Evidence Act (PACE) of 1984. This particular case study involves a 52-year-old male suspected of acts of gross indecency with a nine-year-old female and the suspect is being questioned for the first time following arrest. The suspect admits to the allegations whilst formulating a mitigating narrative which diminishes his own accountability. This case was selected for analysis as it provides a fascinating demonstration of how a police officer, whilst pursuing a description of sexual contact, negotiates an account of a paedophilic offence with a suspect who employs a self-serving discourse of personal bonds and emotions.

Transcription

The interview was transcribed using the system of notation developed by Gail Jefferson (see Appendix for transcription notation).[3] The contributions of the interviewer and the suspect to the discursive interaction were recorded using symbols to represent the paralinguistic features of the talk, for example, the beginning and end points of the speaker's turns, overlaps and interruptions, the pace, volume and intonation of speech and the duration and characteristics of pauses and emphasis.

Analysis and discussion

The first mention of the relationship between the suspect and the alleged victim occurs in extract 1, which is preceded only by interview preliminaries such as introductions and details of the location, date and time of the interview. The extract demonstrates the use of emotional discourse, typically associated with the accounts of paedophiles, by the suspect *and* the police officer. The bond between the suspect and the child is delicately characterised by the police officer as an attachment of innocence and 'feelings' in the use of emotive terms and euphemisms, which is then confirmed by the suspect. By attending to past events, the police officer constructs the idea of 'relationship' development, retaining the emotional discourse whilst implicitly suggesting sexual activity.

'Bright little kid'

Extract 1

```
106 DC:   What–what would dictate (1.2) uh whether or not
107       you would be able to see her or get together
108       with her?
109 Susp: Just uh, what–what load I've got on at the park
110       and whether or not I would be able to spend the
111       time (.) going round with her, uh, during that
112       period.
113       (2.0)
114 DC:   Once this had all started then hhh (0.6) when
115       your–when you first started taking to her–her
116       to the park and you got to know the family
117       (1.2) w–what were your feelings towards Lucy.
118       (2.0)
119 Susp: °Bright little kid.° (0.6) uh somebody who's
120       interested in wildlife and I started showing
121       her the wildlife,
122 DC:   And (.) this was about three years ago you say
123       so (1.6) what–take me through that
124       relationship, how did it develop to the point
125       where (0.8) y'know, hhh ( . . . ) here today.
126 Susp: Well she picked up on uh (2.4) I opened my car
127       b–uh–boot one day an–and inadvertently there
128       were some magazine there °and s–she° .hhh <u>very</u>
129       <u>interested</u> in them and <u>curious</u> etc, as °ch–
130       children of that age w–would be I would
131       imagine.°
132 DC:   Mmm.
133 Susp: °Mmm and then it developed from there.°
```

In line 114, the police interviewer adopts relationship discourse to address the emotional association between the suspect and the child. The narrative commences with 'Once this had all started', a formulation which sets the scene and attends to the minimisation and ambiguity characteristic of paedophile discourse. To identify 'this', it is necessary to consider the previous question–answer pairing of lines 106–112. The police officer describes the early activity between suspect and child as 'to see her or get together with her', vague and euphemistic and marked with conversational difficulty in the form of noticeable stuttering and hesitation, 'what–what would dictate (1.2) uh'. This question invites, and is subsequently followed by, an equally innocuous response. The two individuals do not appear to be discussing the particulars of an initial meeting between a paedophile and his victim, more the early stages of an adult friendship.

The suspect confirms the police officer's euphemistic conceptualisation of 'this' by adding 'spend the time (.) going round with her'. It is apparent in the first utterance, 'what would dictate (1.2) uh whether or not you would be able to see her' that the police officer is inviting the suspect to provide externalised reasons for the companionship, '*what* would dictate' rather than '*who*'. This externalisation is demonstrated in the following response, 'what load I've got on at the park'. His role and responsibilities as a park keeper determine whether he meets the child rather than his interest or attraction, the intervention of her family or the preferences of the victim. It is interesting to note the final utterance of the suspect in lines 111–112, 'during that period'. The suspect locates these events, the ambiguity of 'seeing her', 'getting together with her' and 'spending the time going round with her', in the past. This implies a sense of change and development to justify arriving at the present.

The police officer continues in lines 114–116, 'when your–when you first started taking to her–her to the park and you got to know the family', recounting additional events to clarify the historical period in question. The significance of taking the child to the park and becoming familiar with her family once more directs the narrative towards 'relationship' talk, rather than questioning the onset of sexual activity. This is reinforced in 'w–what were your feelings towards Lucy', a question inviting relationship discourse from the suspect. It could be argued that 'feelings' denote emotions beyond that of a friendship with a child. The suspect is not asked *if* he had feelings for the victim, rather *what* were those feelings. The existence of feelings could be perceived as either innocent or sexual, yet the question permits an innocent response. The police officer invites the suspect to recount his feelings towards the victim in a non-threatening question devoid of action and sexual/criminal terminology. This is illustrated by the innocuous response of the suspect in line 119.

Following a significant hesitation in line 118, the suspect responds with 'bright little kid', an appropriate description of a nine-year-old girl. However, considering the police officer's request for 'feelings', the suspect provides a response which avoids *emotions*, for example, the utterance does not commence with 'I feel . . . about Lucy'. The suspect provides a non-criminal and non-sexual account of the child, describing her character and actions whilst detracting from his own, 'somebody who's interested in wildlife'. The description 'bright little kid . . . interested in wildlife' serves to distance him from the potential incrimination of having 'feelings' towards the child.

By constructing an image of an inquisitive, intelligent child, the suspect is imbuing her with curiosity and maturity. This account, coupled with the knowledge that the suspect is a park keeper lessens his responsibility and provides a justification for the encounters. An indirect device for attributing blame is role talk, where acting in line with a particular personality or occupation is discursively deployed as a form of attributional accounting (Edwards and Potter, 1992). As an older, wiser 'guide' he is simply encouraging an inquisitive child and enabling her to benefit from his work experience. The appropriateness of the relationship is suggested by the innocence of the question–answer pairing and the depiction of a 'normal' adult–child companionship.

In line 122, the police officer invites the suspect to provide a further description of the 'relationship', orienting to the emotive discourse of the suspect. The 'bright little kid' account is treated as an appropriate start to the narrative in that the interviewer does not repeat the question or indicate dissatisfaction with the response. The suspect's feelings or the details surrounding the start of the relationship are not challenged. The police officer is more interested in the events leading up to and resulting in sexual contact between the suspect and the child, the reasons for the arrest rather than the feelings of the suspect. It may also suggest that the suspect's avoidance of talking about his explicit feelings and motivations incites the police officer to reformulate the initial question to re-establish intimacy, physical contact and intent.

The police officer resumes the questioning with 'And (.)'. The reformulation of the suspect's account, from 'during that period' into the more explicit 'three years ago', serves to locate the narrative and the concept of 'bright little kid' in the past. This summarising of the 'gist' of a speaker's previous utterance 'is common in institutionalised, audience-directed interaction' (Heritage, 1985, cited in Hutchby and Wooffitt, 1998: 152). The police interviewer constructs a more precise timeframe, 'this was about three years ago you say', as a means of placing information the suspect has clearly provided *off* the record (due to its absence in the interview transcription) *on* the audiotape of the police interview. The rhetorical device of 'recruiting the record' (Antaki and Leudar, 2001) attributes specific detail to the discourse of the conversational opponent, subsequently diminishing the interest and partiality of the surrounding message. The significant pause 'three years ago you say so (1.6)' would have enabled the suspect to interrupt with 'no, I didn't say that' or 'it wasn't three years ago', but he chooses not to deny the allegation and the information is put on the record. In the statement, the police interviewer seeks confirmation that the suspect was aware that the victim was nine years old at the onset of the offending and the relationship between the paedophile and the child endured a 'development' of increased physical closeness.

The police officer's invitation to 'take me through that relationship' indicates knowledge of a 'transition', the idea that the feelings of the suspect towards the victim must have *changed* from 'bright little kid' to justify his arrest. It assumes that the relationship is now less than innocent and invites an account of the events that occurred during the previous three years to the point where the suspect is being questioned for acts of gross indecency. The utterance, 'how did it develop', skilfully addresses the notion of relationship development and of course, if the contact is between a 'mature' male and female there is a suggestion that this contact will be sexual in nature. The police interviewer seeks a physical account, from initial 'feelings' to 'the point where ... here today', whilst avoiding sexual/criminal discourse and adopting the relationship talk characteristic of the suspect. This form of questioning enables the suspect to continue his narrative of friendship and innocence, a more direct question concerning bodily contact almost certainly inviting a denial. The police officer's speech is hesitant and suggests conversational difficulty. The use of euphemisms such as 'it' and 'y'know' avoid sexual or criminal detail, minimise the acts of indecency and imply a shared understanding between the interviewer and the suspect. The interviewer would expect a response portraying a sequence of events culminating in the incident that led to his arrest.

At this point, unless the suspect chooses to deny the allegations, he must provide a narrative account of transition, constructing the development of the role of the victim, his feelings or the relationship to explain how the concept of 'bright little kid' became something less innocent. The suspect treats the question, 'how did *it* develop' as addressing the sexual component of the relationship and the ambiguous 'here today' as representing his arrest for sexual offences. The ambiguous language enables the suspect to tell his story whilst avoiding sexual and criminal discourse. In line 126, the suspect does not commence by describing the requested sequence of events culminating in his arrest. He selects one event to epitomise the transition from innocent to not so innocent, 'Well she picked up on uh ...' immediately portraying the victim as an active agent in the event. However, this utterance is then reformulated 'Well she picked up on uh (2.4) I opened my car b–uh–boot one day.' It can be argued that the original formulation would have depicted the victim as reacting to the behaviour or actions of the suspect, for example, 'she picked up on ... the fact that I had magazines in my car'. The suspect then offers a self-repair following a prolonged pause and reconstructs the event as more factual and normalised, 'I opened my car b–uh–boot one day an–and inadvertently there were some magazines there.' The first mention of sexual activity between the suspect and the child is associated with an accident, when the child 'inadvertently' saw the suspect's pornography.

The use of the rather commonplace 'I opened my car boot one day ...' before recounting an unusual event is a means of grounding it in normality

(Wooffitt, 1992). It is a discursive device for the production of ordinariness in a rhetorical sense, a routine feature of reporting dubious or unusual experiences. It can be likened to Sacks' (1984) 'I was just doing X . . . when Y', a two-part device in spoken recollections of extraordinary experiences used to counter potentially negative or unsympathetic inferences. The 'X' represents the speaker's activity or state, in this case, a normal male opening his car boot, and the 'Y' is a description of the speaker's first awareness of the particular phenomenon, the realisation that a child was looking. This enables the suspect to distance himself, his actions and intentions from the consequences. The normalising utterance 'one day' implies that the day in question could have been *any* day; there was nothing special about this particular day. The 'magazines' are not described as pornography, a more suitable description of the material. However, it is acceptable for a mature male to possess pornographic material, more acceptable than to admit to sexual relations with a child.

The incident is portrayed as accidental, lessening his responsibility and placing the blame on external circumstances. The victim becomes the central character and her reaction to his innocuous opening of the car boot is pivotal to the account, 's–she° .hhh very interested in them and curious etc'. This reinforces his characterisation of Lucy as an inquisitive child. The victim is portrayed as a 'bright little kid', intelligent and *agentic*, whether the suspect is describing her interest in wildlife or the pornography in his car. The suspect lessens the individuality of the victim and normalises the incident by claiming, 'ch–children of that age w–would be'. This attends to common knowledge and the generalised notion of inquisitive children. It also performs the delicate task of ascribing responsibility to the victim (she was very interested and curious) yet she is not entirely blamed (children are like that). The use of 'I would imagine' is used to express doubt and make him seem more 'reasonable' (Edwards, 1997). It is also a defence that implies uncertainty and a lack of knowledge regarding the sexual interest in children. The suspect succeeds in recasting events in which the victim becomes the agent whilst attending to the fallibility of memory and displaying concerns for truth and accuracy. Once again, the suspect describes the actions of the victim in such a way to minimise the seriousness of his own actions.

When invited to take the police officer 'through that relationship', the suspect selects one event which, to him, encapsulates the required 'transition'. It can be argued that one depiction of child eagerness is not an adequate account of the three years leading to his arrest. However, in response to the subsequent repair, 'how did it develop to the point where (0.8) y'know, hhh (. . .) here today', the incident is representative of *change*. The detective constable does not indicate that the response is inappropriate and encourages the suspect to continue his narrative, 'Mmm'. This is followed by 'then it developed from there' in which the euphemistic and externalised 'it' is employed to denote progression to sexual activity.

'There' represents the victim's curiosity following the inadvertent exposure to pornographic material. This is a narrative recounting a transition from innocence to sexuality and the suspect's response indicates that he has indeed interpreted the previous question in this way. The child's interest becomes a pivotal factor in the instigation of sexual activity, a common justification by paedophiles for sexual acts with children (Howitt, 1995). There is no mention of the responsibility of the suspect due to the externalisation of agency and victim-blame.

The previous analysis has demonstrated how, in the skilled use of relationship talk, the police officer encourages the suspect to generate a narrative of innocence, friendship and victim maturity. The police officer then attends to the suspect's account of past events, the innocence of 'getting together with her' in the park, to suggest transition, a sense of change and development to justify arriving at the present. This extract reveals significant movement in both the characterisation of the victim and the description of the relationship. The next extract focuses on a portrayal of the victim which is *more* than 'bright little kid'. As the interest of the victim in wildlife and sexual behaviour 'developed from there', so does her role on the instigation of sexual activity. The suspect's utterance 'it developed from there' implies that there is more of this physical relationship to come, in a narrative that will bring this account up to the present day.

'Just good friends'

Extract 2

```
223 DC:     Right were you flattered b:::y what you saw as
224         the attentions of a much younger (.) [person.]
225 Susp:                                        [I was ]
226         of course I was fla(hh)ttered. (1.0) Very much
227         so.
228 DC:     How did yo::u, how did you view your
229         relationship, with Lucy (.) [as it developed. ]
230 Susp:                                [Just good friends]
231         I mean .hhh we could we could we could go on,
232         n–n–not bother about anything then other times
233         I said how'dya feel and she said oh yeah she
234         was .hhh I'm not saying this as any disrespect
235         towards Lucy but she (.) quite enjoyed being uh
236         the little sessions.
237 DC:     Right you mean the–the sexual ses[sions. ]
238 Susp:                                     [But even] th–
239         that's no excuse for what I did. I must
240         emphasise that, it's no excuse and I know (.)
241         it shouldn't have happened.
```

This extract is pivotal in the exploration of inappropriate descriptions as it represents a shift from the safe discourse of 'bright little kid' to the inference of sexual contact in 'just good friends'. The police interviewer continues the questioning with 'Right', indicating acceptance of the suspect's previous turn and a change of direction, in this case to more recent activities. In lines 223–224, the police interviewer generates a scenario involving the attentions of a younger female for an older male, an utterance devoid of sexual or criminal terminology. The police interviewer employs the notion of flattery to suggest that the victim's interest in wildlife, which would not have induced feelings of flattery in the suspect, has progressed to an interest in *him*. The police interviewer adopts the suspect's strategies of minimisation and normalisation by describing the victim as a neutralised 'younger person' rather than 'Lucy' or 'the child'. This also attends to the common misperception in paedophiles of mutual attraction with a younger sexual partner (Howitt, 1995). However, the footing 'what you saw' read-dresses the accountability of the suspect and distances the police interviewer from the *suspect's* formulation of the incident. The interviewer does not ask, 'was the younger person attracted to you?' a closed question explicitly addressing the agency of the victim, due to the potential for an outright denial on the part of the suspect. The attentions of the younger person are portrayed as *experienced*, and agreement with 'were you flattered' implies agreement with 'what *you* saw as the attentions of a much younger person'. The distinctive event construction of 'what you saw as the attentions of a much younger (.) person.' is delicately managed. The use of the ambiguous 'younger person' implies an individual older and more capable of inspiring flattery than a 'bright little kid'. This normalising description could easily be referring to a romantic partnership between a middle-aged male and a slightly younger female in its avoidance of paedophilia. However, the question is potentially incriminating as the victim is described as 'much younger', in this case, than the 52-year-old suspect, as opposed to being merely 'younger'.

In line 225, the suspect interrupts the police interviewer prior to the completion of his turn. This could have been due to the presence of a pause and subsequent 'transitional relevance place' (Sacks et al., 1978, cited in Nofsinger, 1991) or the suspect hastening to agree. The emphatic 'of course' and 'very' normalise the suggestion, implying that flattery would be a natural response to the sexual advances of a younger person. However, agreeing to feelings of flattery creates difficulty for the suspect and introduces more of a sexual tone than the chastised 'bright little kid' of the previous extract. The sexual interest of a nine-year-old female for a 52-year-old male would typically met by avoidance and concern for the welfare of the child and the suspect must now negotiate the dilemma of conveying the potential recip-rocation of these attentions. The police interviewer treats this response as satisfactory by continuing with the next question.

The police interviewer attends to the suspect's formulation of the incident in lines 228–229 by minimising the contact between the perpetrator and the victim as a 'relationship', rather than 'offence' or 'sexual acts'. The question 'how did you view your relationship with Lucy (.) as it developed.' invites the suspect to explain this attachment whilst managing a topic change from internalised feelings to direct involvement with the victim. The utterance seeks confirmation that the suspect perceived himself to be in 'relationship' ('how did you view') whilst encompassing an accusation (you had a 'relationship with Lucy'). The interviewer avoids asking 'did you have a relationship with Lucy?' due to the potential for an outright denial. Rather, the police interviewer depicts the bond between the paedophile and the child as experienced so that a response to 'how did you view' implies agreement with 'your relationship ... as it developed'. The police officer once again constructs the relationship as enduring a progression, retaining emotional discourse whilst implying the instigation of sexual activity. The question invites the suspect to clarify *his* perceptions of the events culminating in his arrest. The police interviewer also utilises the euphemistic discourse characteristic of the paedophile in 'as *it* developed'. The use of 'it' to represent the sexual contact between adult and child is ambiguous and normalises an abnormal situation.

The seemingly innocuous 'just good friends' in line 230 creates difficulty for the suspect. In an attempt to normalise the bond, the suspect employs a cliché. However, the utterance represents appropriate 'relationship' discourse for the wrong relationship. 'Just good friends' is a denial when the individuals in question are potential candidates for a sexual partnership, 'we're not having sex but we *could* be'. A nine-year-old female and a 52-year-old male are not conventional candidates for either a sexual relationship or a good friendship. The use of the modifier 'just' is a rhetorical defence with a mitigating function, as in *simply* or *only* good friends, a means of downplaying an offence and disclaiming blameworthiness. In 'The semantics of *just*', Lee (1987) differentiated the *contrastive* 'just' which minimises the significance of a focal process by explicit comparison with a referent process, 'I'm not hurting the child, *just* showing love' (Jenkins-Hall, 1989: 209), and the *non-contrastive* 'just', 'One offender told me that the abuse of his daughter happened when he turned round and his penis *just* went in her mouth' (Wyre, 1989: 19). Such rhetorical defences are characteristic of the interpretive framework of the paedophile, enabling them to justify the offending behaviour and construe the motives of the victims as sexual. The utterance 'just good friends' conveys what it strives to deny and the suspect succeeds in both addressing and evading the sexual component of the accusation. In this example, 'just' friendship was introduced as a means of avoiding discussing the existence of a sexual relationship. The more the suspect attempts to minimise the act, the more the paedophile and child are portrayed as more than 'just good friends'. The suspect minimises the offence using a euphemistic 'anything' to denote sexual contact and avoids agency by suggesting mutuality, 'we could go on, n–n–not bother about anything'. However, in an effort to downplay the contact as occasional, the suspect implies that sometimes they *could* bother about 'anything'. The previous justification succeeds in incriminating the suspect as he explains how the child and himself are 'just good friends' because they sometimes have sexual contact.

The police interviewer avoids directly asking the suspect about physical contact, yet the suspect provides, with considerable conversational diffi-culty, a description of a sexual encounter. It is a non-sexual account and the suspect's role in the instigation of sexual activity is confined to a casual, non-threatening, 'how'dya feel?' The responsibility is placed solely with the seemingly willing victim in agreeing to the act, 'she said oh yeah'. Direct quotation in the guise of verbatim recall or 'active voicing' is commonly used to construct an account as factual and create an impression of perceptual re-experience (Edwards and Potter, 1992). The complex disclaimer, 'I'm not saying this as any disrespect towards Lucy' can be perceived as an attempt to absolve himself from the act of disrespecting his victim. This is followed by a significant repair in lines 235–236 where the child 'quite enjoyed being uh the little sessions'. The utterance 'she quite enjoyed *being*' may have implied that the victim was responding to the actions of the suspect, whilst 'little sessions' is agency-neutralised and suggests mutual participation. The sexual act is admitted by implication as the euphemistic 'little session' and the only detailed actions are attributed to the victim. As with the 'anything' of line 232, the suspect formulates a minimised and playful event with no sexual discourse. The conversational exchange in lines 223–236 could have occurred between any individuals embarking on a mature, romantic rela-tionship. The episode represents a normalised account of flattery in response to the attentions of a younger female, however, in line 230 the suspect contradicts the description he was attempting to construct by claming that they were 'just good friends'. This is an inappropriate expression considering the age of the female and the progression of the narrative; friendship would not induce feelings of flattery. In addition, the utilisation of the child-like 'little sessions' to denote sexual activity in line 236 disrupts the normalised narrative of a mature, romantic relationship.

The utterance in line 237 represents a 'switch' from the police officer's use of emotional discourse to more physical detail, reformulating the contact between the paedophile and the child from '*little* sessions' to '*sexual* sessions'. The police interviewer treats the suspect's terminology as unsatisfactory, employing the first sexual term of the interview to confirm the physical nature of the relationship. The use of 'you mean' indicates the intention of the police interviewer to reformulate the previous utterance, rather than 'do you mean' which would invite the suspect to deny the physical contact. This technique of 'restatement with repair' is common in legal discourse

(Atkinson and Drew, 1979). It is a form of clarification, retaining features of the original account whilst imposing a new agenda. The claim 'you mean the sexual sessions' is also a rhetorical device for recruiting the record (Antaki and Leudar, 2001) and can be likened to the utterance 'this was about three years ago you say' in line 122 of extract 1. For the benefit of the audiotaped interview, this attributes bodily detail to the discourse of the suspect and diminishes the interviewer's interest in depicting the physical nature of the relationship between the paedophile and the child. In line 237, the suspect interrupts the switch in discourses and attempts to manage the dilemma of excusing his own behaviour and blaming the victim by claiming that her 'enjoyment' was no justification for his role in situation. The suspect must construct the account so it will be heard as coming from a sincere, rational individual who is aware of the law, 'it's no excuse and I know it shouldn't have happened'. However, the sexual aspect of the question is ignored and he once again fails to provide detail in the euphemistic '*what* I did' and '*it* shouldn't have happened'. The fact that the suspect is not denying the reformulation of the police interviewer indicates that he is implicitly *accepting* the interpretation.

Conclusion

In the previous extracts, the police officer surrenders the floor to the suspect using emotional discourse and open questioning, 'w–what were your feelings towards Lucy' (line 117, extract 1) and 'how did you view your relationship, with Lucy' (lines 228–229, extract 2). The suspect, permitted to formulate his own self-serving narrative, recounts an elaborate emotional history incorporating victim-blame and minimisation. 'Bright little kid' (line 119, extract 1) is an appropriate description of a child by an adult utilising 'safe' discourse. The suspect depicts the victim as expressing curiosity in the presence of pornographic material, 's–she° .hhh very interested in them and curious' (lines 128–129, extract 1) and the offending behaviour is formulated as an ambiguous 'it developed from there' (line 133, extract 1). In the second extract, the suspect characterises the victim using inappropriate descriptions, 'just good friends' (line 230, extract 2). The suspect attends to the notion of accountability by constructing sexual activity as a consequence of the enjoyment and willingness of the victim, 'she (.) quite enjoyed being uh the little sessions' (lines 235–236, extract 2). The police officer then switches to the use of bodily discourse to reformulate the suspect's innocuous 'little sessions' as '*sexual* sessions' (line 237, extract 2). This enables the police officer to elicit a compromising disclosure from the suspect, 'that's no excuse for what I did . . . I know (.) it shouldn't have happened' (lines 238–241, extract 2).

Police officers and paedophiles describe sexual acts between adults and children differently. While the research supports the previous notion that language clashes shape the progression of the investigative interview (Linell et al., 1993), the findings also offer guidelines about resolving the dilemma of the clash of discourses. The emotional language employed by the paedophile is insufficient for obtaining accurate descriptions of criminal behaviour. However, rather than coercing the suspect to utilise graphic bodily terminology when discussing the paedophilic act, it is more effective for the police interviewer to adopt the relationship talk characteristic of the suspect and encourage the formulation of a justificatory and potentially incriminating narrative. While the current research reinforces the premise that effective police interviewing requires the suspect to generate an uninterrupted account (Mortimer, 1994; Shepherd, 1991), the analysis also reveals that effective interviewing is not simply a case of permitting the suspect to 'tell the story'. The police officer in the previous episodes adopts an 'open' style of interviewing, incorporating the management of conflicting discourses of paedophilia and the use of reformulating questions which move *beyond* the suspect's mitigating account to confirm the occurrence of sexual contact.

A common assertion in police interviewing research is that officers are unable to convince blameworthy individuals to admit their guilt (Milne and Bull, 1999). However, the understanding that the police officer can determine the use of 'open' interviewing, with the suspect reacting discursively to the style of questioning, may offer hope to police officers. The findings suggest that if police officers interview suspects effectively they *can* make a difference to the outcome. If discourse analysis can identify ethical ways of encouraging a guilty paedophile to confess, it has a great deal to offer the study of police interviewing in general.

Notes

1. I would like to thank the Economic and Social Research Council (ESRC) for funding the Postdoctoral Fellowship during which this paper was written.
2. The DSM-IV-TR (Diagnostic and Statistical Manual of Mental Disorders, Fourth Edition, Text Revision, 2000) defines a paedophile as an individual, aged 16 years or older, who experiences 'recurrent, intense sexually arousing fantasies, sexual urges, or behaviours involving sexual activity with a prepubescent child or children (aged 13 years or younger)'. However, not all paedophiles act out their preferences and the practice of paedophilia is not specified as such in criminal law. It can be argued that sexual acts with children are essentially paedophilic in nature and the term 'paedophile' is commonly recognised in the social science research vocabulary of sex offending. Therefore, for the purpose of clarity, this chapter will adopt the definitional system employed by Howitt (1995) and utilise the term 'paedophilia' as 'a generic name for sexual offenders against underage persons' (p. 17).
3. To conform to the ethical requirements of confidentiality, the data was anonymised by removing names and locations which could be attributed to parties involved in the case.

References

Abel, G. G., Becker, J. V. and Cunningham-Rathner, J. (1984) Complications, consent and cognitions in sex between children and adults. *International Journal of Law and Psychiatry*, 7 (1): 89–103.

Antaki, C. and Leudar, I. (2001) Recruiting the record: Using opponents' exact words in parliamentary argumentation. *Text*, 21 (4): 467–88.

Atkinson, J. M. and Drew, P. (1979) *Order in Court: the Organisation of Verbal Interaction in Judicial Settings*. London: Macmillan.

Auburn, T., Drake, S. and Willig, C. (1995) 'You punched him, didn't you?': Versions of violence in accusatory interviews. *Discourse & Society*, 6 (3): 353–86.

Auburn, T. and Lea, S. (2001) Doing cognitive distortions: A discursive psychology analysis of sex offender treatment talk. *British Journal of Social Psychology*, 42 (2): 281–98.

Benneworth, K. (2004) A discursive analysis of police interviews with suspected paedophiles: The implications of 'open' and 'closed' interviewing for admission and denial. Unpublished PhD thesis: Loughborough University.

Billig, M. (1997) The dialogic unconscious: Psychoanalysis, discursive psychology and the nature of repression. *British Journal of Social Psychology*, 36 (2): 139–59.

Billig, M. (2001) Discursive approaches to studying conscious and unconscious thoughts. In D. L. Tolman and M. Brydon-Miller (eds) *From Subjects to Subjectivities: A Handbook of Interpretive and Participatory Research Methods*. New York: New York University Press. pp 290–303.

Ceci, S. J. and Bruck, M. (1993) The suggestibility of the child witness: A historical review and synthesis. *Psychological Bulletin*, 113 (3): 403–39.

Clarke, C. and Milne, R. J. (2001) *National Evaluation of the PEACE Investigative Interviewing Course*. London: Home Office.

Coates, L., Beavin Bavelas, J. and Gibson, J. (1994) Anomalous language in sexual assault trial judgments. *Discourse & Society*, 5 (1): 189–206.

DeYoung, M. (1988) The indignant page: Techniques of neutralisation in the publications of pedophile organisations. *Child Abuse and Neglect*, 12 (4): 583–91.

DeYoung, M. (1989) The world according to NAMBLA: Accounting for deviance. *Journal of Sociology and Social Welfare*, 16 (1): 111–26.

Diagnostic and Statistical Manual of Mental Disorders, Fourth Edition, Text Revision. (2000) American Psychiatric Association. http://www.behavenet.com/capsules/disorders/pedophiliaTR.htm (accessed 09/08/2005).

Drew, P. (1990) Strategies in the contest between lawyer and witness in cross-examination. In J. N. Levi and A. G. Walker (eds) *Language in the Judicial Process*. New York: Plenum Press. pp 39–64.

Drew, P. and Heritage, J. (1992) Analysing talk at work: An introduction. In P. Drew and J. Heritage (eds) *Talk at Work: Interaction in Institutional Settings*. Cambridge: Cambridge University Press. pp. 3–65.

Edwards, D. (1997) *Discourse and Cognition*. London: Sage.

Edwards, D. and Potter, J. (1992) *Discursive Psychology*. London: Sage.

Fisher, R. P. and Geiselman, R. E. (1992) *Memory-Enhancing Techniques for Investigative Interviewing: the Cognitive Interview*. Springfield, Ill.: Charles C. Thomas.

Geiselman, R. E., Fisher, R. P., Hutton, L. A., Sullivan, S. J., Avetissian, I. V. and Prosk, A. L. (1984) Enhancement of eyewitness memory: An empirical evaluation of the cognitive interview. *Journal of Police Science and Administration*, 12 (1): 74–80.

Gudjonsson, G. H. (1992) *The Psychology of Interrogations, Confessions and Testimony*. Chichester: Wiley.

Howitt, D. (1995) *Paedophiles and Sexual Offences Against Children*. Chichester: Wiley.

Hutchby, I. and Wooffitt, R. (1998) *Conversation Analysis. Principles, Practices and Applications*. Cambridge: Polity Press.

Irving, B. L. (1980) *Police Interrogation: a Case Study of Current Practice*. Royal Commission on Criminal Procedure. Research study No. 2. London: HMSO.

Jenkins-Hall, K. D. (1989) Cognitive restructuring. In D. R. Laws (ed.) *Relapse Prevention with Sex Offenders*. New York: Guildford Press. pp 207–15.

Komter, M. L. (1994) Accusations and defences in courtroom interaction. *Discourse & Society*, 5 (2): 165–87.

Lamb, M. E., Sternberg, K. J. and Orbach, Y. (1999) Forensic interviews of children. In A. Memon and R. Bull (eds) *Handbook of the Psychology of Interviewing*. Chicester: Wiley. pp 253–77.

Lea, S. and Auburn, T. (2001) The social construction of rape in the talk of a convicted rapist. *Feminism and Psychology*, 11 (1): 11–33.

Lee, D. (1987) The semantics of *just*. *Journal of Pragmatics*, 11 (3): 377–98.

Linell, P., Alemyr, L. and Jonsson, L. (1993) Admission of guilt as a communicative project in judicial settings. *Journal of Pragmatics*, 19 (2): 153–76.

Linell, P. and Jönsson, L. (1991) Suspect stories: Perspective-setting in an asymmetrical situation. In I. Marková and K. Foppa (eds) *Asymmetries in Dialogue*. Hemel Hempstead: Harvester Wheatsheaf. pp. 75–100.

Marshall, W. L., Hamilton, K. and Fernandez, Y. (2001) Empathy deficits and cognitive distortions in child molesters. *Sexual abuse: a Journal of Research and Treatment*, 13 (2): 123–30.

Milne, R. and Bull, R. (1999) *Investigative Interviewing: Psychology and Practice*. Chichester: Wiley.

Mortimer, A. (1994) Asking the right questions. *Policing*, 10 (2): 111–24.

Nofsinger, R. E. (1991) *Everyday Conversation*. London: Sage.

Perlman, N. B., Ericson, K. I., Esses, V. M. and Isaacs, B. J. (1994) The developmentally handicapped witness: Competency as a function of question format. *Law and Human Behavior*, 18 (2): 171–87.

Pollock, N. L. and Hashmall, J. M. (1991) The excuses of child molesters. *Behavioural Sciences and the Law*, 9 (1): 53–9.

Potter, J. (1996) *Representing Reality: Discourse, Rhetoric and Social Construction*. London: Sage.

Potter, J. (2000) Post-cognitive psychology. *Theory and Psychology*, 10 (1): 31–7.

A Practical Guide to Investigative Interviewing (2000) National Crime Faculty. Bramshill: National Crime Faculty and National Police Training.

Recorded Crime Data: UK (2004) *Home Office Research Development Statistics*. http:www.homeoffice.gov.uk/rds/recordedcrime1.html (accessed 09/08/2005)

Sacks, H. (1984) Notes on methodology. In J. M. Atkinson and J. Heritage (eds) *Structures of Social Action: Studies in Conversation Analysis*. Cambridge: Cambridge University Press. pp 21–7.

Shepherd, E. (1991) Ethical interviewing. *Policing*, 7 (1): 42–60.

Softley, P. (1980) *Police Interrogation: an Observational Study of Four Police Stations*. Royal Commission on Criminal Procedure. Research study No. 61. London: HMSO.

Underwager, R. and Wakefield, H. (1999) Sex offender treatment requiring admission of guilt. Paper presented at the 15th Annual Symposium of the American College of Forensic Psychology, April. http://www.ipt-forensics.com/library/admission.htm. (accessed 09/08/2005)

Watson, D. R. (1990) Some features of the elicitation of confessions in murder interrogations. In G. Psathas (ed.) *Interaction Competence: Studies in Ethnomethodology and Conversation Analysis*. Washington DC: University Press of America. pp 263–95.

Williamson, T. M. (1993) From interrogation to investigative interviewing: Strategic trends in police questioning. *Journal of Community and Applied Social Psychology*, 3 (2): 89–99.

Wooffitt, R. (1992) *Telling Tales of the Unexpected: the Organisation of Factual Discourse*. Hemel Hempstead: Harvester Wheatsheaf.

Wright, R. C. and Schneider, S. L. (1999) Motivated self-deception in child molesters. *Journal of Child Sexual Abuse*, 8 (1): 89–111.

Wyre, R. (1989) Working with the paedophile. In M. Farrell (ed.) *Understanding the Paedophile*. London: ISTD/The Portman Clinic. pp 17–23.

Appendix

Transcription conventions

Symbol	Meaning
(0.5)	A number in parentheses represents an interval of silence occurring within and between speaker's utterances in tenths of a second.
(.)	A dot enclosed in a bracket indicates a pause in the talk of less than two-tenths of a second (0.2)
[ ] [ ]	Square brackets between adjacent lins of concurrent speech indicate the onset and end of overlapping talk.
.hhh	A dot before an 'h' indicates an audible in-breath. The more h's, the longer the in-breath.
Hhh	An 'h' indicates an audible out-breath. The more h's the longer the out-breath. Set off with parentheses if it occurs within a word.
–	A dash indicates the sharp cut-off of the prior word or sound.
:	Colons indicate that the speaker has stretched the preceding sound. The more colons the greater the sustained enunciation.
(. . .)	Parentheses indicate the presence of an unclear fragment on the tape. The more '. . .' s the longer the unclear fragment.
.	A full stop indicates a stopping or falling intonation, which may or may not occur at the end of a turn-constructional unit.
,	A comma indicates continuing intonation, which may or may not occur at the end of a turn-constructional unit.
?	A question mark indicates rising inflection, which may or may not indicate a question.
Under	Underlined fragments indicate speaker emphasis.

(Continued)

Symbol	Meaning
°°	Degree signs indicate that the talk they encompass is quieter than the surrounding talk.
<>	Arrows pointing outwards indicate that the talk they encompass is slower than the surrounding talk.
><	Arrows pointing inwards indicate that the talk they encompass is faster than the surrounding talk.

(Adapted from Hutchby and Wooffitt, 1998: vii)

4

The Questioning of Child Witnesses by the Police and in Court: a Linguistic Comparison

Michelle Aldridge

Introduction

Since the mid 1980s, there has been a growing awareness not only of the large number of children who are, allegedly, being abused but also that their problems can be compounded by the ways in which any disclosure by, or on behalf of, the child is investigated. Historically, the investigative procedure simply was not geared towards children's differing cognitive and linguistic abilities. As noted by Davies (1991: 178–9) children were treated as second-class citizens in the eyes of the law and, not surprisingly, only a small proportion of offenders who sexually abused children were successfully prosecuted.

Fortunately, the last decade or so has seen substantial changes in the UK criminal justice system and similar developments worldwide (see Goodman and Bottoms, 1996 and Davies and Wilson, 1997 for a review) which have attempted to address the need to obtain evidentially valid accounts from child witnesses in a way which is less stressful. It is now more accepted that a child can be a reliable witness given appropriate questioning and legal procedures that take into account their age and vulnerability (Goodman and Helgeson, 1988) but have the changes gone far enough? Focusing on the child witness in England and Wales, the aims, here, are to explore their linguistic experiences during the initial police interview (evidence-in-chief) and cross-examination in cases of alleged child sexual abuse to determine whether the provision for special measures (1999 Youth Justice and Criminal Evidence Act) and the advice given by the Home Office are sufficient to ensure that children have a fair and appropriate hearing.

It is not easy to interview children. They think, for example, that adults know everything and that children ask questions and not adults (Bull, 1992). Very young children often assume that because one adult (the perpetrator) knows what took place, other adults must already know (Toglia, Ross and Ceci, 1992); many children are warned not to speak to strangers and children are generally instructed not to talk about certain topics, sex being one of them. When these facts are combined with the all-too-typical threats that abused children are given if they dare talk to anyone, then, the task of interviewing a child in instances of alleged sexual abuse is, to say the least, difficult.

Quite rightly, since the introduction, in England and Wales, of the *Memorandum of Good Practice on Video Recorded Interviews for Child Witnesses for Criminal Proceedings*, henceforth the MOGP (1992) a great deal of attention has been paid to the linguistic experiences of children in the initial police interview. Many academic researchers (see Aldridge and Wood, 1998; Birch, 2000; Bull, 1995; Davies and Wilson, 1997; Walker, 1994 and Westcott et al. 2002 amongst others for a review of relevant work) have collaborated with interviewing professionals to research the best ways to interview young children during the recording of their evidence-in-chief and it is fair to say that a great deal of progress has been made in this area. Learning from experience, the MOGP was updated in 2002 by Home Office guidelines reported in *Achieving Best Evidence in Criminal Proceedings: Guidance for Vulnerable or Intimidated Witnesses, including Children* (henceforth ABE) and it is now hoped that all vulnerable witnesses will have the opportunity to give their best evidence in criminal proceedings (ABE 1). As noted by Lamb, Strenberg and Esplin (1995: 446) 'the demonstrable fact that investigative interviews with young children can be rendered worthless by inept practice should not blind us to the substantial literature demonstrating that reliable information can be elicited from young children who are competently interviewed'. The study here, then, investigates whether the guidelines in place and the 'special measures' on offer to facilitate interviews with young children overcome the difficulties so often reported by them during the long processes of investigation and justice. Issues considered include investigating whether the training provided for interviewing officers is adequate; whether children have the opportunity to 'tell their story' during the police interview; whether their experiences during this interview prepare them linguistically for what is to come in cross-examination; and whether the recently introduced 'special measures' go far enough to advance the child witness' interests without prejudicing the defendant's position.

The four possible phases (rapport, narrative, questioning and closure) of an interview are considered but the main focus is on the questions asked by police officers and defence lawyers and on children's ability to respond to them during the police interview and subsequent cross-examination. This is done to determine the differences (if any) in language experience between the two settings and to investigate whether the opportunities for change as outlined in ABE are sufficient. In pursuing these goals, section one will give a brief review of the key guidelines in the MOGP and ABE and an overview of the aims of the police interview and cross-examination; section two will describe the study's methodology; section three will linguistically compare and contrast the two settings looking at the three interview phases of rapport, free narrative and closure; section four will focus on the questions used and answered in the initial interview and cross-examination and section five will outline key findings and recommendations.

The memorandum of good practice and achieving best evidence

Following the 1991 Criminal Justice Act, the MOGP was published, in England and Wales, to support the implementation of the video recording of a four-phased approach to interviewing young children which could stand as the child's evidence-in-chief. During the interview, the interviewer was encouraged to (i) build rapport, (ii) give the child the opportunity to give a free narrative account, (iii) ask questions (progressing from open to closed) to elicit missing information and (iv) offer closure which would summarise the interview, give the child opportunity to ask questions and provide the child with details about what would happen next. The Crown Prosecution Service would then decide whether the video could stand for the child's evidence-in-chief. In 1992, the child had to appear live for cross-examination though she[1] could be behind screens or in an adjoining room with a live link facility. In 2002, these Home Office guidelines were updated, following the 1999 Youth Justice and Criminal Evidence Act, by ABE. The phased approach to video-interviewing was maintained and its provision was extended to include vulnerable or intimidated adults. Other special measures were introduced including the removal of wigs and gowns, examination of the witness through an intermediary, the acceptance of aids to communication and video recorded cross-examination (see ABE 2002: 7 for full details). Greater detail was also provided on the planning and conducting of interviews with children and other vulnerable witnesses.

The aims of the police interview and the cross-examination

At least since PACE (1984) the aim of the police interview has been to gather information and to seek a reliable and credible account of events. Certainly, with witnesses, its aim is to be investigative and a variety of communicative strategies are adopted to encourage the witness to speak. The focus, then, is on the witness' story and the communicative behaviour of the interviewing officer is likely to be gentle, encouraging and facilitative. Within the UK's adversarial system, of course, the lawyer leading the cross-examination has a very different agenda. The defendant is his client and is assumed innocent until proven guilty. The lawyer will therefore work hard to challenge everything the witness says and indeed to give limited opportunities for the witness to tell her story. The observation made by Mauet (1992: 23) that 'open-ended questions are disastrous on cross-examination' may be typical of the type of instruction barristers receive.

In recent years, much has been written about the language used in the courts (see Conley and O'Barr, 1998; Drew, 1992; Tiersma, 1999) and the language-behaviour of lawyers aimed at undermining a witness' evidence. The power-tactics and strategies adopted by lawyers, including the use of silence and body language, topic maintenance, question form and timing, the use of repetition and intonation and so forth are well reported (see Matoesian, 1993 and Conley and O'Barr, 1998 for a review) as are the experiences of children in cross-examination (see Brennan and Brennan, 1988; Walker 1993) but of concern here is a direct comparison of the children's linguistic experiences in the initial interview and in cross-examination so that an assessment can be made of whether children are being competently interviewed as Lamb et al. (1995) advised. Remembering that 'the accuracy of a child's account clearly depends on the interviewer's skill and sensitivity to children's special vulnerabilities to questioning' (McGough and Warren, 1994: 14) and 'the skill of questioning is a key issue in effective interviews with children' (Toglia, Ross and Ceci, 1992: 72), the focus here is on question types and responses. A great deal of research and time has gone into the training of police officers in interviewing young children but has this given children false expectations of what to expect throughout the trial? Moreover, while the special measures which have been introduced to help the child through the court process are to be welcomed, are they sufficient to facilitate the giving of best evidence? Or is the legal system still an alien process for children where they still have little hope of being heard and believed? Details of the study are presented below.

The study

The data reported here are taken from 38 court transcripts and 20 police interview transcripts from two separate locations in England and Wales. These involve children aged five to sixteen years, all of whom were prosecution witnesses. The police interviews were transcribed by a researcher[2] by watching the video-interviews, after the event and following appropriate and full consent. The court transcripts were bought from the Court transcription service. They date from before the full implementation of ABE and thus, the children would be responding from behind a screen or from an adjoining room. There was no opportunity for the children to participate in pre-recorded cross-examination. The types of questions (10, 509 in total) asked in the two settings are examined to determine whether they are age-appropriate and whether they give the child the opportunity to answer. The data are quantitatively analysed using appropriate statistical packages[3] and will be qualitatively discussed in sections three and four of this chapter. Section three will focus on rapport, free narrative and closure and section

Table 4.1: Breakdown by age of the children
in the study

Age	Court	Police
5 years	1	2
6 years	4	3
7 years	4	2
8 years	6	1
9 years	5	4
10 years	4	2
11 years	8	2
12 years	2	2
13 years	2	1
14 years	1	1
16 years	1	0
Total	38	20

four will focus on questioning. In the data extracts 'C' will be used to indicate
the child witness, 'P' the police officer and 'L' the lawyer. Table 4.1 shows a
breakdown by age of the children involved in the study

Evidence of rapport, narrative and closure

Since 1992 , and the MOGP, it has been considered best practice in the police
interview to move the discussion through four phases of rapport, narrative,
questioning and closure. Questioning is the focus of section four, here, the
child's experiences during the other three phases are discussed, beginning
with rapport.

The rapport phase

A great deal of emphasis has been placed on the training of interviewing
officers in the strategy of building rapport in the initial interview. ABE,
particularly, lays out ground rules so that children are relaxed by discussion
of neutral topics and reassured that they have done nothing wrong. Similarly, the child will be empowered by a series of ground rules so that she
is reminded that she can say that she doesn't know, that the interviewer
is interested in what the child has to say as she doesn't know everything,
that the child can say anything she wants, using her chosen vocabulary,
that she can ask for a comfort break and so on. Typically, when observing
police interviews, it is clear that time is now spent establishing the aims and
conventions of the interview and relationships are established before more
sensitive issues are introduced. This is in stark contrast to the courtroom
situation where no real attempt at rapport building is made. Of course, there
may have been pre-trial visits to the Court and, most likely, the Judge has

introduced himself to the witnesses, in the presence of the lawyers, before the case begins. However, when the cross-examination begins in Court, there are no pleasantries, the defence lawyer jumps straight into direct questioning. For example, consider the opening lines of the following cross-examinations, taken at random (rather than selected) from the sample of thirty-eight. Here, introductions are kept to a minimum. There is no attempt at rapport beyond the basic check that the child can see and hear what is going on, by means of the live link monitor, and the reminder that she should try to answer honestly the questions asked.

Cross-examination of child aged 12 years

L: Hello Michelle,[4] I am going to ask you some questions. Can you hear me?
C: Yes.
L: I want to try and get some dates in your mind and then to ask you some questions about what went on between those dates.

Cross-examination of child aged 8 years

L: Hi there, Christopher. Can you see me nice and clearly? I am going to ask you some questions today and I'm going to ask you about things that happened last summer, in August, OK.

Cross-examination of child aged 7 years

L: Hello Katrina, I'm going to ask you a number of questions. I'm going to suggest things to you. I'm going to say didn't this happen, didn't that happen and you'll be able to say yes it did or no it didn't. Do you understand?

It is apparent that the child, who is already in an unfamiliar environment, in an often rather small link room, and who is forced to sit still in front of the link monitor is very quickly taken into the questioning phase and this is likely to be intimidating for even the most competent witness. Section five considers the impact of having no rapport-building phase and whether or not the special measures including the possibility of having pre-recorded cross-examination, removal of wigs and so on are sufficient to enable the child to maintain her story.

Free narrative phase
Following the rapport phase, in the initial interview, the interviewer, by use of open, wh-questions rather than more closed questions like yes/no, option and tag forms, will move the conversation into the free narrative phase where the child is given the opportunity to tell her story in her own words.

ABE advises (p. 41) that this phase is the core of the interview and the most reliable source of accurate information. During this phase, the interviewer's role is that of a facilitator and not that of an interrogator. Every effort should be made to obtain information from the child which is spontaneous and free from the interviewer's influence. It is well reported that this is a key phase as the jury is most likely to believe this part of the account as it comes without direction from a professional (Shuy, 1986, reported in Bull, 1992). Here the interviewer is encouraged to be an active listener, giving the child time to tell her story with minimal interruption. The narrative phase is typically introduced with very open questions such as *'what happened?'* and it will be followed by another open question such as *'what happened next?'* so the witness is in complete control of what material is mentioned and discussed and is less vulnerable to suggestion. A great deal of emphasis has been placed on training officers to listen and to let the child pace the interview at this point and again, looking at the police interviews we do see, in most cases, a real attempt to encourage the child to speak unprompted by the use of open questions.

This phase though has mixed success with young children because they can have problems giving information in chronological order and they can fail to give as much information as an adult witness might (see Aldridge and Wood, 1998 for details). Sooner or later, more direct questions will need to be asked. The important point to make, however, is that children are, generally, given the chance to tell their story in their own words. There is no explicit time pressure or constraints, the child has the opportunity to hold the conversational floor and the interviewer is the listener, 'merely' facilitating and providing non-leading prompts for the child to continue.

In contrast, when we look at cross-examination and as we shall see in section four when we look at the range of questions asked, we observe no narrative phase encouraged through open questions. Here, the child is quickly confronted by a series of closed questions. The defence barrister presents with a new style of questioning, at a late stage in the proceedings, which may well disempower the child. It is possible that the very differently-paced and controlled police interview has given the child false expectations about what will happen in court and section five considers whether 'the special measures' can compensate for this distinct lack of narrative oppor-tunity.

Closure

In ABE (p. 47), it is argued that every interview should have a closure phase where information is checked, the child is asked whether she has any ques-tions, is thanked for her time and effort and given appropriate advice on seeking help. The aim of closure should be that the child leaves the interview in a positive frame of mind (ABE p. 48). The following are typical examples of closure from the police-interview data.

Police interview of child aged 8 years

P: Ok. I've got nothing else to ask you now. Are there any questions you would like to ask?

(child speaks)

P: OK. Thank you very much Rhys for coming, you've been brill! The interview is now at an end (formal time details are given).

Police interview of child aged 9 years

P: Ok, that's lovely. There's nothing else I want to talk with you about. Is there anything you'd like to say? You've done very well remembering everything and you've been very good coming to see me. It's not easy with people you haven't met before, is it?

Clearly, as well as formally winding up the interview, the comments are designed to reassure the child, to acknowledge the effort involved in these discussions and to make the child realise that what she has to say is valued. Compare this with typical closure in cross-examination

Cross-examination of child aged 11 years

L: Denis, I have got to say finally just this, that I have to suggest to you that what you have said about Ted touching you in a bad way is just not right.

C: It is.

L: Thank you, that's all.

Cross-examination of child aged 12 years

L: Malcolm has never touched you in this way, has he?

C: He has.

L: He has never offered you alcohol or cigarettes, or anything of that sort, has he?

C: He has.

L: That is all I want to ask you. Thank you very much.

Cross-examination of child aged 12 years

L: Even the spanking of the bottom you were talking about, you never even talked about that to him?

C: No.

L: Thank you. Goodbye.

Even naively ignoring the complex syntactic structures and confusing use of negatives, it is clear that these words are (potentially) damaging to the child's account and of course, to her esteem. Here, the last words the child (and Jury!) hears is the lawyer doubting what she's said. Combining that with no real opportunity to defend her position nor enquire what will happen next (since from a link room, she will be unaware of proceedings), she is likely to be bewildered and disempowered. In section five, the potential impact of no closure is considered Thus far, it has been shown that three of the four phases of the initial interview are either missing or at least handled very differently in cross-examination. The questioning phase is, of course, common to both and a comparison of the use of questions and children's ability to respond to them across the two settings follows.

The questioning phase

At phase three of the initial interview, the child is questioned directly. In cross-examination, the child is questioned directly, so are these phases compatible? Before examining the questioning strategies adopted by police officers and lawyers, a brief summary is given on what is known about children's ability to answer questions. These points are illustrated using child-responses from the police interviews.

Even in everyday conversations, children can be reluctant to answer adults' questions and we are all familiar with children who find it easier to answer '*don't know*' and '*can't remember*' to every question asked. It's not surprising, then, that in the demanding legal setting all interviewers will need to work hard to overcome a child's unresponsiveness, as the following example illustrates.

Police interview of child aged 4 years

P: Where do you do your painting and gluing?
C: I'm not going to tell you.
P: Why aren't you going to tell me?
C: 'Cos I don't like telling people.
P: So who teaches you at school?
C: I'm not telling you.
P: And what are the names of the children in your class?
C: I'm not telling you.
P: We're not going to have much of a chat if you won't tell me anything!
C: I'm bored. Play with those, pretend you are my friend and I've come to tea.

Alternatively, if choosing to speak, children may pragmatically fulfil their turn-taking role by giving stereotypical responses like the following:

Police Interview of child aged 5 years

P: When do you think it happened?
C: Yesterday ago.
P: When did you last see him?
C: Yesterday.
P: Yesterday?
C: I think it was yesterday but I don't know when it was.

This may be because the child is not fully paying attention or does not want to answer the question. It is also well reported (see Ervin-Tripp, 1970; Parnell, Patterson and Harding, 1984; Savic, 1978) that children's ability to answer wh-questions varies with age, so that young children will answer *what, where* and *who* questions earlier than they will cope with *when, how* and *why*. The following is a typical example of a child's responses and her ability to answer wh-questions. *What, where* and *who* questions were answered appropriately but not *when, how* and *why*.

Police-interview of child aged 8 years

P: When did he tickle you?
C: Silence.
P: How did he do it?
C: Silence.
P: Why does it cover that part of your body?
C: Don't know.

Indeed, *why* questions should be avoided with young children as they attribute blame. Similarly, it is well reported that professionals need to use yes/no questions and tag questions with care as the young child is prone to answering 'yes', as the following example, known from the context to be incorrect, illustrates.

Police interview of a child aged 6 years

P: Can you remember my name?
C: Yeah.
P: What is it?
C: Silence.

Police interview of a child aged 7 years

P: You know this room because you've been here before.
C: Yeah.

Police interview of a child aged 5 years

I: I think you went to hospital, didn't you?
C: Yeah.

Police interview of a child aged 6 years

P: You've just moved, have you?
C: Yeah

Likewise, young children are vulnerable to option questions as they can adopt a recency strategy and give the last option as the following examples, known from the context to be incorrect, illustrate.

Police interview of child aged 6 years

I: Do you think it's yellow or orange?
C: Orange.

Police interview of child aged 6 years

I: Was it light or dark outside?
C: Dark.

Police interview of child aged 5 years

I: Were you upstairs or downstairs?
C. Downstairs

And finally, repeat questions should also be avoided as they encourage the child to change her mind as is clear below:

Police interview of child aged 3 years

P: Your nanny, why does she have to put cream on you for?
C: 'Cos I got a poorly bum.
P: Have you? Why?
C: I have.
P: Why is your bum poorly?
C: It is.
P: What do you mean by poorly? What's it like?
C: It's poorly.
P: Does it hurt?
C: No.
P: Why's it poorly then?
C: It isn't poorly.

P: It isn't poorly?
C: No, let's play jigsaws now.

Police interview of a child aged 5 years

I: How did he touch you then?
C: With his hand, I've told you once!

All these facts are well-reported in the child-language literature and are appropriately summarised in ABE (2002, 42–47) as strategies for police officers to adopt during the questioning phase. For example, advice is given such as:

- Ask only one question at a time and allow the child sufficient time to complete their answer before asking a further question.
- Silence may be the best cue for eliciting further information.
- Do not interrupt, interrupting the child may disempower the witness.
- Questions should be kept short and simple.
- Avoid double negatives (such as: Did John not say later that he had not meant to hurt you?)
- Avoid double questions (such as: Did you go next door and was Jim waiting for you?).
- The questioning phase should begin with open-ended questions and this type of question should be used widely throughout.
- Specific questions, the so-called wh-questions will be needed but why should be used with care.
- If a specific question proves unproductive, it may be useful to use a closed question.

Police officers, then, are trained in child language development issues but does this knowledge pass through to practice? And is it heeded by lawyers? This question is addressed in the next section which reports on the types and frequency of questions children experience in the initial interview and in cross-examination and how children respond. In total 10,509 questions are examined. Given that children are less suggestible with open questions; the first calculation measured (cf. Table 4.2) what percentage of questions addressed to the children were open wh-questions in the two settings and Table 4.3 summarises the figures into age bands.

Looking at Tables 4.2 and 4.3 it is clear that the police asked more wh-questions than were asked in court. An independent t-test showed this difference to be highly significant, $t = -17.080$, $p =< .0001$ (police $\underline{M} = 47.417$, $SD = 4.673$, court $\underline{M} = 13.884$, $SD = 4.535$.[5] This substantially greater use of wh-questions suggests that the police are taking more time to elicit the child's story spontaneously, to ask more questions to overcome issues such as the child's reluctance to speak and that they may well be asking more

Table 4.2: Percentage of questions addressed to the children as open wh-questions in the two settings

Age	Police	Court	Total (% open Wh-questions)
5 years	45.19	24.89	38.64
6 years	44.19	13.35	30.57
7 years	43.37	9.43	24.45
8 years	53.16	11.72	19.08
9 years	52.70	11.30	27.14
10 years	48.90	13.91	22.32
11 years	46.91	17.01	24.83
12 years	46.58	17.46	28.48
13 years	54.34	11.25	36.15
14+ years	38.78	9.06	13.64

Table 4.3: Percentage of questions summarised by age bands

Age group	Police	Court	Total
5–7 years	44.25	15.8	31.22
8–10 years	51.59	12.31	22.85
11–13 years	49.28	15.24	29.82
14–16 years	38.78	9.06	13.64

questions to check the credibility of some stereotypical responses. In court, the children's responses are much more controlled in cross-examination by greater use of closed questions which limit what the child can say. This potentially makes the child more vulnerable to suggestion and less convincing to the Jury. In brief, these figures suggest that during cross-examination the lawyer, to a very large extent, determines what the jury hears.

Of course, it is important to evaluate the quality of the questions asked as well as quantity, so the next question to ask is: What percentage of questions (cf. Table 4.4) are answered appropriately[6] by children in this study? Table 4.5 summarises by age bands.

In all age groups, and in both conditions, over 70% of 'wh' questions were answered appropriately but it is clear that the percentage of correct response improved with age in both conditions and the police were consistently better at getting appropriate responses from the witnesses. A Fisher's r to z showed this difference to be statistically significant, with a correlation of 0.721, $p = .0162$.[7] So, in terms of quality of questioning the police interview gives the child the better opportunity to answer questions since they are shown to be superior in obtaining appropriate answers. Perhaps of more interest,

Table 4.4: Percentage of questions answered 'appropriately' by children in the study

Age	Police	Court	Total
5 years	78.73	77.58	78.49
6 years	81.38	72.88	79.74
7 years	88.1	75.36	85.36
8 years	90.1	75.73	83.84
9 years	91.17	82.65	88.97
10 years	91.01	76.25	84.02
11 years	93.64	89.33	91.46
12 years	90.21	86.36	88.74
13 years	97.06	94.44	96.71
14+ years	84.21	78.08	80.77

Table 4.5: Percentage of questions answered 'appropriately' summarised by age bands

Age group	Police	Court	Total
5–7 years	82.74	75.27	81.2
8–10 years	90.76	78.21	85.28
11–13 years	93.64	90.04	92.3
14–16 years	84.21	78.08	80.77

however, is not how much the child is answering appropriately but what is happening when the child doesn't answer a question correctly, because here the 'interviewer' has the opportunity to repair the damage or do serious damage to the child's account. One possibility, illustrated here, is that the child responds inappropriately to the question.

Cross-examination of a child aged 6 years

L: Why was he smacking you?
C: Only on my arm.

Or the child can fail to give a vocal response:

Cross-examination of a child aged 6 years

L: Do you remember watching the tape? You said on the tape, didn't you, that it's very sad if people don't tell the truth, yes?
C: Silence.

Table 4.6: Level of difficulty experienced by children with the different question forms

what	which	where	who	when	why
1.19	1.2	1.23	3.53	5.56	1.75
how manner	how extent	how old	how total		
1.89	2.22	1.37	1.76		
all wh's	yes/no				
1.82	0.27	0.24	2.05	2.52	0.42

It is likely, in these instances, that the child hasn't understood the question and Table 4.6 shows the level of difficulty that children had with the different question forms (figures are percentage incorrect). While the 'incorrect' figures are low, it is noted that some difficulty is experienced with who and when questions and closed rather than open questions, which is something practitioners might wish to bear in mind. Alternatively, of course, the child may be given no opportunity to respond and thus, the jury is 'simply' hearing the officer's/lawyer's account. Here, the child is completely disempowered as the following example shows:

Cross-examination of a child aged 8 years

L: Now, are you sure there is not a light up the stairs before they turn?
C: No.
L: No, okay. So you say there is a light on. Now, your bedroom door, it doesn't open fully does it?
C: Yes.
L: You say it does. Well, think back to last year. The door did not open fully then, did it? (nor) Try to remember. If you can't remember, don't worry. You can say you don't remember.
C: I don't remember.
L: You can not remember, okay. Now, did you say someone came into your room? (nor) You said it was Arwyn, didn't you? (nor) Now would I be right if I said you couldn't really see who it was? (nor) I would suggest that you don't really know if it was Arwyn? (nor) All you could see was a figure coming into the room, that's right isn't it?

If a child can't answer a question, then, she might give a wrong answer or she may remain silent. Or, she may simply not be given the opportunity to answer and it is interesting to note when these options are occurring. Table 4.7 quantitatively summarises the data showing the mean number of questions asked at each age, the mean number of incorrect responses, the mean number of non-responses and the mean number of 'no opportunity

Table 4.7: Means of questions asked at each age, number of incorrect responses, non-responses and 'no opportunity to respond'

Age (no.)	No. of Qs (M)	Incorrect (M)	No Response	NOR
5 years (3)	240.67	5.33	7.33	32
6 years (7)	143	1.71	6.57	18.29
7 years (6)	219.83	2.17	16	15.83
8 years (7)	152.71	1	2.29	11.57
9 years (9)	156	1.23	1.67	8.78
10 years (5)	151.4	1.2	1.6	14
11 years (10)	179.2	1	0.9	10
12 years (4)	202.75	0.5	1.25	13.75
13 years (4)	189.5	0.25	1.25	7.5
14+ years (3)	317.67	1.67	3.33	27
Overall mean	182	1.43	4	14.05

Table 4.8: Means of questions asked at each age, number of incorrect responses, non-responses and 'no opportunity to respond', grouped into 3-year age bands

Age (no.)	No. of QS	Incorrect	No response	NOR
5–7 years (16)	189.75	2.56	10.25	19.94
8–10 years (21)	153.81	1.14	1.86	10.95
11–13 years (18)	186.72	0.72	1.06	10.28
14–16 years (3)	317.67	1.67	3.33	27
Overall mean	182	1.43	4	14.05

to respond'. These figures are further clarified, in Table 4.8, by grouping the children into 3-year age bands.

These tables again show that the legal system must be sensitive to age as inappropriate responses were greatest in the youngest groups as was failure to respond. The under-sevens are particularly vulnerable. It is also noted here that there were significantly more instances of 'no opportunity to respond' than of 'inappropriate responses' or 'no response' by the child. Indeed, 'no opportunity to respond' accounted for over 72% of the questions which were not answered appropriately. This is a serious observation as the child is blocked from telling her story and it is important to know when this is happening. The two settings will now be compared.

The effect of the environment

Table 4.9 shows the proportion of 'wh' and 'other' questions for which there was 'no opportunity to respond' in the police and court setting. This table

Table 4.9: Proportion of 'wh' and 'other' questions with 'no opportunity to respond' in the police and court setting

Category	Police	Court	Total
Wh questions	6.92%	14.85%	9.49%
Other questions	6.49%	7.3%	7.09%
Total	6.69%	8.31	7.71%

shows that the total number of 'no opportunity to respond questions' was higher in the courtroom than in the police interview. This is particularly so in the case of 'wh'questions, where the lawyers were twice as likely to ask them and for which there was no opportunity to respond. It seems that the lawyer is dominating the exchange in this respect, giving the child little chance of responding.[8]

Summary

There is a clear-cut difference between the questioning style used in the courtroom and that used by the police. Many have spoken before (for example Birch, 2000; Brennan, 1995; Carson, 1995; Walker, 1993) about how questioning styles vary significantly between video-recorded examination-in-chief where the examiner moves away from asking the sorts of questions which may compromise the evidential value of the answer and the cross-examination which can thrive on leading questions and we still see no change here. While the children's linguistic experiences in the police interview are generally positive, this certainly is not the case in the courtroom. The predominant trend in the corpus of court cross-examination was the presentation by the defence barrister of a series of statements without the child having any opportunity to respond. At the end of a series, the child was asked to agree or disagree. This is a very dominating, repetitive style where the child is disempowered and the jury is led by the lawyers' questioning. Much of the time, the child has no opportunity to speak and when she does it is a simple yes/no response. In brief, the data here suggest that child witnesses are having the opportunity to tell their story in the initial interview. It does appear to be the case that the training received in the last decade has significantly helped police officers interview children. In stark contrast, in cross-examination, when the barrister challenges her video-evidence, there is little (if any) opportunity for the child to defend her account. So, the jury is likely to judge the events according to the barrister's account.

Conclusions and recommendations

This study examined children's linguistic experiences during police interviews and cross-examination in cases of alleged sexual abuse and has reported that both arenas can be very challenging for the linguistically maturing child. There is no doubt that a great deal has been achieved with the MOGP, ABE and the introduction of the provision of special measures but do these reforms go far enough? Carson (1995) noted that major problems still existed in the adversarial system and in the trial lawyers' questioning techniques and we wonder whether in the last decade anything has really changed. Much has been written about the changes in the initial interview and no one would doubt that the police are now interviewing children in a much more age-appropriate way. The phases of rapport and closure offer a good framework for reassurance and guidance and now the interviewers are scheduling their questions through active listening from open to closed. The courtroom, however, remains a linguistically hostile environment where the child is denied the reassurance of rapport and closure, there is little attempt at open questions and so much of the cross-examination is achieved through a series of closed questions where to a large extent the child has no opportunity to respond. The special measures are to be welcomed, particularly because as Birch noted (2000: 223) 'their provision means that witness-vulnerability is no longer the prerogative of youth' and indeed the removal of wigs, the opportunity for an intermediary, as examples, may ease some of the tension for the child but the fact remains that, irrespective of how the lawyers are dressed, whether the child is supported by an intermediary or whether the cross-examination is pre-video-recorded, the lawyers' closed questions remain unchallenged. It disappoints the author that much reported in Carson's (1995) and Birch's (2000) work remains the same. A decade later, there is still little incentive for the lawyers to offer a less linguistically-challenging cross-examination for the witness. A set of criteria need to be adopted in court which removes the witness from the powerless position of merely being allowed to answer statements whose validity may be questionable. It remains the case, as noted by Carson (1995) and Birch (2000) that the courts (Judges) will have to take a more controlling role with regard to the form of questions if children are to function effectively as witnesses.

Notes

1. I acknowledge fully that boys are victims of child abuse but for ease of presentation I will use she as the pronoun for child witnesses.
2. Thanks go to Joanne Wood for transcribing the child witness–police interviews.
3. Thanks go to Dr Margaret Bell for her help with the statistical analysis of the data. As the groups were unequal it was not appropriate to adopt inferential statistics such as chi-square thus results were obtained through an independent t-test and Fisher's r to z.
4. For reasons of anonymity all names and locations have been changed.
5. This statistical procedure gives us a measure of the likelihood that the difference between two arithmetic means has occurred purely by chance rather than being the result of some same genuine difference between, in this case, the number

of wh-questions asked in the two settings. Here, the value of 'p' (probability or likelihood) has a value of just 1 in 10,000 so the results are highly significant.
6. Here appropriately is taken to mean a (an acceptable) response to the question asked which may be a linguistically accurate response (we can't comment on the truth value) or a nod. Incorrect/inappropriate answers include a mis-match between question form and answer as illustrated below, no response and no opportunity to respond.
7. This shows a measure of the closeness of the relationship between two variables; in this case the age of the child and the accuracy of responses. A perfect correlation would be 1.0, of course, but the obtained result shows that the two variables are strongly related to each other, with the probability of chance occurrence being about 16 in 1,000.
8. It would have been interesting and informative to look at the length of pauses in the NOR category but given that the study is based on written court transcripts where the length of pauses were not given, such an analysis was outside the scope of this investigation.

References

Aldridge, M. and Wood, J. (1998) *Interviewing Children: a Guide for Child Care and Forensic Practitioners*. Chichester: Wiley.

Birch, D. (2000) A better deal for vulnerable witnesses? *Criminal Law Review*, Apr: 223–50.

Brennan, M. (1995) The discourse of denial: Cross-examining child victim witnesses. *Journal of Pragmatics*, 23(11): 71–91.

Brennan, M. and Brennan, R. (1988) *Strange Language: Child Victims under Cross-examination*. Wagga Wagga, NSW: Riverina Murray Institute of Higher Education.

Bull, R. (1992) Obtaining evidence expertly: The reliability of interviews with child witnesses. *Expert Evidence: the International Digest of Human Behaviour, Science and Law*, 1, 3–36.

Bull, R. (1995) Interviewing children in legal contexts, in R. Bull and D. Carson, (eds) *Handbook of Psychology in Legal Contexts*. Chichester: Wiley. pp. 235–46.

Carson, D. (1995) Regulating the cross-examination of children. Paper presented at BSandL Network conference.

Conley, J. and O'Barr, W. (1998) *Just Words: Law, Language and Power*. Chicago and London: University of Chicago Press.

Davies, G. (1991) Children on trial? Psychology, video-technology and the law. *Howard Journal of Criminal Justice*, 30(3), 177–91.

Davies, G. and Wilson, C. (1997) Implementation of the Memorandum: An overview. In H. L. Westcott and J. Jones (eds) *Perspectives on the Memorandum Policy, Practice and Research in Investigative Interviews*. Aldershot: Arena. pp. 1–12.

Drew, P. (1992) Contested evidence in courtroom examination: the case of a trial for rape, in P. Drew and J. Heritage (eds) *Talk at Work: Interaction in Institutional Settings*. Cambridge: Cambridge University Press. pp. 2–65.

Ervin-Tripp, S. (1970) Discourse agreement: How children answer questions. In J. Hayes (ed.) *Cognition and the Development of Language*. New York: Wiley. pp. 79–109.

Goodman, G. S. and Bottoms, B. L. (1996) *International Perspectives on Child Abuse and Children's Testimony: Psychological Research and Law*. Thousand Oaks, Calif.: Sage.

Goodman. G. S. and Helgeson, V. (1988) Children as witnesses: What do they remember? In L. Walker (ed.) *Handbook on Sexual Abuse of Children*. New York: Springer-Verlag. pp. 109–36.

Home Office (1984) *Police and Criminal Evidence Act* (s66): Codes of Practice. London: HMSO.

Home Office and the Department of Health (1992) *Memorandum of Good Practice on Video Recorded Interviews for Child Witnesses for Criminal Proceedings*. London: HMSO.

Home Office, Crown Prosecution Service and Department of Health (2002) *Achieving Best Evidence in Criminal Proceedings: Guidance for Vulnerable or Intimidated Witnesses, including Children*. Home Office Communication Directorate.

Kranat, V. and Westcott, H. (1994) Under fire: Lawyers questioning children in criminal courts. *Expert Evidence*, 3 (1), 16–24.

Lamb, M., Strenberg, K. and Esplin, P. (1995) Making children into competent witnesses: Reactions to the amicus brief in re: Michaels. *Psychology, Public Policy and Law*, 1(2), 438–49.

Matoesian, G. (1993) *Reproducing Rape: Domination through Talk in the Courtroom*. Chicago: University of Chicago Press.

Mauet, T. (1992) *Fundamentals of Trial Techniques*. Boston: Little, Brown and Co.

McGough, L. and Warren, A. (1994) The all-important investigative interview. *Juvenile and Family Court Journal*, 45(4), 13–29.

Parnell, N. M., Patterson, S. S. and Harding, M. A. (1984) Answers to wh-questions: a developmental study. *Journal of Speech and Hearing Research*, 27(2), 297–305.

Savic, S. (1978) Strategies children use to answer questions posed by adults. In N. Waterson and C. Snow (eds) *The Development of Communication*. New York: Wiley. pp. 217–25.

Tiersma, P. (1999) *Legal Language*. Chicago: London: University of Chicago Press.

Toglia, M., Ross, D. and Ceci, S. (1992) The suggestibility of children's memory. In M. Howe, C. Brainerd and V. Reyna (eds) *The Development of Long-Term Retention*. New York: Springer-Verlag. pp. 217–41.

Walker, A. (1993) Questioning young children in court: A linguistic case study. *Law and Human Behaviour*, 17, 59–81.

Walker, A. (1994) *Handbook of Questioning Children: a Linguistic Perspective*. Washington: ABA Center on Children and Law.

Westcott, H. L., Davies, G. M. and Bull, R. H. C. (eds) (2002) *Children's Testimony. A Handbook of Psychological Research and Forensic Practice*. Chichester: Wiley.

5

The Language of Consent in Rape Law[1]

Peter M. Tiersma

The issue of consent is one of the most difficult problems in rape law. In the past, the identity of the perpetrator was frequently an issue. Yet recent advances in genetic testing will almost inevitably result in the question of 'who did it' receding into the background. As a consequence, the question of whether the woman consented is likely to receive even greater attention than it does today.

For ease of discussion, I am going to assume that rape and other sexual crimes take place between a man and a woman. To some extent I also will assume a rather stereotypical worldview in which men are sexually more aggressive, and are therefore more likely to be the rapist or perpetrator, and that women are more likely to be the victim of that aggression. Obviously, this is not always true. Sometimes women are the aggressors. And sexual crimes often enough take place when both perpetrator and victim are of the same sex. I will also leave out of consideration the special difficulties that can arise when the victim is a child. This is consistent with the existing literature, which for the most part has dealt with cases in which a man and woman have sexual intercourse, and the woman later claims that she was raped or sexually assaulted. In such cases, consent is almost always the critical issue.

I would like to begin this chapter by illustrating just how difficult the issue of consent can be. In the late 1990s I was visiting London and, finding myself with some time on my hands, decided to observe a trial at the Old Bailey. Purely by happenstance, the trial that I chose to watch involved a very interesting rape case. For ease of reference, I will call it *Regina* v. *Doe*.

Regina v. Doe

The defendant, whom we shall call Dennis, was a stocky young man, perhaps in his mid-twenties. He was born in the United Kingdom but his family came from Barbados, where he had lived for a number of years on various

83

occasions. Dennis was a university student who worked part-time to support his studies. He was also a devoted bodybuilder. He was accused of engaging in sexual penetration of the complaining witness during a specified night. The complaining witness, like the defendant, had ancestral ties to Barbados. I will refer to her as Connie.

Although jury trials are becoming less common in England, they are still used in criminal cases like this one. The jury consisted of twelve people. Based on appearances, there was one black woman, six white women, one woman who may have been mixed race or Asian, and four white men. The judge and counsel (a prosecutor and one defence lawyer) were all older white men wearing the customary horsehair wigs. The cast also included ushers and some other officials. The latter were a more diverse group than the bench and bar.

Since I was just an informal observer, I was not able to make or obtain a transcript of what exactly was said, or how it was said. In fact, for much of the trial I was forbidden by an usher to take contemporaneous notes and had to scribble a few annotations during breaks. In any event, it is not my purpose to analyse the discourse at trial. What I would like to do is to summarise the evidence that came out at the trial bearing on the issue of whether Connie consented to the intercourse with Dennis.

The undisputed facts, which the judge called *common ground* during his summation, were essentially as follows. Dennis and Connie had known each other for some time and had a relationship, which included sexual relations, during at least some of this period. At some point the relationship ended. At around this same time, Connie became increasingly active in an evangelical church.

One evening, after the relationship had ended, Connie came to visit Dennis in his flat. They ended up in his bedroom and he began to kiss various parts of her body. Apparently she did not kiss him back. He then engaged in an act of penetration. During this act of penetration, she still had her panties on. And Dennis put on a condom before the intercourse. Connie left soon thereafter. She did not make a report to the police immediately, but was convinced by a friend and member of her church to do so a few days later.

Dennis and Connie were the only people who were present during this encounter, so the 'common ground' regarding what happened can only be based on their testimony. Not surprisingly, he claimed that the sex was consensual and she claimed it was not. It would be up to the jury to decide who was telling the truth.

There were a few other witnesses, however, who presented the jury with additional information that might have relevance on the issue of consent. A friend of Connie's testified that she had persuaded an initially reluctant Connie to go to the police several days after the acts in question occurred. For the defence, a striking blond woman took the stand; she ran the gym where Dennis worked out. She was also his personal fitness trainer. She testified that on the night in question, shortly before Dennis and Connie had had intercourse, she had put Dennis through a *very* rigorous training session. In her opinion he would not have had enough energy remaining when he arrived home to force himself upon an unwilling woman. A former girlfriend also took the stand and stated that she had known Dennis for some time and that she did not consider him the type of person who would commit a rape.

After the evidence was presented, the barristers made their closing arguments. What is interesting is how little these arguments revolved around the facts. The most important facts – that they had sexual intercourse, and that Dennis was the responsible party – were not in dispute. Most of the discussion about what happened that night concerned the amount of physical pressure Dennis used in accomplishing the act and how to interpret the pressure that he applied. For example, there was argument about the relative positions of their bodies and the implications thereof. Was he holding his own body *up* to keep it from falling on her, or was he holding her body *down* to keep her from leaving or resisting? Clearly, Connie and Dennis had radically different interpretations of what transpired. From the point of view of the jurors it must have been almost impossible to know whether one was telling the truth and another was lying, or whether perhaps both were telling what was true in their own eyes, or whether their actions were inherently ambiguous.

Because many of the crucial details of what happened in the bedroom that night were so unclear and open to conflicting interpretations, there was a fair amount of attention paid in the closing arguments to the credibility of the witnesses, and in particular the credibility of Connie and Dennis. In a sense, it was a classic 'he said/she said' scenario. The prosecutor pointed out that Connie had cried on the stand, suggesting that this display of emotion indicated that she was sincere and her testimony to be believed. Dennis's defence counsel emphasised that both the fitness trainer and a former girlfriend had testified under oath that he was a good person who would not lie on the stand and would certainly not forcibly rape someone, which would – if the jury believed it – bolster his credibility.

Because there was so little hard evidence on the issue of consent, the lawyers were forced to argue that the jurors should draw certain inferences regarding consent – or lack of it – from the facts. One of those suggested inferences, for example, was based on the fact that the fitness trainer had worked Dennis so hard; the inference that his lawyer asked the jury to draw from this fact was that he would not have had enough energy to force himself on Connie after his workout. Defence counsel also argued that rapists do not wear condoms, which would also support an inference that this was not rape. The prosecutor, on the other hand, focused on the fact that Connie had not reciprocated in kissing him while he was kissing her. This would support an inference that Connie did not consent. In addition, the prosecutor laid a great deal of emphasis on the fact that her 'knickers', as he referred to her panties, had remained on during the intercourse. This fact, he argued to the jury, supported the inference that Dennis just wanted to quickly 'have his way' with her.

There was an additional circumstance that led to a very interesting set of competing inferences: the fact that she had become an active member in an evangelical church, and more particularly, the fact that members of the church considered it sinful to have intercourse outside of marriage. The prosecutor pointed to this fact and suggested that because of her religion, she would never have consented to having sex with Dennis. In addition, he used her religion to try to enhance her credibility, since lying would clearly be sinful.

Dennis's lawyer drew a sharply contrasting inference from exactly these same facts. He pointed out that if she had engaged in consensual intercourse with Dennis without being married to him, members of her church would regard her as a sinner, which would be highly embarrassing to her. He suggested that to rescue her self-image in the church community and to avoid having to confess she had strayed from the straight and narrow, she was under great pressure to accuse Dennis of rape.

I have gone on at some length about this example because it illustrates how difficult the issue of consent can be in the context of a rape trial. There may not be much evidence that bears directly on the question. In addition, the evidence is often contradictory: the man testifies that she consented, the woman testifies that she did not. Whether jurors should believe that evidence often boils down to credibility. Even after jurors conclude that certain facts are true, those facts by themselves may not answer the question of whether the woman consented. Rather, since consent is a state of mind, the issue usually must be decided based on inferences drawn from the evidence, and that evidence, as mentioned, may be limited and subject to dispute. Moreover, the strength of the inferences can vary greatly, and often the same fact can support directly contradictory inferences.

During his summation, which followed the arguments of the lawyers, the judge (as is customary in England but not the United States) summarised the evidence and pointed out some of the inferences that could be drawn from it. He also gave some brief instructions on the law, although in far less detail than we generally see in the United States. He did tell the jury that an essential element in a rape charge is that not only must there have been sexual intercourse, but the woman must not have consented to it.

A large part of the reason why the issue of consent has been so problematic in rape law springs from this requirement: that the woman must not have consented. The implications are profound, especially in cases of acquaintance rape. Because lack of consent is an element of the crime, rather than merely being an affirmative defence, the prosecutor has the burden of proof on this issue. The jury must presume that the defendant is innocent unless and until the prosecution has presented sufficient evidence to convince the jury that the woman did *not* consent. This means, first of all, that the prosecutor has to prove a negative. Secondly, and more importantly, it means that where the evidence is conflicting and the jury cannot decide who is telling the truth, the defence wins. Because there is often so little hard and fast evidence in cases alleging acquaintance rape, the fact that the prosecutor has the burden of proof will often be determinative. Not only must the prosecution prove its case, but it must do so beyond a reasonable doubt. In *Regina* v. *Doe* the judge expressed this standard by telling jurors that they must be 'sure' of their verdict.

So, what happened to Dennis? After the jury was sworn and left to deliberate, I had little time left in London and had to leave the Old Bailey behind me. I had chatted during breaks in the proceedings with a local court watcher, however. She was a native-born Londoner who was probably in her early sixties. I gave her my address and told her I would appreciate it if she would let me know what the outcome was. Her own views were clear: a 'good girl' would not have gone to his bedroom with him, and Connie therefore had only herself to blame. Several weeks later I received a postcard from England with a photo of Big Ben on the front and a message on the back. She was pleased to inform me that the jury had found Dennis NOT GUILTY.

Efforts to reform consent

As the facts of *Regina* v. *Doe* make clear, the issue of consent can be a difficult one. It is not the only hurdle to obtaining convictions, of course. Another major problem is that there used to be, and perhaps still is, a common belief that women tend to lie about their sexual experiences and that therefore their testimony in court might be suspect. Several American jurisdictions at one time had rules that a man could not be convicted of rape on the uncorroborated testimony of the complainant (Estrich, 1987: 42–53). There may be some truth to the assertion that women sometimes lie about sex, but there is no reason I can think of that women would lie more often about this topic than men do. It may well be that the reverse is true. The defendant in a rape case would seem to have an even more compelling reason to lie about what happened, especially at the time during which the corroboration rule was in effect: if convicted, he might well have faced the death penalty. Even today, there can be substantial penalties for rape.[2] The corroboration rule is now largely a thing of the past, although – as we will see below – the issue of the credibility of the victim refuses to go away (see also Spohn and Horney, 1992: 25).

Another issue that has drawn a great deal of criticism and scholarly attention is the admission of evidence of the woman's previous sexual conduct. It is true that a woman's sexual history may sometimes logically have some limited relevance on the issue of consent. This is especially true if the woman had never engaged in sexual relations and intended to remain a virgin until marriage. Somewhat less relevant is the fact that she had previously had a sexual relationship with the defendant. Obviously, the fact that a woman has consensual sexual relations with a man in May does not mean that it was consensual when they again had sex in June.

Even more problematic is evidence of the victim's sexual history with other men. Such evidence was often used by defence attorneys to suggest that because the woman had consented to sex with men on *other* occasions, the jury should infer that she consented on *this* occasion. Of course, the evidence is at least as susceptible to a competing inference: if a woman knows how to say 'yes' to so many men, without complaining later that she had been raped, why would she claim to have been raped on this occasion unless it was true? Because of persistent criticism that evidence of sexual history had the effect of putting the victim on trial, most states have enacted rape shield laws that limit the admissibility of evidence about sexual history.[3]

Another object of reform has been the notorious resistance requirement. At the beginning of the previous century, most American jurisdictions required proof that the woman had resisted her attacker. The reason for this require-ment was that resistance produced clear evidence that the victim did not consent, which is one of the requirements for conviction. Often, however, courts required not just that the woman verbally resist by saying 'no', but demanded that the resistance be physical, or sometimes even that the woman resist to the utmost (Estrich, 1987: 29–41).

An egregious example of the 'utmost resistance' requirement is *People* v. *Dohring*, decided in 1874. A fourteen-year-old girl was working as a 'servant' for the defendant. While working in a hay barn, he locked her inside and began to sexually assault her. When she tried to get up, he held her down and had intercourse with her. The girl testified that she cried out and tried to get away, but that the defendant physically prevented her from leaving. New York's highest court held that the jury, which convicted him of rape, had not been properly instructed on resistance; the correct rule was that the girl must have resisted to the utmost of her ability before they could find that she did not consent:

> The resistance must be up to the point of being overpowered by actual force, or of inability from loss of strength longer to resist, or from the number of persons attacking resistance must be dangerous or absolutely useless, or there must be duress or fear of death. . . . In the case here, there is no evidence of inability from loss of strength longer to resist; there was but one for the prosecutrix to oppose, and he a man in years; there was no duress nor reason to fear death; there were no threats, instead thereof there were promises and words of palliation and persuasion; there was nothing to show that resistance was absolutely useless; she had possession

of her faculties of mind and body, and retained her consciousness; she was then capable of resistance up to the point of being overpowered by actual force . . . [4]

This seems like an awful lot to expect from a girl who is merely fourteen years old.

Not all courts went to this extreme. As the Oregon Supreme Court observed at the beginning of the last century:

[T]o make the crime hinge on the uttermost exertion the woman was physically capable of making, would be a reproach to the law as well as to common sense. Such a test it would be exceedingly difficult, if not impossible, to apply in a given case. A complainant may have exerted herself to the uttermost limit of her strength, and may have continued to do so till the crime was consummated. Still, a jury, sitting coolly in deliberation upon the transaction, could not possibly determine whether or not the limit of her strength had been reached.[5]

Despite differences of opinion regarding exactly how much resistance was necessary, however, the requirement remained a formidable obstacle well into the twentieth century.[6]

Of course, the ultimate issue was consent. To be more exact, the prosecutor had to prove that the victim did not consent. There is no doubt that utmost resistance is excellent proof of nonconsent. But an obvious problem is that it may expose the woman to the danger of greater physical harm. Another problem with resistance is that it is not the only way in which lack of consent can be proven. It should normally be enough for a woman to say 'no,' as many scholars have pointed out. And the emphasis on resistance placed the spotlight on what the woman did or did not do, rather than concentrating on what the defendant did. The argument that rape law put the woman on trial was well founded.

A common reform has been to eliminate the requirement that nonconsent must be proven by resistance and, in the process, to place greater emphasis on what the defendant did. In California, for instance, one type of rape occurs when sexual intercourse is accomplished 'against a person's will by means of force, violence, duress, menace, or fear of immediate and unlawful bodily injury on the person or another'.[7] While the references to force, violence, and so forth, focus on the defendant's conduct, the requirement that the intercourse be 'against a person's will' essentially maintains the traditional requirement that the prosecution must prove nonconsent. This is made explicit by the jury instruction on this type of rape, which defines the phrase 'against that person's will' as meaning 'without the consent of the alleged victim'.[8] Another California statutes addresses circumstances where the victim 'is prevented from resisting by any intoxicating or anesthetic substance, or any controlled substance . . . '[9] This provision, at the very least, presupposes that the victim would have resisted, or should have done so, had she not been intoxicated.

Some states have gone further, completely eliminating any references to consent in their statutory definition of rape. The Michigan law, for instance, does not contain the word *consent*. It begins by stating that there has been 'sexual penetration'. Of course, engaging in intercourse by itself is not criminal, so there must be an additional element or elements to turn it into a crime. Traditionally, of course, this additional element was proof that the woman did not consent or that the acts were against the will of the victim. To address this issue, the Michigan statute has substituted a number of options to replace the nonconsent requirement. One is the status of the woman: if she was under a certain age or mentally incapacitated. Other options focus on the nature of the defendant's act. For example, if he engaged in intercourse with a woman while he was armed with a weapon, or used force or coercion that led to physical injury, he has committed first degree criminal sexual conduct.[10]

This statute seems to do a relatively good job in shifting the focus of inquiry from the conduct of the victim to the conduct of the perpetrator. For this reason, the Michigan law is often held out as a model for other states (Spohn and Horney, 1992: 26–7). But even in Michigan, the issue of consent has snuck in through the back door. In response to a defendant who appealed his conviction because there was no specific instruction at his trial requiring the prosecution to prove nonconsent, a Michigan court of appeals stated that '[t]he court's instruction requiring the jury to find that penetration was accomplished by force or coercion implicitly required the jury to find that the complainant did not consent to sexual intercourse before it could find defendant guilty'.[11] This allows a defendant to try to prove that the woman consented in an effort to negate the element of coercion. In addition, Michigan appellate courts have held that it was reversible error for the trial court not to have instructed the jury on the issue of consent if the man's defence was that he reasonably believed the woman consented to the intercourse.[12] This means that while the prosecutor no longer has to prove nonconsent, which is a substantial improvement, defence counsel can raise the issue either to negate the prosecution's case, or as a defence.

The issue of consent refuses to go away. It probably never will. The reason is simple. If we leave out cases of underage victims or people with mental problems, consent is what distinguishes rape from ordinary sex. For that reason, we move on to examine the notion of consent more closely. Rather than try to avoid consent, as some commentators have suggested, I suggest that we should confront it head-on.

The language and linguistics of consent

Perhaps the most important feature of the word *consent* is that it describes a state of mind. It is not primarily a performative verb. Of course, it is possible to consent by saying 'I consent.' So it might be more accurate to say that *consent* can be used in either a descriptive or performative sense. For our purposes, the critical point is that a person can consent without saying so, as reflected in the adage 'silence is consent'.

Compare consenting to promising. Promising is not a mental state. If I commit myself mentally to doing something for you, I have not promised, except perhaps in the derivative sense of promising myself to do something. Generally, for me to promise something, I have to communicate my commitment to the recipient of the promise. I do not, of course, have to use the word *promise*. But I do have to use words of some sort, or use actions that can communicate prepositional content. To consent, on the other hand, it usually suffices to have the right state of mind. *Consent* is like *believe* or *think*. I can say that I believe or think something, but I can also just believe or think it, without communicating my belief or thought to anyone.

Of course, there are many situations in which consent is expressed in words or actions. In fact, it may be legally required for consent to be expressed, sometimes orally, and sometimes also in writing. By way of illustration, the words 'written consent' occur over 850 times in the statutes of California.[13] Rape law, in contrast, does not require written consent, or even express consent (that is, consent in words). It merely requires a certain state of mind.

It is instructive to compare the verb *consent* with *agree*. Consenting usually involves submitting to someone else's initiative or plan. It suggests that one person is proposing a course of action and that the other is going along with it, or at least allowing it to happen. Although it need not invariably be the case, the person who consents often takes a relatively passive role. As Anna Wierzbicka (1987: 112) has pointed out, 'consent implies a position of dependence on the part of the addressee'. In contrast, she observes that agreeing generally involves a more symmetrical or reciprocal relationship. At the same time, she notes that *consent* does not just involve allowing an act to take place: '*consent* implies a more active kind of support than *permission*' (1987: 113). The latter distinction is important, because some courts seem to believe that it is enough for a woman to permit a man to carry out his sexual plans. Indeed, in many ways the resistance requirement is more consistent with permission, which is not the legal standard, than it is with consent.

In any event, the notion of consent remains problematic because, even if it is viewed as requiring support for the man's plan, the act of consenting is a mental state that may or may not be expressed verbally. Perhaps some of the difficulties with consent in rape law could be solved by requiring that consent must be made explicitly in words (see Remick, 1993). As we have seen in *Regina* v. *Doe*, it can be very challenging to determine a person's mental state by means of inferences from his or her conduct.

Yet there are some serious drawbacks to this proposal. One is that the language that people use to discuss sexual matters is typically vague and indirect. Although our society is no doubt changing in this regard, many people in western society still consider it taboo to talk explicitly about sexual acts, even when they are engaging in them. In English we have a huge number of euphemisms for sexual acts. Moreover, some people seem to consider direct talk about sexual relations unromantic, especially in a dating situation.

Thus, many people in our society typically discuss sex – if they do so at all – by means of euphemism, double entendre, innuendo, or subtle suggestion. At least at the current stage of human development, it seems unlikely that the legal system could require men to obtain verbal consent, with the penalty for not doing so being a prosecution for rape.[14] There is, in addition, the consideration that if a man can force or intimidate a woman into having sex with him, he can certainly force or intimidate her into saying 'I consent.' In that case, the issue at trial would be whether she *really* consented, or whether she just *said* she consented because of pressure from the defendant. We would essentially be back where we started: debating whether the woman had a state of mind described by the word 'consent'.

We might also place the burden on women to verbally object if they do *not* consent. Under this approach, woman could stop any unwanted sexual advances by saying 'no' or 'stop'. If the man continues, he would be guilty to some kind of sexual crime, depending on what he did exactly. If he stops, he would be safe from prosecution. Like requiring express consent, this proposal would simplify matters by creating a bright-line rule. In that sense, it is similar to the former 'physical resistance' rule. But it is unrealistic for the same reason that requiring verbal consent is unrealistic: it is not consistent with behaviour in our society; people do not always speak so clearly. It also places an unfair burden on women, who may be too intimidated by a man to verbally object.

If verbal standards are ultimately unworkable, we are left with a situation in which people often communicate consent indirectly, or where they signal their intentions by their actions, and perhaps even their silence. This may require that the man, and subsequently the jury, infer the woman's mental state from what she says or does. We have already mentioned some of the problems of using inferences to determine consent or lack thereof. There is also a substantial literature containing linguistic or sociolinguistic analyses of rape trials that highlight the problems associated with inferential reasoning in this situation. Susan Ehrlich, for instance, reports on alleged cases of date rape, involving the same man but two different women, that took place on or near a college campus in Canada. She points out that defence attorneys and, in this case, members of a university disciplinary tribunal, often interrogated the women about what they did *not* do or say. Why did one of the women not cry out or yell, for instance, when there were people around who could have helped her? Why didn't she explicitly tell the man that she did not want to have sex with him, rather than saying merely that she had a class in the morning and he had better leave? (Ehrlich, 2001: 79; 86–7). Ehrlich concludes that the utmost resistance requirement is still discursively present, even if no longer explicitly required by law (2001: 92).

Yet it seems that as long as consent remains an element of rape law, we will have to use logical inferences to decide the woman's state of mind. The fact that a woman does not scream or yell or try to leave is at least somewhat relevant in this endeavour; these facts support an inference that she consented. In a situation where there is little coercion, where the man is not intimidating, the door is unlocked, he has no weapons and makes no threats, and there are other people nearby, it seems natural to draw a fairly strong inference of consent if a woman does not scream, yell, say 'stop', or try to leave. As the environment becomes more coercive, that inference becomes correspondingly weaker or disappears entirely. If a man is holding a gun to a woman's head, it seems ludicrous to infer consent from her failure to cry out.

That we use inferences to determine consent is unavoidable. What is often objectionable is that in the context of rape law, these inferences may rest on questionable or offensive (some would say: patriarchal) assumptions. These include the fact that a woman was hitchhiking, wore sexy clothing, invited the man to her room, was sexually experienced, and so forth (Estrich 1987: 121–48). A particularly egregious example is a recent case in which a Texas judge determined that a woman's request that a man use a condom was evidence of consent, despite the fact that he had threatened her with violence (see Da Luz and Weckerly, 1993).

One solution to the problem is to limit the jury's access to facts from which questionable inferences could be drawn. Rape shield laws are an example: they typically exclude certain facts from evidence. This is a rather paternalistic response, of course, because it suggests that the jury cannot be trusted with the information. And the suspicion that relevant evidence is being withheld from them may make the jury speculate about what they are missing. Nonetheless, it is not the only type of information that is withheld from jurors, and in the case of rape shield laws it seems like the right thing to do.

A somewhat different approach is to admit the facts into evidence, but to warn the jury to be cautious in drawing an inference from them. Following the notorious 'condom' case in Texas, the California legislature enacted a statute that provided as follows: 'evidence that the victim suggested, requested, or otherwise communicated to the defendant that the defendant use a condom or other birth control device, without additional evidence of consent, is not sufficient to constitute consent.'[15] Nonetheless, although such rules of evidence are helpful, they cannot solve the many uncertainties surrounding consent. There are just too many inferences that can be drawn from too many differing factual situations.

A final observation that I would like to make about consent is that it can be either voluntary or involuntary. At first, the notion of involuntary consent might seem to be an oxymoron. Isn't consent voluntary by definition? Most of us have the notion that consent at least *ought* to be a matter of free will, uninfluenced by force, intimidation, or other pressure. That is certainly the ideal. But sometimes we can, by the exercise of our free will, consent to have something happen that we would rather not have happen. We do so because preventing the undesirable act would have even worse consequences than allowing it. In that case, we might say that although we consented, it was not really voluntary. And if the event or state of affairs that induced us to consent was coercive or illegal, we could later argue that our consent should not be considered valid.

Lest this discussion seem a bit esoteric, let me give an actual legal example: consent to search. In the United States, police may search a person or a person's car or house only under specified circumstances. Otherwise the search would be illegal. If the police have no legal basis for a search, they can request consent to search. If the person consents, what would otherwise be illegal is now acceptable, and any evidence found during the search is admissible.

The obvious danger with consensual searches is that people may consent because they believe they have no real choice in the matter, especially if a uniformed police officer requests their permission alongside a busy highway in the middle of the night. The United States Supreme Court has addressed this concern by holding the government must show that the consent was voluntary. Elsewhere, Lawrence Solan and I have discussed some of the linguistic problems raised by consensual searches and the voluntariness requirement (Tiersma and Solan, 2004). My point here is merely that the legal system recognises that consent can be either voluntary or involuntary.

Of course, whether someone consents involuntarily, or does not consent at all, can be a subtle distinction. It might even seem to be a trivial distinction. Normally, it does not matter whether a driver refuses to consent to a search, for instance, or consents involuntarily. In either case, the subsequent search is invalid.

But sometimes the distinction between nonconsent and involuntary consent matters. An illustration is the distinction between robbery and extortion. The prototypical robbery occurs when the perpetrator stops someone on the street and threatens that person with violence unless the person gives the perpetrator money or some other item of value. Extortion, on the other hand, usually takes place in private and involves the perpetrator threatening to expose a secret about someone unless that person gives the perpetrator money or some other item of value. These crimes closely resemble each other, but there is an interesting difference with respect to consent. The California Penal Code defines robbery as 'the felonious taking of personal property in the possession of another, from his person or immediate presence, and *against his will*, accomplished by means of force or fear'.[16] California law defines 'against a person's will' as 'without consent'.[17] Extortion, on the other hand, is defined as 'the obtaining of property from another, *with his consent*, or the obtaining of an official act of a public officer, induced by a wrongful use of force or fear, or under color of official right'.[18] Thus, robbery involves obtaining property from someone *without consent*, whereas extortion involves obtaining property *with consent*.

Rape and other sexual crimes are almost universally defined as being 'against the will' of the woman or 'without her consent'. Thus, while the law in other areas distinguishes between acts done *without* the consent of the victim, and acts done with the *involuntary* consent of the victim, the law of rape has traditionally not drawn this distinction.

To summarise our discussion so far, consent (at least in rape law) is essentially a mental state, not a speech act. Because what goes on in a person's mind is not directly observable, a person's mental state must be determined by inferences based on the person's speech and conduct. The inferences that people draw are dependent on their beliefs about how people act or should act in specific situations. In the context of rape law, such inferences may be based on incorrect information or might be objectionable for other reasons. As a consequence, the law's dependence on consent, which persists even after widespread reform, is problematic. Finally, I have argued that consent can be either voluntary or involuntary.

Despite all these difficulties, we cannot eliminate consent completely, it seems to me, because consent is ultimately what distinguishes a very ordinary human activity from a serious crime. I will therefore suggest that the legal system should acknowledge that consent is critical, rather than try to avoid it, but at the same time redefine the crime of rape so that consent plays a very different role.

Managing consent

Part of the traditional definition of rape is that the woman did not consent to the intercourse. In cases of sexual violence, especially by a stranger, it seems to me that this is the correct assessment. To the extent that a man physically forces himself on a woman, it is perverse to say that she consented. This is true even when she does not actively resist. In the face of imminent violence, there is no time to think and reach a mental state that we would rationally label 'consent'.

In the typical date rape scenario, however, the threat – although it may be just as real – may be less immediate. Consequently, it seems to me that a woman who submits to a man in this situation is often consenting – not because she wants to, but because it seems like the best choice under the circumstances. She has weighed her options, and the threat of violence if she refuses, or the possibility that her boss might retaliate against her, or whatever other coercive circumstance exists, leads her to decide that she should consent rather than resist. Yet as in the case of extortion, her consent is involuntary.

The result is that in cases where a woman involuntarily submitted or involuntarily consented to intercourse, her consent is no longer an issue. The prosecution does not need to prove that the woman did not consent; it can concede that the woman consented. Any evidence that relates to the woman's consent or nonconsent should be irrelevant. The only thing that matters would be the amount of force, threat of force, or other coercive device that the defendant used and whether this rendered her consent involuntary. Because the fact of consent could be taken for granted, this approach would help focus the inquiry on the perpetrator's conduct, which is where it properly belongs.

But there is an additional problem with rape law as presently constituted: all of the emphasis is on the woman's mental state, not the man's. It seems to me that consent, and particularly the voluntariness of consent, are very relevant to rape law. But the critical question is not whether the *woman* failed to consent, but rather whether the *man* knew or should have known that this was the case. Virtually all crimes require not only that the defendant have done some act (the *actus reus*), but also that he have had a particular intent or state of mind while performing the act (the *mens rea*). As Susan Estrich has pointed out, rape may be unique in not requiring that the perpetrator have a particular intent.[19]

I would therefore redefine the crime of rape as follows. First, as with current law, there must be a specified sexual act. In addition, I would require that either:

(1) the defendant knew, or reasonably should have known, that the woman did not voluntarily consent to the sexual act; or

(2) the defendant knew, or reasonably should have known, that the woman consented to the sexual act only because of threats, intimidation, or fear caused by the defendant.

The second option could be expanded to include situations where a woman consents because of misrepresentations the man made, for example, or where the man knew or should have known that a woman was not mentally competent.

Rather than avoid consent, my proposal takes it on directly. In cases where a woman resists or says 'no', she clearly does not consent, and the man should know it. The fact is that often enough, women *do* resist or refuse to submit voluntarily. Or they make it clear in words that they do not consent. In those cases, consent should not be a major issue and a prosecutor should not normally have trouble convincing a jury to convict. In addition, it reaffirms that where a woman resists or communicates to a man that she is not interested in sex, her actions should count for something in the legal system.

On the other hand, there are situations where, in the face of a man's sexual aggression, a woman is intimidated into doing nothing, or passively goes along with the defendant's wishes because she fears the consequences if she resists or says 'no'. My proposal essentially neutralises the issue of consent in this context, where it has traditionally been most problematic, by simply admitting the woman consented. It also strikes me as the best description of what is actually happening. Essentially, women in this situation often make a rational choice: that it is better to submit to the defendant's aggression than to risk the possibility of a more severe injury if they refuse. In such cases, it does not matter that she did things that the defendant might argue seemed to him like consent. The critical issue would be whether he reasonably should have known that she consented because of fear or intimidation.

The other advantage to my proposed reformulation is that it directs the inquiry not to what was going on in the woman's mind, but on what the defendant knew or believed, a point also made by Estrich. Not only is this more consistent with other crimes, but it potentially has some other advantages. Issues regarding the victim's credibility continue to be a major concern in this area of the law.[20] At least in theory, requiring that the man have a certain mental state, rather than the woman, should focus more attention on the man's credibility, and less on the woman's. Finally, my proposal might make men more careful in ambiguous situations. If the issue is what the man knew, or reasonably should have known, men will have a greater incentive to make sure that their potential sexual partner is in fact acting voluntarily, rather than blithely assuming that as long as a woman isn't physically resisting him, he can, in the words of the prosecutor in *Regina* v. *Doe*, 'have his way' with her.

Some caveats and a conclusion

It would be naïve to believe that my suggested reformulation of rape law would solve the multitude of problems in this area. Even if it were successfully implemented, there are inevitably going to be roadblocks to any comprehensive solution. In fact, I would like to suggest that there are three main caveats to any proposed solution to rape law: consent, cognition and the Constitution. The points regarding the Constitution may seem self-evident or even pedantic to experts in criminal law. I mention them nonetheless because it is my impression that the social science research seldom takes them into account.

We have already discussed consent, so I will not belabour the issue. It is possible to minimise the role of consent, as recent statutes have attempted to do, or to manage it, along the lines that I have suggested, but it is impossible to eliminate the issue entirely. Whether we look at whether the woman consented, or whether the man knew that she did not consent, we inevitably inquire into the mental state of a human being, with all the attendant difficulties.

As to cognition, it is important to note that *rape*, like many other words, invokes prototype effects. A *prototype* refers, roughly speaking, to a typical member of a category. In contrast, a *definition* of a word attempts to state the conditions that are necessary and sufficient to describe it. Quite possibly, we store both definitions and prototypes in our mental lexicons (Solan, 1995). Take the word *automobile*. The *American Heritage Dictionary* (1970: 90) starts its definition with necessary and sufficient conditions ('a self-propelled land vehicle'), and it then continues by providing a prototypical example ('as a four-wheeled passenger vehicle propelled by an internal-combustion engine'). Although the notion of a prototypical car will differ somewhat from person to person, it is probably true that most people envision an automobile as having four wheels, being capable of carrying passengers, and probably having a gasoline-powered engine. If confronted with a self-propelled vehicle that carries passengers but has only three wheels, however, most people would still consider it to be an automobile, although they might begin to waver. If the three-wheeled vehicle becomes small enough, some people would probably begin to say that it is an odd type of motorcycle or some other contraption. Likewise, a vehicle that looks like an automobile but is powered by solar panels on its roof will probably still be called an automobile by most speakers. But if it is powered by a large sail, many people would become less sure.

Psychologist Vicki Smith (1991: 861) has confirmed the importance of prototypes in the legal context. She asked her research subjects to list the features that they associated with various crimes, such as kidnapping. The two most common features that participants listed for a kidnapping were that there was a ransom demand (63%) and that the victim was a child (60%). The legal definition of kidnapping requires neither of these features. But it seems that the prototypical kidnapping involves the abduction of a child for purposes of obtaining a ransom demand from the parents. If someone were to abduct an adult for other reasons (for example, to force the adult's family to repay a valid debt owed to the abductor), juries might be more reluctant to convict the defendant because his action strayed from their prototypical image of a kidnapping. In addition, it seems to me that the prototypical kidnapping also involves an abduction by someone who is a stranger to the victim. For this reason, it is difficult to convince people that a kidnapping has occurred when a noncustodial parent does not return his or her child to the parent who has legal custody.

The prototypical rape also involves strangers, It occurs when a stranger jumps out of the bushes or some other hiding place and forces himself on an unsuspecting victim. At the same time, acquaintance rape clearly falls within the legal definition, which generally requires that a man have sexual intercourse with a woman without her consent. The problem is that while the legal definition of *rape* plainly covers date rape or acquaintance rape, most speakers consider this type of behaviour to be a more marginal (less prototypical) member of the category, or they might to consider it to fall outside of the category entirely. Thus, even if a jury were to overcome the evidentiary hurdles that we have discussed, and decide that the defendant's actions meet the legal definition of rape, they might still hesitate to convict because the acquaintance rape scenario deviates too far from their image of a prototypical rape. Smith's research suggests that it can be extremely difficult to dislodge commonly held prototypes that are at odds with legal definitions, even if the judge gives very explicit instructions.

The importance of prototypical thinking has been acknowledged by at least one legal commentator on the subject, Susan Estrich, although she does not refer specifically to the linguistic and psychological research. The focus of her book, *Real Rape*, is that the legal system deals seriously with a prototypical or 'real' rape that is committed by a stranger, but is relatively indifferent or even hostile to claims of rape committed by someone that the victim knew, or where the victim's behaviour or dress is felt to have somehow contributed to her situation (Estrich, 1987).

Estrich refers to the classic study of the jury by Henry Kalven and Hans Zeisel (1966: 249–54). Kalven and Zeisel distinguished between 'aggravated rape', which involved violence, multiple assailants, or a lack of a prior relationship between the defendant and the complainant, and 'simple' rape, where these factors were absent. Their research found, not surprisingly, that juries were four times more likely to convict in cases involving an aggravated rape, which is essentially a prototypical rape.

Recent studies confirm that, even today, people are more likely define an encounter as rape depending on the amount of force used by the man, or the extent of the woman's resistance, the degree of physical injury, and whether the man was a stranger. Some scholars have viewed such studies as evidence that popular attitudes toward rape have changed very little over the years (Taslitz, 1999: 39). It does seem to be true that it is not easy to dislodge deeply-embedded prototypical thinking. At least in our lifetimes, it seems unlikely that ordinary people in the English-speaking world will agree that all unwelcome sexual contact should be branded as 'rape'.

Some jurisdictions have addressed this issue by subdividing rape into a number of different crimes, reserving the term *rape* for more serious crimes and alternative language (like *unlawful sexual intercourse* or *sexual assault*) for lesser offences. Or they avoid the term *rape* entirely (as in Michigan, which has substituted *criminal sexual conduct*).[21] In *Regina* v. *Doe* the operative term was *rape*, which may in part explain the jurors' reluctance to convict.

One way to address these problems is to eliminate the jury entirely. Kalven and Zeisel's research suggests that in cases of simple (nonprototypical) rape, judges are substantially more likely to convict than juries (1966: 254). That brings us to what may be the most important caveat: the Constitution. I will limit myself to protections extended to criminal defendants in the American Constitution, but most of the world's nations have similar provisions.

The first constitutional barrier is the presumption of innocence and the related doctrine of proof beyond a reasonable doubt.[22] A defendant in the United States must be presumed innocent until the state proves him or her guilty beyond a reasonable doubt. As we noted in the discussion of *Regina* v. *Doe*, the effect of the presumption of innocence, which places the burden of proof on the prosecution, is that where the evidence is roughly equally weighted, the man must be acquitted. In what is often a 'he said-she said' situation, this principle can explain the outcome in many cases.

Not only do prosecutors have the burden of proving that the complaining witness did not consent, but they have to convince the jury beyond a reasonable doubt. In the United States, there are varying definitions this standard. For instance, juries may be told that they must have an 'abiding conviction' in the truth of the charge, that they must not 'waver or vacillate', or that they should be 'firmly convinced' that the defendant is guilty.[23] Regardless of which formulation is used, it is a formidable barrier for the prosecution. Defence attorneys do not have to show that their client is innocent; all they have to do to get an acquittal is to raise a reasonable doubt that one of the elements of the crime has been met. In virtually all acquaintance and rape date cases, what they will argue is that there are reasonable doubts about consent. In other words, about all they have to do to win their client's freedom is to get jurors to think: 'Well, maybe she did consent.'

Because of this formidable burden on the prosecution, many people who are guilty of crimes are likely to remain free because the evidence against them is not strong enough. This is expressed by the maxim that it is better for ten guilty people to go free than for one innocent person to be convicted. That may seem a noble sentiment, but it necessarily implies that it is better for ten guilty rapists to go free than for one innocent person to be convicted of rape. There is no rape exception in the protections that the Constitution affords to criminal defendants.

Also embedded in the Constitution is the right to a jury trial in criminal cases. One of the great strengths of the jury system is that jurors are ordinary people who take their common sense and life experiences with them into the courtroom, as well as serving as a bastion against government oppression (Levy, 1999: 69–105). Of course, one person's common sense is another person's patriarchal narrative. We have discussed some of the ways in which courts can try to exclude evidence upon which jurors might draw questionable inferences, or to caution them to draw certain inferences with caution. But jurors will inevitably use their experiences and view of the world in reaching a verdict. Short of abolishing the jury system, I see no way of avoiding this entirely.

The final constitutional consideration is that a person accused of a crime has the right to confront the witnesses against him. In the typical rape case, this means that the defendant's lawyer has the right to cross-examine the victim. Many of the criticisms by scholars like Ehrlich and Matoesian regarding what happens to women at trial – that they are essentially revictimised – are really complaints about the behaviour of defence lawyers. Of course, it is the adversarial legal system that enables these lawyers to act as they do. Judges could be more vigilant in reining in abusive cross-examination, especially with a vulnerable witness. Another deterrent to aggressive defence lawyers is that jurors are likely to take an unfavourable view of their clients if they seem to be unfair to the victim. But as long as the defendant – through his lawyer – has the right to cross-examine the prosecution's star witness, rape trials will not be a pleasant experience for the woman. If all goes well, however, convicting the rapist and seeing justice done will make the experience worthwhile in the long run.

Rape law has come a long way since the days of the 'utmost resistance' requirement a century ago. At the same time, there is plenty of room for further reform of the legal system, even if the proposal that I have put forth shifts the focus to the defendant's actions and state of mind. Yet the most important improvements, in my view, will only come if we learn to reform ourselves.

Notes

1. Thanks to Heidi Brooks, a student at Loyola Law School, for research assistance. I would also like to thank my former research assistant, Kelli Walsh, for a paper that she wrote as an independent study project, which provided me with several useful references.
2. A recent case in Ventura, California, involved a man who lived in a beach-front house and met young women in local bars. In at least three cases he invited them to his house, offered them drinks laced with a drug known as GHB, had sex with the essentially unconscious women, and videotaped the proceedings. He created an excellent evidentiary record for the prosecution and was sentenced to 124 years in prison. Dawn Hobbs, *Luster Lured Women from State Street Bars*, Santa Barbara News Press, 19 June 2003, at A1.
3. For an overview, see Bienen (1980); Spohn and Horney (1992).
4. *People* v. *Dohring*, 59 N.Y. 374, 382 (1874).
5. *State* v. *Colestock*, 67 P. 418, 420 (Or. 1902).
6. For another egregious example, see *Vaughn* v. *State*, 110 N.W. 992 (Neb. 1907).
7. Cal. Pen. Code § 261(a)(2).
8. California Jury Instructions, Criminal, 10.00 (1996).

9. Cal. Pen. Code § 261(a)(3).
10. Mich. Comp. Laws § 750.520b (2003).
11. *People* v. *Johnson*, 341 N.W.2d 160, 163 (Mich. Ct. App. 1983).
12. *People* v. *Hearn*, 300 N.W.2d 396 (Mich. Ct. App. 1980); People v. Thompson, 324 N.W.2d 22 (Mich. Ct. App. 1982).
13. Westlaw search for the words 'written consent' conducted on the database CA-ST on June 26, 2003.
14. It may be possible to do so in more cohesive communities, as has happened at Antioch College in Ohio. See Francis, 1996: 135.
15. Cal. Penal Code sec. 261.7. The same is true of evidence regarding a 'current or previous dating relationship'. Id., sec. 261.6.
16. Calif. Penal Code § 211 (emphasis added).
17. Calif. Jury Instructions, Criminal, 9.40 (1996).
18. Id., § 518 (emphasis added).
19. See Estrich (1987: 92–104). Estrich argues that the intent of the man should matter, although the exact standard she would propose is not entirely clear to me.
20. See, for example, Matoesian (1993) and Taslitz (1999).
21. Mich. Comp. Laws § 750.520 (2003).
22. See *Estelle* v. *Williams*, 425 U.S. 501, 503 (1976).
23. For a discussion of the various standards, along with experimental data on how people understand them, see Horowitz and Kirkpatrick (1996) and Solan (1999).

References

American Heritage Dictionary of the English Language (1970) Boston: Houghton Mifflin.
Bienen, L. (1980) Rape III – National Developments in Rape Reform Legislation, *Women's Rights Law Reporter*, 6(3): 170–213.
da Luz, C. M. and Weckerly, P. C. (1993) The Texas 'condom-rape' case: caution construed as consent, *UCLA Women's Law Journal*, 3: 95–104.
Ehrlich, S. (2001) *Representing Rape: Language and Sexual Consent.* London and New York: Routledge.
Estrich, S. (1987) *Real Rape.* Cambridge, Mass.: Harvard University Press.
Francis, L. (1996) *Date Rape: Feminism, Philosophy, and the Law.* University Park, Pa.: Penn State University Press.
Horowitz, I. A. and Kirkpatrick, L. C. (1996) A concept in search of a definition: The effects of reasonable doubt instructions on certainty of guilt standards and jury verdicts, *Law and Human Behavior*, 20(6): 655–70.
Kalven, H. Jr., and Zeisel, H. (1966) *The American Jury.* Boston: Little, Brown and Co.
Levy, L. W. (1999) *The Palladium of Justice: Origins of Trial by Jury.* Chicago: Ivan R. Dee.
Matoesian, G. M. (1993) *Reproducing Rape: Domination through Talk in the Courtroom.* Chicago: University of Chicago Press.
Remick, L. A. (1993) Read her lips: An argument for a verbal consent standard in rape, *University of Pennsylvania Law Review*, 141(3): 1103–51.
Smith, V. L. (1991) Prototypes in the courtroom: Lay representations of legal concepts, *Journal of Personality and Social Psychology*, 61 (December): 857–72.
Solan, L. M. (1995) Judicial decisions and linguistic analysis: Is there a linguist in the court?, *Washington University Law Quarterly*, 73(3): 1069–80.
Solan, L. M. (1999) Refocusing the burden of proof in criminal cases: Some doubt about reasonable doubt, *Texas Law Review*, 78(1): 105–48.

Spohn, C., and Horney, J. (1992) *Rape Law Reform: a Grassroots Revolution and its Impact*. New York: Plenum Press.

Taslitz, A. (1999) *Rape and the Culture of the Courtroom*. New York: New York University Press.

Tiersma, P. M., and Solan, L. M. (2004) Cops and robbers: Selective literalism in American criminal law. *Law and Society Review*, 38: 229–66.

Wierzbicka, A. (1987) *English Speech Act Verbs*. Sydney: Academic Press.

6
The Repertoire of *Complicity* vs. *Coercion*: the Discursive Trap of the Rape Trial Protocol

Diane Ponterotto

Introduction

In the 1970s, both in the UK and the USA, the conduct of rape trials and the treatment of complainants in court began to become an issue of juridical as well as political concern. As a consequence, there has been some improvement in legislation and in jurisprudence on these questions. For example, in May 2002, in an effort to address the accusation of insufficient understanding and inadequate sentencing, especially of non-stranger rape, the Sentencing Advisory Panel of the UK invited the Court of Appeal to revise the guidelines on rape cases. The result of this move was the publication of new guidelines adopted in the case of *Millberry*.[1] The case and the label *Millberry* has since become the current framework for sentencing (see Rumney, 2003).

Nonetheless, the dissatisfaction with the conduct of rape trials persists and this dissatisfaction, albeit for various and differentiated reasons, is shared alike by victims, social advocates, counsellors, lawyers, feminist associations and juridical bodies. According to Temkin (2000), there has been continuing criticism of the way barristers prosecute and defend in rape trials. The failure of judges to control defence excesses to the disadvantage of the victim has been likewise signalled.

The problem: the trial as a form of reiterated abuse

Many serious psychological reactions are experienced by women in the aftermath of sexual violence, especially during the victim's contact with social institutions.[2] These reactions have often been referred to as 'time suspended, being "on", the rape relived, betrayal, and allaying silent suspicion' (Holmstrom and Burgess, 1978: 229; see also Berger, 1977). For the rape victim, the trial becomes a second traumatic experience. Due to the rhetorical conventions of trial examination protocol, in fact, the victim is obliged to:

- relive the violent experience of physical and psychological trauma;
- give an 'objective', 'neutral' and entirely physical description of an experience marked, on the other hand, by intense emotional and psychological stress;
- recall details of the event posed especially by the cross-examiner in a sometimes 'sordid' way: for example: 'Did you or did you not have your pantyhose on when speaking to Mr X?'

What remains particularly upsetting about sexual assault is the fact that the victims are not protected by legislative, police and judicial practice. On the other hand, sexually abused women find themselves further endangered. They risk being transformed into the persons accused;[3] they risk loss of psychological serenity; they risk attack on their sexual and personal dignity. In other words, the rape trial reiterates the scenario of abuse.

Perhaps for no other crime has society been so lenient. Perhaps for no other crime has legislation been so slow in the clarification of right and tort. Perhaps for no other crime has jurisprudence been so lax in the assignment of due punishment.

Aim: the description of rape trial discourse

From an observation of rape trial transcripts, it is apparent that a certain scenario continually recurs, albeit re-enacted with variations determined by the specifics of the reported event of violence. A somewhat fixed protocol seems to exist for the rape trial proceedings, a kind of *a priori* semantic script which directs interpretation of the events and thereby heavily conditions judgment and sentencing. As Rock (1993: 83), cited in Temkin (2000: 230) notes:

> Defence and prosecution counsel do not devise utterly new forensic methods for every trial in Crown Court . . . They rely on standard stories, stories in which they may actually have little trust themselves.

Thus, in rape cases, as Temkin (2000: 231) comments: 'certain tactics are routinely employed and certain stories routinely told'.

The aim of this study is to describe some aspects of this routinised story in Anglo-American juridical culture, to reveal its discriminatory format and to make manifest its covert ideological underpinnings. The study will argue that the common script of rape trial discourse is founded on the display of the semantic opposition *Complicity* vs. *Coercion*. It will claim that this institutionalised repertoire is biased in favour of male offenders, offensive to female victims, reproductive of patriarchal ideology and ultimately detrimental to the administration of justice.

Verbal interaction in the courtroom and its implications for the rape trial

The specific rape case routine is based on a relatively simple discursive strategy. Whereas prosecutors aim at confirming the victim's accusation of sexual abuse, defence counsel aims at confirming the alleged rapist's denial of abuse. We shall now attempt to analyse the typical discursive strategy used in the interrogation of victims in rape cases. Following previous research on the relation between language and the law in rape trials (see, among others, Cotterill, 2003; Ehrlich, 2001; Matoesian, 1997), the analysis will utilise the tools of DA (discourse analysis) and CA (conversation analysis) to uncover the typical discursive strategies used by cross-examiners to undermine the testimony of rape victims.

Courtroom dialogue

As a first point, it is to be noted that the discursive praxis of courtroom procedure in the Anglo-American judiciary is particularly aggressive. As Drew (1997: 51) notes, especially of cross-examination conventions:

> In the adversarial Anglo-American criminal judicial system, cross-examination is essentially hostile. Attorneys test the veracity or credibility of the evidence being given by witnesses, with questions which are designed to discredit the other side's version of events, and instead to support his or her own side's.

This means that the defence attorney must aggressively challenge the claimant's words in order to discredit them for the sake of defending his client. Significantly, it is the cross-examiner who selects the facts which become the major topics of the interrogation. It is the cross-examiner then who conducts the discourse strategy, controls the direction of the testimony and therefore orients the perceptions of judge, jury and public. As emphasised by Matoesian (1997: 137):

> Above all else, the art of trial cross-examination prescribes a cardinal rule for impeaching the credibility of witnesses and discrediting their testimony . . . Never ask a question to which you do not know the answer . . . As a corollary to the cardinal rule, law texts advise attorneys to 'control' testimony through the use of short, leading questions designed to elicit a single discrete fact to which the witness must agree. Attorneys employ such questions to 'stretch', expand and emphasize a piece of evidence over the course of several questions or even several minutes rather than exhausting the topic in a single question or two, a bit-by-bit or detailing to death procedure . . . In so doing, attorneys may construct a piece of

evidence cumulatively over time though a series of questions so that the fact in issue assumes a level of unusual and striking importance.

Natural vs. courtroom dialogue

The direct and cross-examinations in the courtroom have the form of a dialogue, very often couched, in fact, in an almost conversational style. Obviously, the dialogue is significantly different from spontaneous inter-action, having a kind of semi-fixed format determined both by normative courtroom strategy and specific rape case routines.

The dialogic strategy of courtroom examination has one particularly determining feature: it is, contrary to everyday conversation, asymmetrical. In other words, there is a fixed, question–answer pattern whereby only the prosecutor or the defence attorney has the right to ask questions, while the witness on the stand can only answer them. This puts the questioner in control of the discourse strategy (see Kebbell, Deprez and Wagstaff, 2003). Normal dialogic conventions like topic and turn-taking patterns are non-existent. Thus, the communicative event called direct or cross-examination has the form, but not the function, of the conversation text. The primary function of conversation, which seems to be, as many linguists have pointed out (see for example, Tannen, 1989), affiliative participation and joint nego-tiation of meaning, is by no means the objective of courtroom dialogue. On the contrary, barristers never ask questions for which they do not know, *a priori*, the answers. They conduct the examination so as to highlight previously selected information and to force the witness to acknowledge as truthful the specific, pre-selected evidence deemed useful in order to win the case.

The convention of questioning strategies in rape trials has been forcefully critiqued by Kebbell, Deprez and Wagstaff (2003: 54) who conclude:

> These question–answer forms increasingly constrain witness's responses ... The use of such closed questioning also means that the examination takes the form of the lawyer asking a question and the witness giving a brief answer, the lawyer asking another closed question and so on. This format allows only a short time between question and answer and the next question giving little opportunity for the witness to elaborate or extend an answer. Also and more importantly, this format ensures that the evidence is directed by the lawyer rather than the witness. The only information that is elicited is that which is requested.

A textual example

A look at any transcript of a rape trial cross-examination will therefore reveal that, independently of the specific event and the individual forensic style of the examiner, the argumentative movement seems to be routinised. To give an illustration, we shall report a mock interrogation of a rape victim, whose purpose was to prepare her for the likely cross-examination she would have to undergo in court. The example is taken from the video of a forensic seminar, held by Charles Reynard, prosecutor, judge and chairman of Continuing Legal Education for the Illinois Prosecutors Committee, addressed to students of law. By way of explanations, discussions and role-play performances, the juridical education video aims to demonstrate the usual discourse routines in court proceedings concerning non-stranger rape and thereby make future legal practitioners aware of the discursive trap which victims almost invariably face.[4]

In the video, Judge Reynard teaches the students how to prepare the victim for the trial, how to conduct a direct examination that builds credibility for the victim, how to anticipate the cross-examination of the defence attorney and finally how to prepare a convincing closing speech which can win the jury over to the victim's perspective. The video segment we have chosen is entitled:

ANTICIPATING THE CROSS / PRACTICE CROSS:
Demonstration 8
(LOCATION: Prosecutor's Office)
(Practice Cross-Exam with Prosecutor playing Defence)
Demonstration 8

The prosecutor first informs the victim (Amanda Brown in the transcript) that he is going to stage the cross-examination of the rapist's defence attorney, saying: 'Amanda – today I want to go over the cross-examination that we talked about. And as I explained already, I will pretend that I am a defense attorney and actually cross-examine you. Do you understand?' The segment of the text (pp. 78–80) that will be used for our analysis follows, with the participants indicated as *prosecutor playing the role of defence attorney* (P as D) and *victim* (A):

Participants:

P as D: The Prosecutor imitating the anticipated cross-examination
            of Defence Counsel
A: The Victim

            . . .

1. P as D: Ms Brown, on the night in question you went up to my
            client's – Michael Cates' – dorm room, correct?
2. A: Yes, yes I did.
3. P as D: Well, ma'am, isn't it true you voluntarily went up to
            Michael's room?
4. A: Yes.

5. P as D:	And it was just the two of you when you went off with him, correct?	
6. A:	Yes.	
7. P as D:	Isn't it true you'd never so much as gone on a date with my client before you went to his room with him that night?	
8. A:	Yes.	
9. P as D:	And isn't it true that you only knew Michael casually from school activities when you went up to his room with him?	
10. A:	Yes.	
11. P as D:	Isn't it also true that you went up to his room with him at night?	
12. A:	Uh, yes.	
13. P as D:	I'm sorry – what did you say?	
14. A:	Yes, that is true.	
15. P as D:	As a matter of fact, it was 10:30 at night when you voluntarily went up to his room, correct?	
16. A:	Yes.	
17. P as D:	And isn't it true that you finished two drinks that night with Michael?	
18. A:	That's true.	
19. P as D:	And isn't it also true that you started a third drink?	
20. A:	Yes.	
21. P as D:	And you went up to my client's room – a man you did not know very well – at 10:30 at night, isn't that what happened?	
22. A:	Well, yeah, I mean, that was the time, I think.	
23. P as D:	You think? Would you like me to call another witness who saw you in the lobby of the building to help you with the time?	
24. A:	No, it was 10:30 at night.	
25. P as D:	And you went up to Michael's dorm room – which is pretty much just a room with a bed and a refrigerator filled with beer – alone with him, right ma'am?	
26. A:	Yes, we went up to his room alone.	
27. P as D:	And isn't it true that other people in your theatre group went home because it was a school night but you went straight to Michael's room and started drinking with my client, right ma'am?	
28. A:	Yes, but I had finished my finals that day. I was done with classes –	
29. P as D:	That is a yes or no question ma'am.	
30. A:	Yes, I went to his room, and we had a few drinks there.	
31. P as D:	And now after you've had sex with him and after all this drinking you are going to try to tell this jury that you didn't want to have sex with Michael?	

32. A: Oh, I didn't have any intention –
33. P as D: That's a yes or no question ma'am.
34. A: No . . . Yes . . . He raped me.
35. P as D: Isn't what really happened is that you found my client Michael attractive, went home with him, partied with him, had sex with him, and then after a few months, you realised that this was not going to be this relationship that you had hoped for – then you decided that you were going to go after him and give him a hard time – isn't that what this is really about?
36. A: No – definitely not.
37. P as D: Ma'am didn't you start calling Michael a few days after the two of you had sex?
38. A: I called him once.
39. P as D: But that phone call was two days after you had sex with him, isn't that true?
40. A: Yes.
41. P as D: You went up to his room at night and started a night of drinking and drugs with him. After one drink the two of you then had another drink and then another, and then you smoked pot – isn't that true?
42. A: Yes, it's true.
43. P as D: And there were plenty of people on his dorm floor weren't there, ma'am?
44. A: There were people around.
45. P as D: And not one of these people heard you cry out that you were being attacked, did they ma'am – yes or no?'
46. A: No, they didn't.
47. P as D: And that's because you didn't cry out, isn't that true – yes or no?
48. A: Yes, that's true.
49. P as D: You went up to his room at night, had a drink with him and then you kissed him, isn't that true?
50. A: Yes, I kissed him
51. P as D: You went to this good looking young man's dorm room, you started drinking with him – one drink after another – smoked pot – started fooling around with him – and later you start calling him up – and now you want these twelve good men and women to believe that you are not simply just angry at Michael because he didn't start dating you?
52. A: No – he raped me.
53. P as D: You knew exactly what you wanted when you went up to Michael's room, didn't you?'
54. A: Yes, I did.
55. P as D: Nothing further of this witness.

Analysis

Let us try to analyse this courtroom dialogue by focusing on its syntactic and lexical characteristics as well as its specific discourse strategies. On the basis of evidence in previous studies (Cotterill, 2003; Ehrlich, 2001; Matoesian, 1997), as well as the fact that it was created by an experienced prosecutor, judge and professor of prosecutor education as an example of a classic direct examination of rape victims, the text can be considered a typical scenario of courtroom behaviour in rape trials. We shall therefore try to describe the discursive strategy which emerges from the text as a typological representation of cross-examinations of women in rape cases.

Discourse structure

According to the Birmingham model elaborated initially by Sinclair and Coulthard (1975) to describe classroom dialogue, a conversation usually consists of a series of three-part exchanges: question/answer/follow-up; for example: *What time is John arriving? /Oh about ten, I think./ That's good.* As demonstrated by subsequent research on natural conversation, along with a somewhat routinised structure, spontaneous dialogue evolves with a complex alternation of turns and a subtle flow of topic variations. It is also characterised by hedging and overlapping. Hedging, which is a kind of hesitation or slowing down of information delivery, is considered by many linguists to have two primary functions in conversation: a *cognitive* function, as a kind of pause to plan subsequent moves and a *social* function, as a kind of overture to the participant's position, a kind of tuning-in to the interlocutor. Overlapping also is a cooperative movement whereby interlocutors speak simultaneously in an effort either to gain the floor or to complete the utterances of others. In either case, however, the effect is commonly affiliative, the result of co-participation and joint message negotiation.

Courtroom dialogue presents a highly structured format which lacks the characteristics of spontaneous conversation. When that format is applied to sexual violence proceedings, it can provide the framework for what I have termed the 'discursive trap of the rape trial protocol'. The format usually consists of only two parts: question(Q) /answer(A), with (A) being limited to an exclusively *yes/no* alternative and with no overlapping, leaving little discursive space to the victim-witness. The textual example, reported on pages 108–10, reveals the typical, fixed Q – A pattern, with the examiner in complete control of the discursive strategy and therefore of event interpretation. We can note that an apparent overlap occurs twice – first in turns 27 and 28, and then in turns 31 and 32, when the victim attempts an extension to the yes – no question in the form of a clarification. The cross-examiner's move (turn 29 and then again in turn 33) *'that's a yes – no question, ma'am'* is an interruption (rather than an overlap), aimed first of all at keeping control of the conversation flow and secondly, at preventing the victim from finding a way out of a leading question. By limiting the witness's moves to exclusively yes – no questions as in turn 47: *P as D. And that's because you didn't cry out, isn't that true – yes or no?* the witness is deprived of discursive mobility and can only answer: *A. Yes, that's true.*

Hedging, a normal conversational feature which participants use to gain time to think is immediately targeted by cross-examiners as a hesitancy which covers up a non-truth. Cross-examiners often highlight the victim's hedges in order to cast doubt on her testimony. For example, let us focus on this part of the exchange:

21. P as D: And you went up to my client's room – a man you did not know very well – at 10:30 at night, isn't that what happened?
22. A: **Well, yeah, I mean**, that was the time, **I think**.
23. P as D: **You think?** Would you like me to call another witness who saw you in the lobby of the building to help you with the time?

Here, participant A, the victim, produces various hedges, *'well'*, *'yeah, I mean'*, *'I think'*, which the cross-examiner pounces upon adding the subsequent insinuation of untruthfulness, *Would you like me to call another witness who saw you in the lobby of the building to help you with the time?* Another example occurs in this segment:

11. P as D: Isn't it also true that you went up to his room with him at night?
12. A: Uh, yes.
13. P as D: I'm sorry – what did you say?

In this exchange, the victim is probably aware of the insinuation behind the cross-examiner's phrase *'at night'*. Drew (1992: 470) makes the point that victims do not answer questions of the cross-examiner. They answer the *presupposition* or the *inference* that they think may be detrimental to them, what is 'behind the question', or what they think the examiner is 'getting at'. In fact, Drew (1992: 470) notes:

> When being cross-examined, witnesses are, of course, conscious of the purposefulness behind the questions they are asked.. They are alive to the possibility that a question or a series of questions may be intended to expose inconsistencies in their evidence, and hence to challenge or undermine it. This awareness on the part of witnesses is manifested in the guarded and defensive ways in which they answer certain questions.

This awareness leads witnesses to pause or produce contradictory responses. In turn 12 of the foregoing exchange, the victim utters the hedge *Uh*, which the cross-examiner immediately highlights as a hesitation indicating insincerity. The cross-examiner aims thus at projecting what Matoesian (2001: 39) has called 'a covertly gendered doubt about the victim's account' seeking to expose the victim's apparent lack of logic.

The last lines of the dialogue are indicative of the dominance strategy of the cross-examiner who, after a leading question '*You knew exactly what you wanted when you went up to Michael's room, didn't you?*', followed by the victim's response '*Yes, I did*', moves to closure, '*Nothing further of this witness*' thereby creating, for judge and jury, the inference of the victim's intention (*what you wanted was sex*) and precluding the possibility for the victim of further clarification.

Functional pattern

Although the speech act pattern in everyday conversation is complex and heterogeneous, courtroom dialogue implies institutionalised functional routines. Obviously, the main speech act activated by the cross-examiner is *challenging* – challenging the veracity of the victim's testimony. Given the discursive rigidity of the courtroom dialogue as explained above, the only speech act left open to the victim, on the other hand, is *self-justifying*. In the rape trial, this determines the reversal of the offender/victim roles. The victim becomes the offender and is expected to explain her sexual behaviour – a sexual behaviour which is presupposed by the cross-examiner's argumentative moves to be socially deviant, in the sense that it does not conform to society's norms of acceptability (see Ehrlich 2001, 2002).

An observation of the discourse strategy developed by the cross-examination leads to an awareness of the role reversal effected by the implications that the victim was promiscuous and therefore, not only an accomplice in the sexual act, but, in reality, its initiator.

Firstly, the cross-examiner uses the second person singular for the events leading up to the violence, insinuating that the decisions were made by the woman rather than by the man or by both parties. All the actions, in fact, are expressed as the structure: YOU DID X WITH HIM. For example:

- you started drinking with my client
- you started a night of drinking and drugs with him
- you partied with him
- you went up to his room with him.

This strategy obviously shifts the responsibility of the sexual activity to the victim.

Secondly, the cross-examiner selects the structure '*You went up to his room*' in order to enact two related strategies, which are typical of defence lawyers' cross-examination of victims. The structure '*You went up to his room*' is repeated twelve times. It seems therefore to be used as a spatialisation frame for the construction of the cross-examiner's narrative perspective. Matoesian

(1997), in fact, mentions the repetitive use of *there-existential* in his data (*there's a door, right . . .*), which serves the function of 'controlling the witness through a spatialized object merely because it exists'. Moreover, this structure is repeated each time with the addition of a detail which compounds the negative image of *'going up to (a man's) room'*.

- you went **up to his room with him?**
- and you went up **to my client's room?**
- you went up to **his** room **with him?**
- you **voluntarily** went up?
- you went to his room with him **that night?**
- you went up to his room **at night?**
- **it was 10:30 at night** when you **voluntarily** went up to his room . . . ?
- but you went **straight to** Michael's room?
- you went up to his room at night **and started a night of drinking and drugs with him?**
- and you went up to Michael's **dorm** room – **which is pretty much just a room with a bed and a refrigerator filled with beer** – **alone** with him . . . ?
- you went to **this good looking young man's dorm room** . . . ?
- and it was **just the two of you** when you **went off** with him . . . ?
- you went **home with him, partied with him, had sex with him?**

The phenomenon of repetition in courtroom cross-examination has been identified by Matoesian (1997: 137) as a means to 'emphasize and dramatize referential content of evidence in testimony in order to thereby organize and intensify the inconsistencies in the victim's account into a cumulative web of reasonable doubt'. Moreover, it serves to give attorneys complete control of the witness.

Furthermore, this segment is illustrative of the complexity of typical repetition strategies often adopted in rape trial cross-examination. Following Matoesian (1997), we can observe the presence of different patterns for the syntactic structure which appears repeatedly in our example. *'Isn't it true that you did X?'*:

Contrastive:

27. P as D: **And isn't it true that other people in your theatre group went home** because it was a school night **but you went straight to Michael's room and started drinking with my client, right ma'am?**

Incremental:

17. P as D: **And isn't it it true** that you finished two drinks that night with Michael?

18. A: That's true.
19. P as D: **And isn't it also true** that you started a third drink?
20. A: Yes.

After numerous questions the cross-examiner goes back to the structure producing the following turn:

Resumptive:

41. P as D: You went up to his room at night and started a night of drinking and drugs with him. After one drink the two of you then had another drink and then another, and then you smoked pot – **isn't that true**?

This strategy of repetition summarises and highlights what the cross-examiner intends as the basic message for the jury, judge and public, which is that the victim acknowledges having misbehaved *'Isn't true that you did X?'* Moreover, this repetition pattern of fixed structure plus variation lends a sense of automaticity to the accusation and therefore a connotation of veracity. Following the argumentation found in Tannen (1989), we could add that the repetition strategy activates recall of a conventionalised social frame or routine, that of the accusatory script common to rape trials. In fact Tannen (1989: 37) notes the position of Becker (1984: 435) who holds that:

The actual a-priori of any language event – the real deep structure – is an accumulation of remembered prior texts; ... our real language competence is access, via memory, to this accumulation of prior text.

Thus, the repetition pattern of our example based on a pre-patterning, composed of an alternation of fixed and varied utterances, triggers memory of previous rape scripts. In the 'rape trial frame', sexual violence is always the result of the victim's misconduct. This 'prior text' is in a sense the 'deep-structure' of patriarchal discourse, which means that the female victim is guilty and the male offender is innocent.

Lexis

The lexical choices of the cross-examiner create a web of associations which are designed to negatively represent the woman's behaviour.

Use of adjectives, nouns and verbs
(insinuating promiscuousness)

You found him **attractive**
With a **bed**
Alone with him
fooling around

Use of adverbs:
(insinuating complicity)

You **voluntarily** went up to his room
(insinuating promiscuousness)
You only knew Michael **casually**

Use of nouns from the semantic field of alcohol and drugs
(insinuating substance abuse)

Drinks, beer, pot, drinking

Use of quantifiers
(insinuating excess and intoxication)

two drinks
a **third** drink
one drink **after another**

Use of intensifying phrases
(insinuating excess and intoxication)

filled with beer
a night of drinking and drugs

Use of dynamic verb groups
(insinuating assertive will and determined action in promiscuity)

You **had sex** with him
You **partied** with him
You **smoked pot** with him
You **called** him

Use of dynamic verb negation
(insinuating omission – and therefore consent)

You **didn't cry out**

Use of stative verbs
(insinuating awareness, conviction and sexual desire)

You **knew** what you **wanted**

Thus, in almost all the grammatical categories, the lexis is loaded with implicit accusations of sexual promiscuousness. Moreover, the basic sentence structure [You DID X], featuring dynamic verbs, along with nouns, adjectives and adverbs which are negatively stereotyped and socially stigmatised behavioural descriptors, casts the woman in a pro-active task, defined as energetic, intentional and competent 'whoring'.

Antagonistic scripts: the discourse of *complicity* v. the discourse of *coercion*

The perspectives of offender and victim can be presented as antagonistic: the former activating the script of *complicity* while the latter activating the script of *coercion*.

The male script of female complicity

On the basis of the analysis given above, we can summarise the cross-examiner's discourse strategy as follows (Table 6.1a):

Table 6.1a: The cross-examiner's script

Accusing	Discourse strategy
Commission	'You went up to his room ...'
Omission	'You didn't cry out ...'
Consent	'You kissed him ...'

It is a script of accusation, which reverses the offender–victim positions and casts the woman in the role of promiscuous provoker. The script is exemplary of the classical defence counsel strategy of demonstrating the victim's complicity in the sexual activity and thereby disclaiming the male offender's responsibility. As Scully (1990: 42) so clearly explains:

> Patriarchal ideologies reproduce rape as a systematic social fact by furnishing the topical content of courtroom talk ... Patriarchal domination – a system organized around the subordination and sexual control of women – propels a second set of signification and legitimation structures: the patriarchal meanings that define how females should act and behave as legitimate victims during the rape incident ... At the surface, membership categorizations are organized around the V's complicity in the rape: that she had consented to sex with her assailant, that she was a willing participant in the very state of affairs she is complaining about and for which she is blaming others, or at the very least, that she had 'asked for it' through her actions and inactions, her acts of commission and omission.

The cross-examination of the victim by the alleged offender's attorney stages the male perspective of the violent event. This male version is also society's perspective. Rumney (2003: 837) repeats a point made by Moody (1995) that rape trial protocols are influenced by specific stereotypes about the sexual behaviour of women. These stereotyped images correspond to traditional patriarchal views of gender roles and relationships.

Juridical institutions like most social institutions have created operative frameworks based on misguided conceptions which turn out to be discriminatory and consequently unjust towards women. According to Smart (1989), the legal process with regard to rape has embraced male interests and ignored women's representations of the experience of violence. The narrative which is normally salient is the male narrative. Through what Matoesian (2001: 39) calls the 'rhetorical efficacy of poetic talk in courtroom discourse', the rape trial tells the male story. The conversational, grammatical and ideological structures are reorganised as 'rhythms of domination'(Matoesian 2001: 39), an institutionally sanctioned male domination.

The last task of the defence counsel is to give the court a convincing explanation of why the victim is lying. And to do so, since motivations are commonly seen to involve the emotional plane, the male script activates the topos of revenge. The victim becomes at one and the same time a woman scorned and a femme fatale, intent on destroying her lover. So, we could add to the male script the accusation of revenge as follows in Table 6.1b:

Table 6.1b: The cross-examiner's script

Accusing	Discourse strategy
Commission	'You went up to his room . . . ',
Omission	'You didn't cry out . . . '
Complicity	'You kissed him . . . '
Emotion	Discourse strategy
Revenge	*'You were going to go after him and give him a hard time . . . '*

Thus, sexual identities are renegotiated and reconstructed by the reiterated institutionalised script of female complicity and consent. Holmstrom and Burgess (1978: 229) in fact speak of 'situated practices of discursive interaction through which sexual identities are improvisationally assembled, transformed and naturalized into a relevant object of legal knowledge to accomplish practical tasks in the rape trial context'.

The female script of male coercion

Contrary to what occurs for the male perspective, the female script does not always emerge forcefully in the courtroom. The victim's story is reconstructible on the basis of a series of institutional encounters that precede the trial: the police report, the medical examination, the telephone calls to help lines, the moments of psychological counselling, and so on. An overview of women's statements in these institutionalised communicative moments reveals an antagonistic script, one of sexual assault and aggression, imposed against her will, by psychological and physical coercion. When we study the female script, a different picture emerges. First of all, due to the conventions of rape trial dialogue, the woman is obliged to activate self-justification as her primary speech act; secondly, her story is one of submission, imposition and dissent as summarised here in Table 6.2a:

Table 6.2a: The victim's script

Self-justifying	Discourse strategy
Submission	'He invited me up to his room . . .'
Imposition	'He raped me . . .'
Dissent	**'*I said no* . . .'**

Moreover, the female script is interlaced with the intensity of traumatic recall, the representation of the overwhelming emotion of FEAR. Some (although insufficient) attention has been paid to this aspect of the rape experience in legal research and practice. According to Holmstrom and Burgess (1978: 233):

> Victims' main emotional reaction at the time of the rape is fear. They report being scared that they would be killed. The rape clearly is experienced by them as a life-threatening event.

Rumney (2003: 874) also states:

> Women's reactions during rape are varied. What is apparent, however, is that fear, or sometimes terror, is a major component part of rape whatever the identity of the perpetrator.

Thus, the counterpart of the male's claim of female revenge is the female experience of fear, which during the sexual aggression is more often than not wordless.[5] The victim is muted[6] by the overwhelming terror of physical, sexual and life-threatening violence, as can be seen in Table 6.2b:

Table 6.2b: The victim's script

Self-justifying	Discourse strategy
Submission	'He invited me up to his room . . .'
Imposition	'He raped me . . .'
Dissent	'I said no . . .'
Emotion	Discourse strategy
Fear	(**silence**)

Some comparisons

A comparative table (Table 6.3) of the two perspectives of the abusive event would thus appear as follows:

Table 6.3:   Male script vs. female script: *complicity* **vs.** *coercion*

	Male script: complicity			Male script: coercion
Commission	*'You went up to his room ...'*	vs.	**Submission**	*'He invited me up to his room ...'*
Omission	*'You didn't cry out ...'*	vs.	**Imposition**	*'He raped me ...'*
Consent	*'You kissed him ...'*	vs.	**Dissent**	*'I said no ...'*
Revenge	*'You were going to go after him and give him a hard time ...'*	vs.	**Fear**	*(silence)*

A related aspect is the fact that society's expectations of women in her defence against assault do not coincide with the reality of the rape experience. Women, who do not have equal physical strength, are overpowered, often caught psychologically unprepared to counteract male aggression, and blinded to submission and inaction by the oppressive sensation of fear. Matoesian (2001: 40), moreover, notes that *'there is an inconsistency between the victim's version of the events and the expectations of patriarchal ideology governing victim identity'*. We could summarise this discrepancy as follows in Table 6.4:

Table 6.4:   Societal expectations of victims vs. reality of victims' experience

Societal expectations of female behaviour expected during the assault	vs.	Reality of female behaviour during the assault
Forceful resistance		Physical powerlessness
Assertive speech		Unheeded words
Clarity of thought		Confusion
Strong reactions		Inaction due to fear

The courts, which expect women to have acted logically and reacted forcefully, likewise expect them to represent that action under examination in a rigidly rational and coherent way.

Thus, there is a behavioural protocol which women must adhere to during the rape trial itself. Yet, there is a subtle variation here. Expected to demonstrate strength, resistance and determination in the rejection of her assailant, the victim is contrarily expected in court to respond to the stereotype of the feminine ideal: demure, polite, soft-spoken and passive. With this 'powerless' discourse style, however, she is expected to demonstrate in a convincingly forceful way that she actively resisted the offender. Her discourse is expected to feature 'power'; it is expected to convince the court that she was assertive and aggressive in 'fighting off' the male attacker. We could present the difference as in Table 6.5.

Table 6.5: Societal expectations of women's behaviour in court

Expectations of women's self-representation	vs.	Expectations of women's representation of the event
Non-aggressiveness		Physical force
Non-assertiveness		Assertive speech
Indirectness		Directness
Passivity		Action

But what representation of logical behaviour and reasoning can a woman give of an event experienced through betrayal, assault and terror? In courtroom discourse, little account is really made of the victim's fear. Little account whatsoever is made of her physical and psychological powerlessness.

The ideological foundations of rape trial discourse

The *Complicity* vs. *Coercion* dichotomy is a discursive trap for victims of sexual assault. How is such an injustice to be explained? How can one account for such inadequacy in juridical cultures which have democratic foundations and consolidated, century-old traditions of juridical practice in crime prevention and treatment? The source of the inadequacy of rape trial practice can be suggested to be found not in the legal and judicial process but in the ideological foundations of gender-related issues in contemporary society. In other words, the only answer can be in the nature of the crime itself. The inadequacy derives from an ideological aspect of the problem, specifically, the fact that we are dealing with criminal acts which are gender-specific, within a patriarchal culture.

For example, Matoesian (2001: 37) responds to the court's expectation of rational behaviour on the part of the victim as follows:

But what precisely is the logic that the victim's logic must fit? Just how does this logic organize inconsistency – an incongruity among facts – in acquaintance rape trials? Is this inconsistency just a generic or neutral form of commonsense legal logic, a linguistic technique of impeachment? Or could it possibly, at particular moments in specific trials, activate, embody, or interact with hegemonic forces of culture? Can legal realities such as inconsistency emerge not just from logical, rational, or natural juxtaposition of contradictory issues of evidence but also from an interaction between cultural ideologies and linguistic resources in the trial context?

Thus, his argumentation points to the ideological underpinnings of gender-related issues in legal practice, which are carried, reinforced and disseminated through language and the conventionalised discourse patterns which are discriminatory towards women. The summary of his critical stance (Matoesian (2001: 37–8) aptly frames the entire question:

> I show how inconsistencies in the witnesses' testimony are constituted both interactionally and culturally through a poetic interlacing of grammatical, sequential, and ideological resources. I argue that courtroom participants construct and resist the legal facticity of rape allegations through symbolically mediated narratives. I demonstrate how language, law and power interpenetrate the institutional field of trial talk to create a richly layered logic, of patriarchal and legal domination, and which are naturalized (made to appear self-evident or commonsensical), and which are, in turn, incrementally produced through the imposition of symbolic power: the power to create reality through language.

It is thus that the male script becomes the dominant discourse, the ideologically constituted mainstream repertoire for the social representation of rape, a repertoire marked by linguistic and discourse features which are inherently abusive towards women. This discourse of abuse is reiterated in institutional discourse, in all those socially sanctioned sites which are called upon to deal with victims of sexual violence but become instead loci of gender discrimination.

Reforming the *complicity/coercion* repertoire

Given the aforesaid premises and analyses, it is obvious that change is not merely the responsibility of the legal and juridical institutions. We can advance two points as evidence for this position.

First of all, if in Western democracy the accused has a right to defence, it may seem obvious that the only way that defence counsel can argue the case for their client is to disclaim the act of rape and try to prove that the sexual activity was consensual. Moreover, from the defence counsel's point of view, this may necessarily require demonstrating that the victim is sexually licentious. Thus, even if legislation has improved so that, in most Anglophone cultures, it disallows evidence of prior sexual history or questioning the victim's moral character, defence attorneys usually resort to insinuating the victim's sexual promiscuousness, as was demonstrated so aptly by the cross-examination scenario reported above.

A second point of evidence can be taken from observations that judges and attorneys are themselves conditioned by gender stereotypes. One of the declarations of the barristers interviewed by Temkin (2000: 225) is exemplary of the sexism inherent in the cognitive perspective, discourse strategy and language use of judicial professionals:

> I tend to size up the complainant and decide whether the more aggressive approach is required or whether the softly-softly approach. If you've got a sort of tarty woman then you're not going to get the softly-softly approach. I mean if you've got a tarty little number with a mini-skirt round her neck who's brassy and will give as good as she gets then you'll be fine with her but if you've got some little mouse then you'll treat her gently and sympathetically because you'll get more out of her.

Perhaps the inroad to improvement in legislation and jurisprudence on questions of sexual violence should be sought above all in the direction of social research and engagement. In other words, it is the social denunciation of sexual discrimination which will rightfully inform institutional practice, raising awareness of the need for change in ideological perspective and therefore in legislative and juridical process.

Thus, new movements in social science research have a role to play in this effort. Forensic linguistics is a case in point. By unmasking the covert workings of social and institutional discourse on gender-related crime, forensic linguistics can foster judicial equity and thereby make a significant contribution to the elimination of violence against women.

Notes

1. *R* v. *Millberry* (2003) 1 WLR 546.
2. As emphasised for example in the First Report (March 1980–December 1981) of the Manchester Rape Crisis Line, p. 5: 'A women who has been raped should be able to expect sympathy, support and understanding from friends, relatives, doctors and police, but the reactions she is most likely to encounter are in fact blame, shock, disbelief and embarrassment.'
3. The First Report (March 1980–December 1981) of the Manchester Rape Crisis Line, p. 15, likewise notes that police questioning of the victim (for fear of 'false complaint' !?) is harsh and lengthy, sometimes lasting from six to ten hours.
4. The transcript of the complete four-day curriculum, entitled *Understanding Sexual Violence: Prosecuting Adult Rape and Sexual Assault Cases*, includes 95 pages and was

124   *The Language of Sexual Crime*

found at: www.nowldef.org/html/njep/directexam/transcript.pdf. It is also available on the Department of Justice Office on Violence Against Women website:
www.vaw.umn.edu/FinalDocuments/usvpros.asp.
5. Rape victims have been documented to have difficulty in verbalising the traumatic experience. In fact, the First Report (March 1980–December 1981) of the
Manchester Rape Crisis Line records a large percentage of *silent* calls to the crisis
line, that is women who dial but are unable to speak.
6. Analogously, on the silencing of victims of domestic abuse, cf. Ponterotto, 1997
and Cotterill, 2003: 54.

References

Becker, A. L. (1984) The linguistics of particularity: Interpreting superordination in
a Javanese text. *Proceedings of the Tenth Annual Meeting of the Berkeley Linguistics
Society*. Berkeley, Calif.: University of California. pp. 425–36.
Berger, V. (1977) Man's trial, woman's tribulation: Rape cases in the courtroom.
Columbia Law Review, 77(1): 1–103.
Cotterill, J. (2003) *Language and Power in Court: a Linguistic Analysis of the O. J. Simpson
Trial*. Basingstoke and New York: Palgrave Macmillan.
Drew, P. (1992) Contested evidence in courtroom cross-examination: The case of a trial
for rape. In P. Drew, and J. Heritage, (eds), *Talk at Work: Interaction in Institutional
Settings*. Cambridge and New York: Cambridge University Press. pp. 470–520.
Drew, P. (1997) Contested evidence in courtroom cross-examination: The case of a
trial for rape. In M. Travers, and J. F. Manzo, (eds) *Law in Action: Ethnomethodological
and Conversation Analytic Approaches to the Law*. Aldershot: Ashgate/ Dartmouth.
pp. 51–76
Ehrlich, S. (2001) *Representing Rape: Language and Sexual Consent*. New York: Routledge.
Ehrlich, S. (2002) Discourse, gender and sexual violence. *Discourse and Society*,
13(1):5–8.
Holmstrom, L. L. and Burgess, I. W. (1978) *The Victim of Rape: Institutional Reactions*.
New York: John Wiley.
Kebbell, M. R., Deprez, S. and Wagstaff, G. (2003) The direct and cross-examination
of complainants and defendants in rape trials: A quantitative analysis of question
type. *Psychology, Crime and Law*, 9 (1): 49–59.
Matoesian, G. M. (1993) *Reproducing Rape: Domination through Talk in the Courtroom*.
Cambridge: Polity.
Matoesian, G. M. (1997) 'I'm sorry we had to meet under these circumstances':
visual artistry (and wizardry) in the Kennedy-Smith rape trial. In M. Travers, and
J. F. Manzo, (eds) *Law in Action: Ethnomethodological and Conversation Analytic
Approaches to the Law*. Aldershot: Ashgate/ Dartmouth. pp. 137–82.
Matoesian, G. M. (2001) *Law and the Language of Identity: Discourse in the William
Kennedy Smith Rape Trial*. Oxford and New York: Oxford University Press.
Moody, S. 1995 Images of women: sentencing in sexual assault cases in Scotland, in
J. Bridgeman and S. Millns (eds) *Law and the Body Politics: Regulating the Female Body*.
Aldershot: Dartmouth/Ashgate. pp. 213–39.
Ponterotto, D. (1997) Battering: the silencing of women. *Working Papers in Gender,
Language and Sexism*, 7(2): 5–24.
Rock, P. (1993) *The Social World of an English Crown Court: Witness and Professionals
in the Crown Court Centre at Wood Green/Paul Rock*. Oxford: Clarendon Press and
New York: Oxford University Press.

Rumney, P. (2003) Progress at a price: The construction of non-stranger rape in the *Millberry* sentencing guidelines. *Modern Law Review*, 66(6): 870–84.

Scully, D. (1990) *Understanding Sexual Violence: a Study of Convicted Rapists*. Boston: Unwin Hyman.

Sinclair, J. and Coulthard, M. (1975) *Towards an Analysis of Discourse*. Oxford: Oxford University Press.

Smart, C. (1989) *Feminism and the Power of the Law*. London: Routledge.

Tannen, D. (1989) *Talking Voices: Repetition, Dialogue and Imagery in Conversational Discourse*. Cambridge: Cambridge University Press.

Temkin, J. (2000) Prosecuting and defending rape: Perspectives from the bar. *Journal of Law and Society*, 27(2): 219–50.

7
Normative Discourses and Representations of Coerced Sex

Susan Ehrlich

Introduction

Recent formulations of the relationship between language and identity, following Butler (1990), have emphasised the performative aspect of identity. Under this account, language is one important means by which identities are enacted or constituted; identities are something individuals *do* – in part through linguistic choices – as opposed to something individuals *are* or *have* (West and Zimmerman, 1987). While the theorising of identity as 'performative' has encouraged language and identity researchers to focus on the agency and creativity of social actors in the constitution of gender, race, ethnicity, and so on, there has been less emphasis placed on another aspect of Butler's framework – the 'rigid regulatory frame' (Butler, 1990) within which such identities are produced. That is, what has been emphasised in recent work on language and identity is the linguistic and interactional agency of speakers in constructing different kinds of identities. What has received less attention, to my mind, are the limits and constraints on speakers' agency in constructing these identities.

For Butler and other post-structuralist theorists, identities are never outside the established meanings or discursive practices within a culture, but rather are determined by the 'subject positions' that particular discourses make available. As Shotter and Gergen (1989) argue, identities are always embedded within discourses and such discourses 'lay out an array of enabling potentials, while simultaneously establishing a set of constraining boundaries beyond which selves cannot be easily made' (Shotter and Gergen, 1989: Preface). What is invoked in these comments is a Foucauldian notion of 'discourse', that is, the idea that people's understandings of the world are shaped by culturally available, sense-making frameworks and that these frameworks, or 'discourses', constitute constraints on the kinds of identities individuals are able to easily take up.[1] Indeed, what I explore in this chapter is the force of dominant discourses in structuring the kinds of identities and experiences individuals discursively claim for themselves. Scott (1992), in an essay entitled 'Experience', critiques historical writing that treats 'experience' as a foundational category, ascribing, for example, 'an indisputable authenticity to women's experience' (Scott, 1992: 31). Scott argues instead for an understanding of experience as 'a linguistic event' (p. 34), that is, an event that is always structured in some way by culturally available discourses that circulate in a given time and place.

In this chapter, I draw upon Scott's work as a way of understanding how a complainant in a sexual assault trial represents her experiences and concomitantly her identity. More specifically, by examining data from a Canadian civil trial in which a woman sought compensation for sexual abuse she experienced at the hands of her father, I show the way the representation of her experiences and identities seem to be structured and constrained by culturally available discourses. That is, while in court to seek compensation for sexual abuse, the woman did not generally represent herself as a victim of abusive and coerced sex; rather she typically represented her experiences in the language of consensual sex. The fact that the complainant characterised her experience in this way is testimony, I argue, to the very restricted discursive frameworks culturally available for the representation of sexual violence and abuse.

Normative discourses and violence against women

Susan Estrich's (1987) book, *Real Rape*, provides a compelling argument for the differential treatment of stranger rape vs. acquaintance rape within the American legal system. The question Estrich explores in her book is why many cases of rape in the United States that meet the statutory definition (that is, acquaintance rapes) are often not considered as such by police, prosecutors, judges and juries. That is, Estrich argues that the law differentially prosecutes perpetrators and differentially protects the interests of victims. And paradoxically, it is the cases of rape that are least frequent that the law treats most aggressively. In cases of stranger rape, what Estrich calls 'real rape', in which the perpetrator is an armed stranger jumping from behind the bushes and, in particular, a black stranger attacking a white woman within the context of the United States, Estrich argues, the law is likely to arrest, prosecute, and convict the perpetrator. By contrast, in cases of what Estrich calls 'simple rape' – that is, when a woman is forced to engage in sex with a date, an acquaintance, her boss, or a man she met at a bar, when no weapon is involved and when there is no overt evidence of physical injury – rapes are much less likely to be treated as criminal by the criminal justice system. Put in slightly different terms, the discourses that surround the prosecution of 'real rape' vs. 'simple rape' cases in the criminal justice system (for example the discourses of police, lawyers and judges) bring into being definitions of what constitutes a well-founded complaint, a believable or legitimate victim and a plausible or legitimate perpetrator. Legitimate or plausible perpetrators, for example, are strangers to their victims, carry a weapon and inflict physical injury upon their victims beyond the sexual violence; legitimate or believable victims are women that are raped by precisely these kinds of perpetrators. The discourses of rape that surround the criminal justice system's treatment of rape, then, construct stranger rape as 'real rape' and render the vast majority of rapes invisible.

Research on the language of sexual assault trial judgments (see Coates, Bavelas and Gibson 1994, Coates and Wade 2004) within the Canadian context is strikingly consistent with Estrich's findings within the American legal system. That is, in investigating judges' decisions in Canadian sexual assault cases between the years of 1986 and 1992, Coates, Bavelas and Gibson (1994) found judges to have extremely limited 'interpretive repertoires', or discourses, in the language they deployed in describing sexual assaults. In describing 'stranger rapes', judges employed a language of assault and violence; however, in describing cases where perpetrators were familiar to their victims and often trusted by their victims, the language judges used was often that of consensual sex. For example, the unwanted touching of a young girl's vagina was described as 'fondling' in one trial judgment; in another, a judge described a defendant as 'offering' his penis to his victim's mouth. Expressions such as 'fondling' and 'offering a penis' conjure up an image of affectionate, consensual sex, thereby situating the violent acts that were at issue into a framework of normal sexual activity. Coates et. al. (1994) argue that such linguistic representations are 'anomalous' because they are inconsistent with both Canadian law and the experiences of the victim. That is, in spite of the fact that Canadian statutory reforms in 1983 explicitly reconceptualised sexual assault as a crime of *violence* rather than a crime of sex, most cases where the perpetrators were known to the victims (even in cases where the accused was convicted) were described by judges in a language of erotic, affectionate and consensual sex. Like Estrich, then, Coates et. al. found that non-stranger rape was often conceptualised and represented as consensual sex.

It is not only the legal system, however, that has some difficulty in characterising non-stranger rape in a language of violence and abuse. Bergen (1996), for example, found that women used the term, 'rape', in partner relationships only to describe extremely violent sexual acts that made their partner's behaviour unrecognisable to them. Likewise, Wood and Rennie (1994), based on open-ended interviews with women who had been raped by dates or acquaintances, showed that the women had great difficulty naming their experiences as rape, because, Wood and Rennie argue, the women saw two different ways of representing their sexual experiences – as rapes or as dates – but neither of these corresponded terribly well to the women's own experiences. While the characterisations of non-stranger rape described by

Bergen (1996) and Wood and Rennie (1994) occurred in interviews with researchers, what I describe below suggests that even women who are in court to seek compensation for sexual abuse can have difficulty representing themselves as victims of violent and abusive sex when their perpetrators are individuals they know and trust.

Data

The data I present below come from a civil trial involving sexual abuse that is part of a larger collection of civil trial data that I am collecting and analysing. While my previous work (for example Ehrlich, 2001) has focused on sexual assault trials within the criminal justice system, I have more recently turned to investigating comparable cases within the civil system because of the limited advocacy complainants seem to have in the criminal system. Within the Canadian criminal justice system, as is the case in all legal systems deriving from the English common law, complainants are not directly represented by lawyers of the state; rather, state lawyers, called Crown attorneys in Canada, represent the state and complainants assume the role of witnesses for the state. For a number of feminist legal theorists in both Canada and the United Kingdom, the lack of agency exercised by complainants who are merely witnesses for the state and not directly represented by the state is noteworthy – and problematic. Within the Canadian context, Busby (1999) comments on the heavy caseloads of Crown attorneys, precluding careful preparation of witnesses for trial. Complainants do not generally have any input regarding plea bargains; moreover, if an accused is acquitted, complainants have no involvement in determining whether an acquittal should be appealed or not. In Busby's (1999: 268) words, 'in law's Official Version, a complainant has no interest in the outcome of criminal proceedings'. Lees (1997) makes similar comments about complainants' status within sexual assault trials in the British criminal justice system. Even more significant, perhaps, than the limited representation and advocacy complainants receive from prosecuting lawyers are the ideological perspectives that they themselves embrace or embody on behalf of the state. Lees (1997: 57), for example, suggests that prosecuting lawyers in Britain are 'inept at countering myths and prejudices about women' put forth by defence lawyers; indeed, according to Lees, 'they often share them'. By contrast, complainants who seek damages for sexual abuse or sexual assault within the Canadian civil legal system have their own legal representation; indeed, they can be represented by lawyers who self-identify as feminists. As Sheehy (1994: 214) says of women seeking compensation for sexual harms against them: 'In a tort suit the woman . . . has an attorney representing her own interests, and not simply the Crown as overworked and sometimes ambivalent advocate for the state.' Sheehy (1994: 205) further elaborates on the agency women are able to exercise within the civil system (in contrast to the criminal justice system) in the following excerpt:

> A woman who has been raped may have many reasons to pursue compens-
> ation. It may be the most empowering action available to her, especially
> if the criminal process has derailed, as it so often does. Compensation
> may be the only process which *she* gets to drive, instead of respond to;
> it may be the only time when the legal system focuses on *her* needs;
> and it may be the only state acknowledgement of a wrong against her
> that she will receive. (emphasis in original)

Given, as Sheehy remarks, that civil trials constitute a forum that victims of violence seem to 'drive, instead of respond to' with lawyers that represent their own interests, I have speculated that they may also provide a site for the emergence of counter-hegemonic or alternative discourses regarding violence against women, that is, sense-making frameworks that do not conceptualise and represent non-stranger rape and abuse in the language of consensual sex. (See Ehrlich, 2002 for some work on this issue).

Marciano v. *Metzger and Metzger (1985)*: The complainant in the case that forms the focus of this chapter was a victim of incest. (I will refer to the complainant as K. M.) The incest began with her father fondling her on a regular basis and after the age of ten or eleven involved sexual intercourse.[2] K. M.'s cooperation and silence were elicited by various threats that the complainant had reason to take seriously, according to a number of judicial rulings. She was also rewarded with soft drinks, potato chips and money. Over time, K. M.'s father gave her the responsibility for initiating the sexual contact. The complainant tried several times to disclose the abuse but without success. At age ten or eleven she tried to tell her mother and at age sixteen she told a high school guidance counsellor, who referred her to a school psychologist. Her father forced her to withdraw her accus-ations to both the school psychologist and a lawyer for the local school board. Other disclosures that she made after leaving her parents' house amounted to nothing until she attended meetings of a self-help group for incest victims and realised that her psychological problems as an adult were caused by her experience as a victim of incest. With additional therapy, the complainant came to realise that it was her father who was at fault and not the complainant herself. In 1985, at the age of 28, the complainant sued her father for damages arising from the incest and for breach of a parent's fiduciary duty. A jury found that the defendant had sexually assaulted the complainant and assessed damages at $50,000. The trial judge ruled, however, that the action was barred because the statute of limitations period for civil cases had expired. This ruling was subsequently overturned by the Supreme Court of Canada and the complainant was awarded the damages.

K. M.'s lawyer began her direct testimony by asking questions of K. M. that imputed to K. M. allegations and complaints regarding her father's sexual assault/sexual abuse. Consider (1) below, which is illustrative:

1. Q: You allege in your statement of claim that your father sexually assaulted you.
   A: Yes.
   Q: That he sexually abused you for a period of approximately eight years.
   A: Yes.
   Q: How old were you when your sexual abuse began?
   A: I believe I was eight.

In this example, the lawyer's first two questions seek confirmation that K. M. has made allegations to the effect that her father sexually assaulted and sexually abused her; both of these questions are confirmed by K. M. The third question then treats the sexual abuse as presupposed information – in other words, information whose truth is taken for granted – given its presence in the temporal clause 'when your sexual abuse began'.[3] Subsequent questioning by the lawyer also presupposes that sexual abuse has taken place. In (2), for example, the lawyer presupposes that K. M.'s father had begun to sexually abuse her and inquires as to how it began.[4]

2. Q: How did it happen that your father began to sexually abuse you; how did it begin?
   A: When I was about eight I was sitting on the couch with him, Mom wasn't home and he had just sent the other kids to bed.
   Q: Where was your mother?
   A: At work doing twine and he was asking me, after the kids went to bed, if I knew what different parts of the body were called.
   Q: And did you?
   A: No.
   Q: And did he tell you?
   A: Yes.
   Q: And what did he say to you?
   A: He said that – He pointed between my legs and said that that was called a cunt.

While it is hardly surprising that K. M.'s lawyer names her father's behaviour as sexual abuse and treats the abuse as information that should be taken for granted within the discursive space of the trial, what *is* perhaps surprising is that K. M. very rarely named her experiences with her father as sexual abuse or sexual assault. For example, in the following sequence about K. M. disclosing her father's abuse to a high school guidance counsellor and to a doctor at the Kitchener-Waterloo hospital, K. M. twice describes the abuse as 'my father/dad was having sex with me' (italicised below).

3. Q: Now then, we know that you told your mother what you did when you say you were about eleven?
   A: Yes.
   Q: And then later did you have another conversation with some other person and made a disclosure?
   A: Yes. I told my school guidance counsellor when I was in grade 10.
   Q: What was his name?
   A: Mr Rys.
        (a few intervening turns)
   Q: What did you tell him?
→ A: *That my father was having sex with me.*
   Q: This is when you were in Grade 10, that would be 1973.
   A: Yes.
   Q: And what did Mr Rys do?
   A: He phoned my father.
   Q: And were you also referred to the Kitchener-Waterloo hospital?
   A: Yes.
   Q: And did you see Dr McKie?
        (a few intervening turns)
   Q: And what did you tell him?
→ A: *That my dad was having sex with me.*

While in both italicised sentences above K. M.'s father is the referent of the subject noun phrase (in other words, my father, my dad) and thus interpreted as taking a more active role in the activity (Eckert and McConnell-Ginet, 2003), it is also the case that the predicate representing the activity, 'have sex with X', is not one that conjures up images of coerced or forced sex. Rather, it is a predicate that denotes consensual sex. One piece of evidence for this claim is the fact that the predicate can occur in reciprocal constructions such as 'They had sex' and 'They had sex with each other.' That is, 'have sex with X' is a predicate designating an activity that is 'engaged in by two people on the basis of mutual desire' (Cameron and Kulick, 2003). Indeed, K. M. also uses one of these reciprocal constructions, 'we had sex', in representing events that took place between her and her father at a point in time when her mother was hospitalised for childbirth. Consider example (4) below:

4. Q: Was your mother hospitalised for childbirth for the children that were born after you, do you know?
   A: She had to go into the hospital to have Rosie, I remember that.
   Q: And when she went into hospital to have Rosie where were you?
   A: Well, the night she went in I was sleeping with my girlfriend in a tent and Dad came to the tent to get me to tell me to come home

and then I had to spend one night with my Dad in bed and then make his coffee and his lunch the next morning.

Q: How old were you then?

A: I think ten or eleven.

Q: Rosie was born in 1968.

A: Yes.

Q: You were born in 1957?

A: Yes.

Q: And you said you had to sleep in bed. Whose bed did you have to sleep in?

A: My Dad's.

Q: Did anything occur that night?

→ A: Yes. *We had sex* and then I had to go to sleep and I was scared that one of the kids might see me in there.

In using the reciprocal construction, 'We had sex', K. M. is highlighting the mutually consensual aspect of the activity, and not its forced, coercive nature. In addition to using this reciprocal construction to represent the sexual abuse she suffered at the hands of her father, K. M. also used the construction 'have sex with X' with herself as the referent of the subject noun phrase (as opposed to her father as the referent of the subject noun phrase as in (3) above). Consider example (5) below:

5. Q: You met Mr Miersma in November of 1983.

   A: Yes.

   Q: And what did you think of that relationship?

   A: He was a very nice man. He was very kind and he liked to just talk.

   Q: And did you make a disclosure to him?

   A: Yes.

   Q: Do you know when it was in the relationship that you made a disclosure to him?

   A: I think it was a month after I had known him.

   Q: Why did you make this disclosure to him?

   A: Because I didn't want to lose him and I wanted him to know right away what I had done so if he didn't love me or didn't think he could love me he could leave right away.

   Q: What had you done?

→ A: *I had had sex with my dad.*

   Q: Now, having made this disclosure to Mr Miersma did he make some suggestions to you, following which you made some enquiries?

As stated above, the referent of the subject of 'have sex with X' is interpreted as taking a more active role in the activity than the referent of the object of the preposition 'with'. Thus, in this articulation of the events, K. M. represents herself as an active participant. While it could be argued that K. M. is the topic of this sequence (she is being asked what *she* did, not what her father did) and hence information structuring factors would account for K. M.'s position as subject (that is, discourse topics often assume subject position), there are alternative ways of representing K. M. as subject. For example, K. M. could have responded with 'I had been sexually abused by my dad' rather than 'I had had sex with my dad', thereby maintaining herself as topic (in subject position) *and* depicting the forced and abusive nature of the events.

Perhaps the most striking – and disturbing – dimension of K. M.'s representation of the sexual abuse she endured was the fact that her representations of so-called consensual sex with other men were articulated in precisely the same way. That is, in keeping with the very restricted discourses available for depicting violence against women, and non-stranger rape and abuse in particular, K. M. employed the language of consensual sex for both sexual abuse and so-called consensual sex. Consider examples (6) and (7) below, where K. M. is describing relationships that she had with men other than her father.

6. Q: Following your separation from your husband did you associate with other men?
   A: Yes.
   Q: And would you describe your association with these other men?
→ A: *We had sex.*
   Q: You say 'we had sex'. You had sex with other men?
   A: Yes.
   Q: With what frequency?
   A: Some were married, so whenever they could come to my house they would come, so it always varied.

7. Q: Are you frightened of your father today?
   A: Yes.
   Q: Are you able to have reasonably healthy and meaningful relationships with men? You told us about the relationship with Peter being a good one, but before that had you had any reasonably healthy and meaningful relationship?
→ A: *I could have sex with them.* I don't know what 'healthy' –
   Q: Let's deal with your relationship with Steven. You told us you didn't love him when you accepted his proposal of marriage; you didn't love him when you married him.

Notice that in both of these examples – where K. M. describes sexual relations with men other than her father – she uses constructions identical to those she has used in depicting her sexual abuse: the reciprocal construction 'We had sex' and the 'have sex with X' construction with K. M. as the subject noun phrase 'I could have sex with them.'

Conclusion and implications

A problem to emerge from these data concerns the fact that a woman who is seeking compensation for sexual abuse does not generally represent herself as a victim of coercive and forced sex but rather as a participant in consensual sex. For Coates, Bavelas and Gibson (1994), whose work I have cited earlier, this problem is, in part, a discursive problem. For example, they speculated that the tendency for judges to describe non-stranger rape in the language of consensual sex was, in part, the result of the absence of a well-developed sense-making framework or discourse (what they called an 'interpretive repertoire') for the conceptualisation and description of non-stranger rape. This conclusion was undoubtedly influenced by the fact that judges used the language of consensual even in judicial rulings that *convicted* perpetrators. In the case of K. M., given that she was not raped or abused by a stranger with a weapon (in other words her situation did not match the prototypical case of rape), she no doubt had difficulty deploying a language of abuse, force and violence, not recognising her experiences in this language. Moreover, Gavey (1999) has made the point that the dominant (and restricted) discourses about women, men and sexuality under discussion here are as much about normative heterosexuality as they are about rape. To elaborate, when dominant notions of heterosexual sex include women 'as the passive recipients of an active male desire' (Gavey 1999: 60), then on a continuum of victimisation, non-stranger abuse (such as that experienced by K. M.) may have more in common with such representations of normative heterosexuality than it does with stranger rape. Indeed, this commonality may account for K. M. representing her experiences of sexual abuse in precisely the same terms that she represented her experiences of 'normal' heterosexual sex. While clearly the process of *naming* an experience as sexual abuse is an important and complex aspect of coming to terms with the abuse, I am suggesting something further: that the lack of a well-developed discourse for representing sexual abuse by non-strangers whom women trust probably does not facilitate this process of formulation and naming. (See also Wood and Rennie, 1994 for discussion.)

A recurring theme in the work of critical legal scholars, including those who focus on the language of the law (see Conley and O'Barr, 1990, 1998), has been the way that lay litigants' voices are silenced or rendered unrecognisable by the hegemonic discourse of the law. That is, when disputes enter the legal system, lay litigants' accounts are transformed and reformulated so that they conform to relevant legal categories and to the general conventions of legal discourse (Conley and O'Barr, 1990: 169). For example, much research on courtroom language (*inter alia* Woodbury

1984; Walker 1987; Drew 1992; Ehrlich 2001) has highlighted the way that lawyers' questions – especially in cross-examination – structure and constrain witnesses' testimony, preventing the emergence of witnesses' *own* stories and *own* voices. Indeed, because the narratives that emerge in trial discourse (especially in cross-examination) are determined to a large extent by the questions that lawyers ask of witnesses (for example their controlling of topics, their selective reformulating of witnesses' responses, and so on), Cotterill (2002: 149) argues that courtroom narratives are best characterised as 'dual-authored texts', 'with the emphasis on the voice of the lawyer as the primary and authoritative teller'.

Thus, for scholars such as Conley and O'Barr, the project of recovering the 'missing voices' in the legal system has meant investigating 'talk' in the legal system and, in particular, 'talk' that is unmediated by legal professionals and/or legal conventions. In particular, Conley and O'Barr (1998: 67) have investigated lay litigants' narratives in a setting – small claims courts – because this is a setting 'where lay people can assert legal claims in a relatively informal environment, usually without the advice or assistance of lawyers'. Taslitz (1999), a legal scholar and lawyer, goes even further than Conley and O'Barr to the extent that one of his recommended reforms to the adversarial system in rape trials is allowing the rape victim to tell an *uninterrupted narrative* of her abuse (emphasis mine). Taslitz (1999: 116) explains: 'The solution is to permit the victim to speak in an uninterrupted narrative. She should be free to tell her tale in a way closer to what is natural for her and relatively free of defense counsel intimidation.' My own work on sexual assault trials in the criminal justice system (see Ehrlich, 2001) has similar implications: I found that cross-examining lawyers strategically exploited dominant and discriminatory notions about male/female sexuality through their questioning of complainants, severely constraining and distorting the kinds of narratives complainants were able to tell. Thus, work by Conley and O'Barr and Taslitz (among others) has been critical in focusing our attention on the *mediated* nature of litigant voices in the legal system, whether such voices are structured by legal categories and concepts or by discriminatory cultural narratives intended to impeach the credibility of witnesses. However, at the same time, the data and analysis in this chapter demonstrate that there is a danger in unduly privileging narratives or accounts of experience that are *unmediated* by lawyers' advice and questioning strategies as 'natural' or 'true'. That is, the complainant's lawyer in the case described in this chapter represented K. M.'s experiences as sexual assault and sexual abuse (see, for example, excerpts (1) and (2) above), yet K. M. often represented these same experiences in the language of consensual sex. Thus, it would be difficult to argue that K. M.'s 'voice' was structured by the lawyer's intervention and influence. Rather, it is my claim, following Scott (1992), that K. M.'s interpretations of her experiences are themselves in need of interpretation: they are structured and mediated by culturally hegemonic meanings. As Cameron and Kulick (2003: 12) argue, 'The language we have access to in a particular time and place for representing sex and sexuality exerts a significant influence on what we take to be possible, what we take to be "normal", and what we take to be desirable.' In other words, representations of identities and experiences will always be mediated in some way by culturally available discourses, and, in this particular case, by the very restricted discourses for conceptualising and describing non-stranger rape and abuse.

Notes

1. I adopt here Foucault's (1972: 49) well-known definition of 'discourses' – 'practices that systematically form the objects of which they speak'. Following Cameron and Kulick (2003), I will not attempt to distinguish between a Foucauldian definition of discourse and a linguist's definition of discourse – socially situated language use – because I assume that socially situated language use in a context such as the courtroom is inextricably connected to the construction of 'discourses' in the Foucauldian sense.
2. The 'facts' of the case are taken from the Ontario Court of Appeal and Supreme Court of Canada judicial rulings.
3. Temporal clauses have been identified as presupposition triggers, that is, as syntactic constructions that are sources of presuppositions (Levinson, 1983).
4. The Wh-construction in English is conventionally interpreted such that the information after the Wh-word (for example *What, Where, How*) is interpreted as presupposed, that is, is already known to be the case (Yule 1996: 28–9).

References

Bergen, R. K. (1996) *Wife Rape: Understanding the Response of Survivors and Service Providers*. Thousand Oaks, Calif.: Sage.

Busby, K. (1999) 'Not a victim until a conviction is entered': Sexual violence prosecutions and legal 'truth', in E. Comack (ed.) *Locating Law: Race/Class/Gender Connections*. Halifax, Nova Scotia: Fernwood Press. pp. 260–88.

Butler, J. (1990) *Gender Trouble: Feminism and the Subversion of Identity*. London: Routledge.

Cameron, D. and Kulick, D. (2003) *Language and Sexuality*. Cambridge: Cambridge University Press.

Coates, L., Bavelas, J. and Gibson J. (1994) Anomalous language in sexual assault trial judgements, *Discourse & Society*, 5(2): 189–206.

Coates, L. and Wade, A. (2004) Telling it like it isn't: Obscuring perpetrator responsibility for violent crime, *Discourse & Society*, 15(5): 499–526.

Conley, John and O'Barr, William (1990) *Rules versus Relationships: the Ethnography of Legal Discourse*. Chicago: University of Chicago Press.

Conley, John and O'Barr, William (1998) *Just Words: Law, Language and Power*. Chicago: University of Chicago Press.

Cotterill, Janet (2002) 'Just one more time . . . ': Aspects of intertextuality in the trials of O. J. Simpson, in Janet Cotterill (ed.) *Language in the Legal Process*. Basingstoke: Palgrave Macmillan. pp. 147–61.

Drew, Paul (1992) Contested evidence in courtroom examination: The case of a trial for rape, in Paul Drew and John Heritage (eds), *Talk at Work: Interaction in Institutional Settings*. Cambridge: Cambridge University Press. pp. 470–520.

Eckert, P. and McConnell-Ginet, S. (2003) *Language and Gender*. Cambridge: Cambridge University Press.

Ehrlich, S. (2001) *Representing Rape: Language and Sexual Consent*. London: Routledge.

Ehrlich, S. (2002) (Re)contextualizing complainants' accounts of sexual assault, *Forensic Linguistics*, 9(2): 193–212.

Estrich, S. (1987) *Real Rape*. Cambridge, Mass.: Harvard University Press.

Gavey, Nicola. (1999) 'I wasn't raped, but . . . ': Revisiting definitional problems in sexual victimization, in S. Lamb (ed.) *New Versions of Victims: Feminists Struggle with the Concept*. New York: New York University Press. pp. 57–81

Foucault, M. (1972) *The Archeology of Knowledge and the Discourse on Language*. New York: Pantheon Books.

Lees, S. (1997) *Ruling Passions: Sexual Violence, Reputation, and the Law*. Buckingham: Open University Press.

Levinson, S. (1983) *Pragmatics*. Cambridge: Cambridge University Press.

Scott, Joan. (1992) 'Experience' in J. Butler and J. Scott (eds) *Feminists Theorize the Political*. London: Routledge. pp. 22–40

Sheehy, Elizabeth (1994) Compensation for women who have been raped, in J. Roberts and R. Mohr (eds) *Sexual Assault: a Decade of Legal and Social Change*. Toronto: University of Toronto Press. pp. 205–40

Shotter, J. and Gergen, K. (1989) *Texts of Identity*. London: Sage.

Taslitz, A. (1999) *Rape and the Culture of the Courtroom*. New York: New York University Press.

Yule, G. (1996) *Pragmatics*. Oxford: Oxford University Press.

Walker, Anne Graffam (1987). Linguistic manipulation, power and the legal setting, in L. Kedar (ed.), *Power through Discourse*. Norwood, N. J.: Ablex. pp. 57–80

West, C. and Zimmerman, D. (1987) Doing gender, *Gender and Society*, 1(2): 25–51.

Wood, Linda and Rennie, Heather (1994) Formulating rape: The discursive construction of victims and villains, *Discourse & Society*, 5(1): 125–48.

Woodbury, Hannah (1984). The strategic use of questions in court, *Semiotica*, 48(3/4): 197–228.

8
Purposes, Roles and Beliefs in the Hostile Questioning of Vulnerable Witnesses

Ester S. M. Leung and John Gibbons

Introduction

Legal background and terminology

In the Hong Kong legal system, as in many Common Law systems, the crime of 'rape' has been abolished and replaced with various categories of 'sexual assault'. Where a person below the age of sixteen is the complainant it is called 'sexual assault on a minor'. Until assault is proved, the legal term for the person who does the sexual assault is 'the accused' and the person who is assaulted is 'the complainant'. After the accused is convicted, the respective terms become 'assailant' and 'victim'. In the cases we discuss today the male accused were found guilty, so we will occasionally use the term 'victim' when discussing this participant, although we will mainly use the neutral 'witness' when it is being referred to in the context of the trial itself. In sexual assault cases in Hong Kong, the complainant must prove beyond reasonable doubt that s/he did not consent, even if s/he is a minor.

Ideologies

In cases of sexual assault there are two competing ideologies in the courtroom. One is that the complainant has in some way provoked or is complicit in the sexual act – one loaded way of referring to this is 'blaming the victim'. Particularly when sexual assault on a minor is involved, the competing ideology is that the complainant is not responsible. In a court case, it is the role of the prosecution to adopt the second view, and that of the defence (of the accused) to adopt the first view. The defence therefore is likely to adopt a hostile stance toward the complainant. In this chapter we shall examine how these ideologies are manifested in the language behaviour of the various parties, not just Counsel, but also the interpreter and the judge. Philips (1998) provides a carefully argued data driven analysis of how judges' ideology affects their courtroom behaviour, and in chapter 4 shows how their courtroom procedures can be less or more 'witness friendly' as a result. Solan (1993) shows how judges frame their judgments as interpretations of the wording of the legislation, but in reality deploy their personal views and morals.

Purposes

The major players all have different, and sometimes conflicting purposes within the courtroom. For opposing counsel, their purposes are in open conflict. In the Common Law system, a well-established understanding of what happens is that the two sides are attempting to construct competing versions of the same event or state (Bennett and Feldman, 1981), two reconstructions of a reality outside the courtroom. As Cotterill (2003: 9) points out 'the adversarial system is not primarily concerned with establishing the true facts of the case; rather, it involves attempts to persuade the jury that one constructed version of reality is more plausible than another'. In criminal cases, the prosecution counsel is usually trying to construct a version that will prove that the accused person is guilty, while the defence lawyers are usually trying to construct a competing version of the same events that means their client is not guilty, or is worthy of lenient treatment. For example:

> *Mrs X died – Mr Q did/did not kill Mrs X;*
> *Chemical pollution occurred – Company R did/did not release toxic chemicals.*

In other words Mr Q's defence counsel is trying to show that in the events leading to Mrs X's death, Mr Q was not the cause of her death, while the prosecution in its version of those same events is trying to prove that he did. Similarly in the chemical pollution case, the plaintiff's lawyer may be trying to prove that Company R did release toxic chemicals, while Company R's lawyers are attempting to prove it did not.

The opposing parties are also trying to construct two different types of 'fit' to the legislation – one that is more damaging versus one that is less damaging. For example:

> *Mr Q's killing of Mrs X was deliberate murder/the killing was unintentional manslaughter;*
> *Company R's release of chemicals was not punishable under existing laws/it was punishable.*

Assuming that we now know that Mr Q did kill Mrs X, Mr Q's defence lawyer is trying to present a construction of the killing that means that it is manslaughter, while the prosecution is trying to present a construction that means that the killing is deliberate murder, which is a more serious offence. In the pollution case the plaintiff's lawyer will be trying to fit the events to the law in such a way that the release of chemicals is punishable, while the defence lawyer is trying a fit which means that it is not punishable.

A further example illustrates the oppositional nature of cases of sexual assault, where events are similarly disputed:

> *A 14 year-old girl claimed that she was 'raped' by Defendant X in one of the recorded cases that we have collected for this study. The defendant did/did not rape her.*

> *Sexual intercourse happened – The defendant did/did not have the consent of the girl.*

In other words the defendant's counsel is trying to show that in the events leading to the act of the sexual intercourse, the girl has given the defendant the impression that she liked him, while the prosecution in its version of those same events is trying to prove that she had not.

Since Common Law courtroom practice is essentially a form of miniature warfare, the two sides are not only *constructing* competing versions of reality, they are trying to *impose* them. When lawyers cross-examine a hostile witness, they have to play a complex game, where they attempt almost simultaneously to do three things:

(1) **construct** and **support** their version of events
(2) **attack** the version of the other side, and
(3) **attack** the credibility of hostile witnesses. (When examining friendly witnesses they need to **support** their credibility.)

In practice it can be quite difficult to separate out these agendas, since one utterance or question may be serving two or three of them, but in principle the divisions are clear. In each agenda, a hostile witness is attempting to do the exact reverse, so cross-examination is a verbal battlefield between the lawyer and the witness, in which lawyers have the upper hand, since in principle the conventions of examination mean that they are expected to ask the questions, and control the turn taking, while witnesses can only respond. Stygall (1994: 146) states 'For lawyers, the focus of attention to question forms is on how to control witnesses. Their assumption is that by controlling what the witnesses say, they will also control what the jurors think.'

Therefore, one objective of witnesses is to maintain their own version of events – if they are found to have deliberately lied this is perjury – a punishable offence, and they would also wish to avoid the discrediting of their character, since this is a humiliating experience in court, and could also spread to the wider community and affect their lives.

The judge's main purpose is to assure that justice is done, but also to avoid future appeals based on their handling of the case, which could affect their standing in their profession.

Defined roles

The courtroom participants have roles that are defined by the rules of procedure in the courtroom.

- The *judge* is subject to such rules, in particular judges are supposed to be impartial – not favouring either side. Judges also have the role of ensuring that other players follow the rules of procedure.
- The *barrister's* role is also subject to various rules, for example not asking 'leading' questions of some witnesses, and in many legal systems there are limitations on the types of questions that can be asked of vulnerable witnesses. Their role is mostly partial, working for one party only, although in principle they are also working for the court.
- The *witness's* role, as defined by the oath they take, is to tell the truth, the whole truth, and nothing but the truth. If they are not representing themselves as defendants (and thereby taking on some of the lawyer role) witnesses are also placed in the role of 'answerers' – they are not expected to ask questions concerning the secondary reality, although they may sometimes be permitted to ask questions about courtroom procedure. This is made explicit in the following exchange reported by Harris (1994).

Magistrate:	I'm putting it to you again – are you going to make an offer – uh – uh to discharge this debt
Defendant:	Would you in my position
Magistrate:	I – I'm not here to answer questions – you answer *my* question

Similarly in our data, a judge says to a witness:

JE: . . . your function is answering questions

- The *interpreter* according both to court rules and to interpreter ethics, should be a neutral and impartial transferor of meaning from one language to the other, not taking sides or assisting witnesses. For instance the Australian National Accreditation Authority for Translators and Interpreters (NAATI) guidelines state under the rubric of 'impartiality' 'Members shall observe impartiality in all professional situations and shall not permit personal opinion to influence the performance of their work' (National Accreditation Authority for Translators and Interpreters, 1990: 39).

Aggressive questioning and the vulnerable witness

Lawyers support their version of events in two ways. The first way is carefully to structure questions so that they both contain the lawyer's version, and prevent the witness from presenting an alternative – in Gibbons (2003) I call this 'information control'. For those 'victim witnesses' (Eades, 2006) who find the recounting of what was done to them difficult in the first place, this makes it even harder to consistently maintain their version.

The second means of supporting the lawyer's version is to put pressure on the witness to agree with the lawyer's version – in Gibbons (2003) I call this 'control of the person', and in other places it is often called 'coercion'. Various kinds of vulnerable witnesses, particularly children, the intellectually disabled, and people who for social reasons do not resist authority, risk being pressured into agreeing with things they do not believe.

Attacking the other side's version, is often achieved by revealing seeming internal inconsistencies or contradictions within the witness's testimony (sometimes known as the 'contrast' strategy). Attempts to establish inconsistencies with other evidence, or with the assumed schemas of judge and/or jury (such as appeals to common sense) are less common during examination, although they are frequent in final argument at the end of the trial. Information is the object under attack.

Attacking the witness's credibility, is achieved in part by status reduction, by creating a perception that the witness is lacking in intelligence, maturity, morality, emotional control, rationality or reliability. As in the rape cases of this study, all of the victims' intelligence and rationality had been challenged by the defence lawyers' that they should have or should have not behaved in certain ways so as to avoid being raped, for example, they should not have gone to the defendant's home, or they should have put up a serious fight with the defendant to indicate 'non-consent' to the sexual intercourse. In this case it is the person (rather than the information) that is under attack. Victim witnesses who are already traumatised or humiliated by what happened to them, or by having to recount it, are particularly vulnerable to this strategy, and in many jurisdictions the distress caused by it has led to modifications in courtroom procedures for handling vulnerable witnesses.

As Ehrlich (2001) pointed out, counsel often assert their discursive control through different kinds of questioning strategies such as 'the pseudo-declaratives and presuppositions embedded in questions – many of which were reformulations of complainants' previous propositions.' So 'not only do cross-examining questions have the effect of revictimizing complainants, they also perform substantive ideological work' Ehrlich (2001: 76). Similar questioning strategies were identified in the bilingual courtrooms of Hong Kong in our data. However the intervention of interpreters can mean that the actual effects of these strategies are unpredictable and the process becomes more complicated. Some of the questioning strategies are reinforced and others diluted through the interpreting process.

Data analysis

The data

The cases that we will discuss were heard in the High Court of Hong Kong. Hong Kong uses a form of Common Law. The defendants were charged with sexual assault on female minors. The data consist of audio recordings that have been transcribed.[1] The transcription conventions are given at the end of this chapter.

Interpreting took place between English and Cantonese, with the Counsel speaking English and the victims of the assault speaking Cantonese. One linguistic resource available to Cantonese which does not have an exact equivalent in English, is the utterance particle (UP) which appears at the end of most Cantonese utterances, marking speech act functions, the speaker's stance, and revealing the discourse status of the utterance. For more information on utterance particles see Gibbons (1981) and Luke (1990).

Case 1

The victim in this case was a fifteen year old female, and the court found that she had been sexually assaulted at the age of thirteen. The Defence Counsel is defending the assailant, not the victim. The interpreter is female. Our interest is in the Judge's interventions, which seem to reveal hidden beliefs. (See p. 158 for the meaning of the abbreviations BDE, JE, etc.)

Extract 1

12. BDE: now <u>the third occasion</u> (.) you told us (.) that *you were thinking* (.) *that* he was going to take (1.0) other (.) teammates who lived in the same neighbourhood of yours but obviously he did NOT (.) is that correct?
13. JE: pick up (.) pick up pick up
14. BDE: yeah
15. ICT: 嘩至於第三次嘅事件呢你就話當時你以為呢佢係會接埋住係你附近嘅其他嘅隊員嘅咁但係明顯地呢，佢就係無接到其他隊員□ 係咪?

  [now <u>as for the third occasion</u> you said at that time *you thought* he would pick up other teammates who lived in the same neighbourhood of yours however obviously he did not +pick them up+ right?]
16. WC: 係
17. IET: right =
18. BDE: = right(.)

In turn 12 above the lawyer asks a question in a way that attempts to strongly control both the information and the witness.

'*now*'

This normally only prefaces an utterance directed to a participant in a lower status position, for example teacher-to-student or manager-to-worker.

'*you told us that*'

is a form of verbal projection which means that any denial by the witness would involve contradicting her previous testimony.

'*obviously*'

This word makes it difficult to deny the content – it assumes shared schemas.

'*NOT*' and '*is that correct*'

Both the volume and the agreement tag pressure the witness into contradicting herself. The combination of all these linguistic features makes the question highly coercive and hostile, particularly when targeted at a sexually assaulted minor.

However, in this example the lawyer, whose English is not always adequate, says 'take other teammates' rather than 'pick up other teammates'. The Judge, ostensibly in his role of achieving maximum accuracy in the account, corrects him, and the interpreter includes the correction in the interpreted version. Notice however that this intervention takes place after a highly coercive question. The comparatively minor English correction effectively reduces its coercion.

In the following extract the question in Turn 60 is once more coercive since it is prefaced with both 'bear in mind' and 'you told us previously'. It attempts to plant a false and contradictory version of the witness's previous testimony. The Judge actively prevents (Turn 61) the Defence Counsel from doing so (Turn 60). He reminds the Counsel that the witness has already answered 'no' to the question, so the lawyer switches his line of questioning (Turn 63).

Extract 2

60. BDE: bear in mind you told us previously (.) you watched TAPES (.) together with other teammates (.) and TCS

61. JE: but she said no =

62. BDE: = yes I'm sorry my lord

63. BDE: is that right (.) <u>at the TIME</u> (1.0) when he had (4.0) sexual intercourse with you (2.0) you were naked

64. ICT: }當佢同你eh {發生性行爲嘅時候呢當時你係咪乜嘢衫都無著係赤裸 □

[when he and you eh have sexual intercourse at that time you were wearing nothing, you were naked, right?]

65. WC: 係

66. IET: yes

Turn 63 is again coercive, since it is prefaced by 'is that right', and the core proposition takes the form of a declarative. It is also insensitive, given the victim's age and circumstances.

In Extract 3 the Judge is once more ostensibly working on an accurate account by specifying the point at discussion, but also protects the vulnerable witness from mistaking the question of the Counsel.

Extract 3

88. BDE: [whispering] I see (5.0) you told the police (2.5) you were wearing is that right em (2.5) an upper garment (.) with a V neck (.) shape
89. JE: what what (.) at the time
90. BDE: at the time when you went to his house
91. JE: when you first went to his house
92. BDE: the third occasion yes my lord
93. ICT: 當你同警方講第三次事件嘅時候呢你就話俾警方聽話你當日係著住一件V領嘅:上衫去佢屋企□係咪啊

[when you told the police about the third occasion that you told the police that on that day you were wearing an V neck garment to go to his home right?]
94. BDE: 係
95. IET: yes

In Turn 88 the Defence Counsel uses a range of linguistic devices which pressure the witness to agree:
'*I see*'
This is a cohesive device, tying what follows to what has been said.
'*you told the police*'
This is a projection of the witness's own words.
'*is that right*'
This is an agreement tag, and its unusual position in the middle of the utterances gives this turn the appearance of a declarative rather than an interrogative. The Judge intervenes, this time twice (Turns 89 and 91) ostensibly on a point of information, to clarify the particular occasion when the assault took place. Once more however the intervention comes when a coercive question is asked.

In Extract 4 the Judge intervenes on a number of occasions:

Extract 4

91. BDE: [whispering] I see (2.0) [normal] indeed (.) that v neck shaped garment I take it (.) {when you put it on you indeed} have to raise your ARMS (.) to go through (.) through your HEAD
92. ICT: 咁a:你:=
[So a: you]
93. JE: = for you to raise your arms? (1.0) to get it off your head

94. BDE: or to put it on (.) to your body
95. ICT: 咁你嗰件 V 領衫呢係咪過頭凹□要

   [so your V neck garment is it a pullover that you have to]
96. WC: 係啊
97. IET: yes
98. BDE: remember you told the police (1.0) indeed you told us too (1.0) that you tried to STOP him (1.0) to take off your (.) clothes (.) remember you told us?
99. ICT: 嗱你就講過啦話你就同警方呢(.)eh同埋響法庭入面呢都係話當時你有制止佢除你啲衫□係咪？

   [okay Ø you said you told the police and Ø also the court that at that time you did try to stop him from taking off your clothes Ø > is that correct <?]
100. WC: 係
101. IET: yes
102. BDE: indeed (1.0) <u>at one time</u> you told the police (3.0) you (.) HELD ON (.) to your CLOTHES (.) is that correct
103. JE: but she's told us that too
104. BDE: is it (.) yes (.) and you told us you HELD on to your CLOTHES (.) correct?
105. JE: that I grabbed hold of my upper garment to prevent him taking it off (.) that's what she said
106. ICT: 嗱你曾經呢係講過話當(.)eh 佢想除你啲衫嘅時候呢 ∖你就捉實件(.)衫 ges(.) 避免佢除 (.)eh 嚟度 (.) 等佢呢係除唔到你係衫嘅係咪？

   [okay you already said that when he was trying to take off your clothes you grabbed hold of your clothes to prevent him so he couldn't take off your clothes right?Ø]
107. WC: 係
108. IET: right

In Turn 91 the Defence Counsel uses coercive devices:
'*indeed*' (twice)
   which makes the content of the question a logical consequence, and raises the volume. The interpreter has some problems in interpreting the rather bizarre question 'have to raise your ARMS (.) to go through (.) through your HEAD' (almost certainly the Counsel meant 'have to raise your arms to get your head through'). The Judge clarifies and corrects the question (Turn 93).

Turn 98 is a highly coercive question:
'*remember*' (twice)
   is a mental projection, using a factive verb.
'*you told the police*'
   A verbal projection, attributing the words to the witness
'*indeed*'

See above

'*you told us too*'

Another verbal projection, attributing the words to the witness, but repeated with a different audience.

'*you told us*'

Another verbal projection.

In Turn 102 the Defence Counsel asks another coercive and hostile question:

'*indeed*' and '*at one time*'

These assume the witness is saying something different now.

'*you told the police*'

projects the witness's own words, making it hard to deny the proposition

'*is that correct*'

is an agreement tag, and Counsel also uses high volume for the elements he is asserting. The Judge intervenes (Turn 103), ostensibly on a point of procedure, that questions already answered should not be repeated, but one may suspect that he is also protecting the witness from this manner of questioning. The likelihood of protection of the witness is reinforced by a second intervention (Turn 105) after the next question, when it does not seem warranted on procedural grounds alone. Once more Counsel's question in Turn 104 is coercive

'*yes and*'

are used as a cohesive device that makes the question seem a logical continuation of what was said previously

'*you told us*'

is a projection of the witness's own words, and

'*correct*'

is an agreement tag.

Something similar happens in the following section in Extract 5, where the Counsel is following an aggressive and possibly distressing line of questioning concerning the manner in which the girl's clothing was removed and the assault took place (Turns 130–140). Once more the Judge intervenes (Turn 141) on an issue of fact, but it also effectively interrupts the questioning.

Extract 5

130. BDE: of course not only had he removed your (.) shorts but also removed your underpants

131. ICT: 佢唔單止除咗你條短褲啦另外亦都係除咗你條內褲□係咪?

[Ø he not only take off your shorts but also take off your underpants +right+]

132. WC: 係

133. IET: yes

134. BDE: again you (.) do not know HOW he (.) managed to do so

135. ICT: 你亦都唔知道點解佢可以除到口係咪？
[also you don't know how he could have taken it off right?]
136. WC: 係
137. IET: right
138. BDE: all you could tell is he simply lied on top of me =
139. IET: =你只係=
[= you only =]
140. BDE: = he was sitting on top of me
141. JE: well why sitting
142. BDE: sorry em (.) that was (.) on top *what he said was* he was simply on top of you
143. ICT: 咁而根據你所講就話你只係知道呢當時佢響你上面係咪?
[Ø Ø Ø so *according to what you have said* you only knew he was on top of you right?]
144. WC: 係
145. IET: yes

Further Judge interventions are found in Extract 6.

Extract 6

175. BDE: will you agree with ME (.) THIS (.) would AVOID (.) the possibility (.) at least you going over to his house AGAIN?
176. ICT: 咁 辯方指出=
[+so the defence pointed out+ =]
177. JE: =well we have really established <u>there were occasions</u> he said I've got a video at home (2.0) sorry I've I've just got to clarify that
[Ø Ø]
178. BDE: when HE rang you up (.) you told us (.) that (2.0) you were going to watch a video about badminton (.) you understood it was going over to HIS HOUSE =
179. JE: =<u>on the third occasion</u>
180. BDE: on the (.) on the third occasion that he (.) [sounding exasperated] she was coaxed (1.0) I don't think <u>we have any other occasions</u> = my lord =
[Ø Ø]
181. JE: = yeah
182. ICT: 噂 eh 第三:關於第三次嘅時候呢當佢打電話俾你就話呢(.) 睇羽毛球帶嗰陣呢據你嘅理解係去佢屋企睇嘅喏唔喏啊
[+so+ eh +so+ <u>the third about the third occasion when</u> he rang you he said watch the badminton video tape at that time according to your understanding it was going to his house to watch it is that right 啊 [/aa/ (UP)]

183. WC: 啱
184. IET: right
185. BDE: so (.) it never occurred to you on THAT phone chat (.) when
            he told you come over to MY house (3.0) to watch the video
            (.) about badminton (.) that you should (.) at least (.) see if he
            (1.0) he could lend you the video and so that you can watch
            it at home?
186. ICT: 咁意思係咪即係話嗰次 :eh 響電話度當佢同你講呢話 叫你去佢屋
            企一齊睇羽毛球帶嘅時候呢 當時你從來呢都無諗過就話 問佢借嗰
            餅帶等你自己可以係屋企睇你無咁諗過

            [so +it means+ at that time on the phone when he told you
            Ø (you should) Ø (at least) to go to his house to watch the
            badminton video tape +together+ at that time you have never
            thought of >asking him< to lend the tape so that you can
            watch it at home +you have never thought of that+?]
187. WC: 係
188. IET: right
189. BDE: you agree with me (1.0) had you done so (1.0) you wouldn't
            end up in his HOUSE and got raped?
            [some exchanges between the Judge and the barristers on the
            validity of the question]
190. BDE: em ah yin (1.0) is LWL (3.5) a teammate of yours?

In Turn 175 the lawyer uses a range of coercive and possibly intimidating
devices.

175. DC: Will you agree with ME (.) THIS (.) would AVOID (.)the possib-
            ility(.) at least you going over to his house AGAIN?

The neutral version of this question is 'Would this avoid the possibility of
you going over to his house again', without the emphasis by loudness.
'*Will you agree with ME*'
    This projection pressures the witness to agree – it attempts to make the
following utterance 'disagreement proof', in part because it is difficult for a
fifteen year old Chinese girl to publicly disagree with a statuesque barrister.
'*at least*'
    These words are unnecessary. They add a particular connotation to the
content (the least action you could have taken is . . .) and may sound
sarcastic.
'*ME (.)*' '*THIS (.)*' '*AVOID (.) the possibility (.)*' . . . '*AGAIN*'
    Here we have the use of non-verbal resources – loudness, and deliberate
pausing. The emphasis is similarly intended to make it difficult to disagree.

The lawyer's purpose is to pressure the witness into agreeing with his strongly expressed contention, which will then make her failure to adopt this hypothetical course of action appear suspect, and implicitly make her partly responsible for the sexual act. It may also be an attempt to suggest this to the jury.

In Turn 176 the interpreter begins to interpret this utterance, but the Judge intervenes and makes the following point.

> 177. JE: =well we have really established <u>there were occasions</u> *he said* I've got a video at home (2.0) sorry I've I've just got to clarify that

'*We have really established*' and '*I've just got to clarify that*'

These projections are making a seemingly unnecessary point that the defendant had previously stated that he had a video machine. It is made on the procedural ground that this is repetition of existing information, but we may wonder whether there is some other point to this intervention.

> 178. BDE: when HE rang you up (.) you told us (.) that (2.0) you were going to watch a video about badminton (.) you understood it was going over to HIS HOUSE =

'*you told us (.)*'

is a verbal projection of the witness's own words (see the discussion above)
'*you understood*'

is a mental projection that is difficult to deny, stating what it was that the witness believed at the time of the assault. It constitutes in effect a second proposition within a single question. The pausing here and later also adds emphasis.
'*HIS HOUSE*'

adds non-verbal emphasis again.

Finally, this turn is a statement, not a question.

The accumulation of these various linguistic forms makes the two statements very difficult to deny.

Before the interpreter can begin, the Judge interrupts Defence Counsel again

> 179. JE: =<u>on the third occasion</u>

This secondary textual information takes the form of clarification of information, but it is unnecessary, since the particular incident that is under discussion has been established for several turns.

The lawyer's exasperated reaction in Turn 180 shows his awareness of this fact, as does the Judge's agreement with his point in Turn 181.

180. BDE: on the (.) on the third occasion that he (.) [sounding exasper-
            ated] she was coaxed (1.0) I don't think we have any other
            occasions = my lord =
            [Ø Ø]
181. JE: = yeah

We must wonder about the Judge's motives in these interventions: their
ostensible motive is not convincing, and the lawyer's reaction shows this.

189. BDE: you agree with me (1.0) had you done so (1.0) you wouldn't
            end up in his HOUSE and got raped?
            [some exchanges between the Judge and the barristers on the
            validity of the question]

In turn 189 the defence barrister once more uses coercion.
'You agree with me'
Here an assumption is made that the witness does agree – it is in declarative
form – and it is also a form of projection (a denial would be a denial of
agreement, not a denial of the core proposition).
'HOUSE'
Volume adds to the coercion.

The question is also insensitive. But perhaps most importantly (and it
may be this that triggered the judge's intervention) the question blames the
victim for the fact that she 'got raped'.

Also by means of using 'you' as the main subject of the utterance the
barrister has made the victim-witness the action carrier of actions: 'agree',
'had done', 'ended up'. This makes it seem that the victim has every opportunity to play an active role in deciding or affecting what had happened. The
most important of all is the barrister's stringing together all the actions with
the act – 'rape' itself, and embedding it as a passive voice so the responsible
actor himself is not mentioned at all. The focus and the responsibility for
what happened are shifted to the witness.

A key issue that arises from the descriptions given here is whether young
vulnerable victims of sex crimes should be subjected to questions that are
(a) highly coercive or (b) relive in detail the abusive experience or (c) blame
the victim. The Judge is uncomfortable with such questioning and there is
a clear pattern in his interventions. In most cases he does so on an issue
of fact, or of repetition of previous evidence, but these interventions occur
consistently after questions that are particularly hostile, insensitive, or coercive. He obviously does not always feel on safe ground in intervening on
the manner of the questions, so instead he masks his interventions as points
of information, but nevertheless effectively disrupts the hostile questioning.
We may postulate that (like Solan's and Philips' judges) he is in reality intervening on the basis of his objection to aggressive questioning of this young

victim. It does not reflect well on the Hong Kong judicial system if the Judge did not feel able to openly protect a vulnerable witness.

Case 2

This case involved a victim in her early twenties who has worked as a karaoke singer (a job which many Hong Kong people think would involve some form of prostitution). She claimed that she was raped by the friend of a female friend on one occasion when she was staying with both the defendant and her friend in the latter's apartment. The interpreter is a middle-aged male who has been rather disapproving of the victim throughout the trial – he seems to blame the woman for what occurred and this belief affects his role.

In the following extract he intervenes in the examination process.

Extract 7

301. BDE: =would you stop a moment I want to ask some questions I won't stand here and listen to you forever
302. ICT: 等等先吓=
  [hang on =]
303. BDE: = you had your chance
304. ICT: 等等先
  [hang on =]
305. BDE: to tell the whole story
306. ICT: 等等先=
  [hang on =]
307. BDE: = I have a chance to ask you questions
308. ICT: 嗱等等先 X 小姐佢話呢 eh: 佢唔能夠 eh 資深大律師就話佢唔能夠 冇了期咁企喺度聽妳講嘢因爲妳頭先講嘅嘢呢佢有啲問題問妳先嘅. 當然佢係有權咁問問題嘅首先妳頭先講嘅嘢資深大律師有啲嘢要問 吓先嘅吓
  [now (.) hang on a second miss X he said er he couldn't er the senior counsel/the learned counsel said he couldn't stand here and listen to you forever (.) because based on what you had just said there were questions he wanted to ask you first (.) naturally he has the right to ask you questions (.) what you just said the senior counsel has something to ask you first 嘅吓[UP / ge ha/ – denotes the end]]
309. BDE: you probably get that I'll let you go through every stage I've been VERY particular to you miss X don't worry
310. ICT: 咁啊或者妳會諗吓啦 eh:: 妳佢會俾機會妳講每一個 eh 細節啊唔急 妳唔使憂喎妳唔使擔心啊佢呢非常之細膩嘅細膩啊細膩每一個細節 都會問到

> [so perhaps you will think about it er::: you he will give you chance to talk about every detail (.) no rush no worry 喎[UP /woh/] you don't need to worry 啊[UP /a::/] well he will ask you about every tiny tiny (.) tiny (.) tiny little bit of the details]

In Turn 308 the interpreter intervenes on behalf of the lawyer, 'naturally he has the right to ask you questions' explaining the lawyer's right to question to the witness. Similarly in Turn 310 he adds 'he will ask you about every tiny tiny (.) tiny (.) tiny little bit of the details'.

In the next extract, the lawyer is hinting at collaboration between this witness and another witness 'KP'. The lawyer hedges his question carefully to make it seem that there is nothing wrong with the friendship, but in subsequent turns attempts to elicit an admission of collaboration on testimony between the two.

Extract 8

311. BDE:　could you tell me (2.0) that I know KP is your very good frien:d and (1.0) like my learned friend and I: just the difference I've noticed that you have (.) come:: and leave this court together with your best friend (.) nothing wrong with that right it's all about trust

312. IE:　yes

313. ICT:　噂(.)eh 大啫係大家知道啦妳同 KP 啊死黨啦同埋呢呢幾日啊

　　　[now (.) er that we all know 啦[UP /la::/] you and ka po 啊[UP /a::/] are buddies 啦[UP /la::/] also these few days 啊[UP /a::/]]

314. WC:　嗯

　　　[/mm/]

315. ICT:　呢位資深大律師同埋主控官呢亦都留意到妳出入法庭啫係㗎法庭都係同嘉寶一齊嘅 a: [emphasised]冇嘢唔妥吓[normal]只不過講吓啫冇嘢唔妥咁樣做

　　　[this senior counsel and the prosecutor have also noticed that you come and leave the court that you come and leave the court together with ka po 嘅[UP /ge/] THERE'S NOTHING WRONG 吓[UP /ha/] just mentioning it 吓[UP/ha/] there's nothing wrong about doing so]

In Turn 313 the interpreter turns the lawyer's 'I know' into 'we all know', which sounds more conclusive (note that in Turn 315 he adds the parties mentioned in the original question – the defence and prosecution lawyers – to 'we all'). This effect is enhanced by the use of the utterance particle 啦 /la::/ which indicates that the knowledge is already established. In Turn 315, in contravention of interpreting norms, he changes the lawyer's question to the third person and emphasises the counsel's prestige by adding 'this senior counsel'. He deletes the important mitigation 'it's all about trust'. Finally the utterance particle /ha/ is usually found in contexts of power asymmetry, such as teacher to child, or disapproving older generation to younger generation. Its use here reflects disapproval and power asymmetry between the interpreter and witness.

In the following extract the interpreter again takes a patronising stance and takes on the role of the lawyer by adding information to the question.

Extract 9

316. BDE: [speaking in a dull tone] miss X:: isn't the truth of the matter this you know what I'm putting at that you asked ah R:: (1.0) to talk to the defendant that you wanted to have money from the defendant

317. ICT: 係咪咁啊＝
[isn't it like this =]

318. BDE: = to settle this case is this the truth =

319. ICT: ＝係咪咁啊 X 小姐：嘥聽住啦吓
[isn't it like this? miss X now listen]

320. WC: 嗯
[/mm/]

321. ICT: 妳叫R 妳叫R
[you asked R you asked R]

322. WC: 嗯
[/mm/]

323. ICT: 問被告[emphasised]可唔可以俾筆[emphasised][normal]妳大家了斷呢件事和解呢件事係咪
[you asked the defendant to give you an amount of MONEY (.) so everybody settles this matter reconciles this matter, correct?]

324. WC: 唔係
[no]

In Turn 319 the interpreter's 'miss X now listen' in effect tells the witness to be quiet while he is speaking, an inappropriately dominant position and at the same time he assumes an authoritative role over the witness. The effect of this on the witness is obvious, as she responds very briefly and with an /mm/ in her subsequent turns. In Turn 324 the interpreter changes the presupposed content, adding significant information 'so everybody settles this matter reconciles this matter'. He uses the verb 和解

/wo ga:i/ which is a Chinese traditional legal term used to refer to financial compensation in settlement of a dispute. The interpreter also adds
a courtroom specific coercive agreement tag 'correct'. This represents a
significant intervention in the courtroom process – the interpreter is in
effect taking on the lawyer's role, and examining the witness. He is also
clearly against her. These additions of information during the interpreting
are often not obvious to the monolingual participants in the courtroom.
However the cumulative effects of the interpreting on the witness is significant as she was positioned as a 'defendant' rather than a witness, and at
the same time has to take on the submissive role of a listener but not an
extensive speaker. Her version of what had happened was only excerpts
of the events elicited and shaped by the counsel. Though interpreters are
not supposed to assert their personal opinions when interpreting, their
interpretations are often affected by their understanding, experience and
their world view. As the interpreter in this case has assumed the role of
authoritative figure and is dismissive of the witness's behaviour, his additions to the original utterances, though subtle, affected the way the witness
responded to the questions and the role that the witness plays in the
trial.

Conclusions

What we see in these extracts is that the underlying belief structures of the
courtroom players affect the way they play their roles. We have examined
the behaviour of a judge and an interpreter. In the case of the Judge, it seems
likely that his attitude toward the witness is one of sympathy. The questioning by the hostile counsel seems to significantly exceed that normally
permitted by rules of procedure in relation to vulnerable witnesses. However
the Judge clearly does not feel comfortable in openly intervening. Rather
he masks his interventions as points of information. There are two issues
here. One is that aggressive and oppressive questioning of possible victims
of sexual assault are still frequent in Common Law courtrooms. The other is
that reforms of the judicial system have not reached the point of practical
implementation.

In the case of the interpreter, the barrister's open blaming of the witness
for the events is compounded by the interpreter's personal disapproval of
her. On many occasions, using a range of linguistic devices, he makes the
questioning even more assertive and judgemental, and even takes up the role
of opposing barrister. When aggressively hostile questioning is reinforced
and compounded by the interpreter, the judicial process is placed at risk.
Once more the Judge fails to intervene when the behaviour of the barrister is
questionable, and when that of the interpreter is in clear breach of interpreter
ethics.

The conduct of both of these cases is depressingly familiar After the work of many critics of this process, such as Matoesian (1993) and Ehrlich (2001), has revealed the unnecessary suffering that is caused, the legal reforms that would impel judges to intervene openly are long overdue.

Note

1. The transcriptions of the courtroom recordings were performed by Leonard Y. Y. Yip, Eva Y. T. Wong and Yama Y. N. Wong, and were funded by Hong Kong Baptist Faculty Research Grant number FRG/02-03/II-22 and CERG Grant number HKBU2146/03H.

Transcription conventions

In the transcripts

- the original utterance is above
- the interpreted version is below.

Symbol	Description
[. . .]	Our back translations / our comments
(.)	A brief pause
(numbers)	Pause timed in seconds
{ } / } {	Pace (faster / slower)
Ø	Material deleted at this point (by the interpreter)
+. . . .+	Material added (by the interpreter)
>. . . .<	Material changed (by the interpreter)
=	Utterances immediately follow/followed
?	Rise of intonation
(UP)	Utterance particle in Cantonese
CAPITAL LETTERS	Loud
/ . . . /	Phonemic transcription

Abbreviation	Meaning
BPE	Prosecution Barrister's English utterance
BDE	Defence Barrister's English utterance
IC	Interpreter's Chinese utterance
IE	Interpreter's English utterance
ICT	Interpreter's Chinese translation
IET	Interpreter's English translation
JE	Judge's English utterance
WC	Witness's Chinese utterance
WE	Witness's English utterance

References

Bennett, L. and Feldman, M. (1981) *Reconstructing Reality in the Courtroom*. London: Tavistock.

Cotterill, J. (2003) *Language and Power in Court: a Linguistic Analysis of the O. J. Simpson Trial*. Basingstoke: Palgrave Macmillan.

Eades, D. (2006) Interviewing and examining vulnerable witnesses. *Encyclopedia of Language and Linguistics*, 2nd edn. K. Brown (ed.) Oxford: Elsevier. pp 772–7.

Ehrlich, S. (2001) *Representing Rape: Language and Sexual Consent*. London: Routledge.

Gibbons, J. (1981) A tentative framework for speech act description of the utterance particle in conversational Cantonese. *Linguistics*, 18 (9/10): 763–75.

Gibbons, J. (2003) *Forensic Linguistics: an Introduction to Language in the Justice System*, Oxford / Malden, Mass.: Blackwell.

Harris, S. (1994). Ideological exchanges in British magistrates courts. In J. Gibbons (ed.), *Language and the Law*. Harlow: Longman. pp. 156–70.

Luke, K. K. (1990) *Utterance Particles in Cantonese Conversation*. Amsterdam: Benjamins.

Matoesian, G. (1993) *Reproducing Rape: Domination through Talk in the Courtroom*. Chicago: Chicago University Press.

National Accreditation Authority for Translators and Interpreters (1990). *Candidates' Manual*. Canberra, ACT: NAATI.

Philips, S. U. (1998). *Ideology in the Language of Judges: How Judges Practice Law, Politics, and Courtroom Control*. New York/Oxford: Oxford University Press.

Solan, L. M. (1993). *The Language of Judges*. Chicago: University of Chicago Press.

Stygall, G. (1994) *Trial Language: Differential Discourse Processing and Discursive Formation*. Amsterdam: Benjamins

9

The Victim as 'Other': Analysis of the Language of Acquittal Decisions in Sexual Offences in the Israeli Supreme Court[1]

Bryna Bogoch

Introduction

Between the years January 1988 and May 1993, the Supreme Court of Israel[2] heard the appeals of 564 defendants who had been tried for violent offences by various District courts. While some appeals were accepted and sentences reduced or increased,[3] only twelve defendants were completely acquitted by the Supreme Court: ten defendants in eight different cases had their convictions overturned by the Supreme Court, while two others, whose acquittal had been appealed by the State, had their acquittals affirmed. All the victims in these cases in which the defendants were acquitted were in some way marginal figures, and half dealt with sexual offences. It is the purpose of this chapter to examine the language of the judicial decisions in two cases of acquittals of sexual assault. I will analyse the ways in which the language of the decisions constructs the victim as 'other'. I will argue that the characterisation of the victim as 'other' is an important part of the rhetorical strategy used by judges in justifying their decision to acquit.

Victims and judicial discretion

Much scholarship has referred to cultural myths and stereotypes that play a role in the way the legal system processes sexual offences (see Holstrom and Burgess, 1978; Frohman, 1991; Ekstrom, 2003; Bogoch and Don-Yechiya, 1999). Unlike other offences, in which the characteristics of the *defendant* have often been associated with judicial and prosecutorial decisions (see Hood and Cordovil, 1992; Rattner and Fishman, 1998; Crawford, 2000; Daly and Tonry, 1997), in sexual offences, the roles of victim and accused are reversed (see Lees, 1997; Temkin, 1995; Coates and Wade, 2004) and demographic characteristics as well as elements in the victim's behaviour and lifestyle have been found to be associated with low rates of charging, convictions and sentencing (Bogoch, 1999; Bryden and Lengnick, 1997; Frohmann, 1991; Holmstrom and Burgess, 1978; Lees, 1996; Spohn, Beichner and Davis-Frenzel, 2001; Temkin, 1995; Tendayi and Abrams, 2002; Ekstrom, 2003). The 'ideal victim' envisaged by the legal system in general (Christie, 1986) seems to be particularly relevant in sexual offences, where in addition to race or class based stereotypes and biases (Carter, 1988), age, marital status, sexual history and perceptions of morality also affect the claim to victim status by women who maintain they have been raped.

However, victimhood is not solely determined by the objective characteristics of the victim (Larcombe, 2002). Rather, in all offences victimhood is constructed in each particular context (Carter, 1988) through interactional activity and descriptive practices (Holstein and Miller, 1990). In rape cases, Matoesian (1993) has shown that defence cross-examination inevitably 'involves categorization work specifically designed to create a disjuncture between the victim's actions on the one hand, and the requirements of normative and socially structured incumbency in the category victim on the other' (1993: 30). Nonetheless, the complainant on the stand can resist the defence attorney's efforts to deny her victimisation, and through discursive practices, she can reject an unfavorable reconstruction of her self and confirm her status as a 'real' rape victim (Larcombe, 2002; Matoesian, 1993).

While these strategies of resistance may be effective in the courtroom before a jury, there is little the victim can do to alter the *judges'* reconstruction of the events and personalities involved in the case, especially at the appellate level. Appellate judges work with files, documents and decisions made by the courts of the previous instance, and impressions of the credibility of both the victim and defendant are made one step removed, as it were. This analysis of the language of Israeli Supreme Court decisions will show how in certain cases when 'others' claim to be victims, the decision is constructed to deny their victimhood and thus justify the acquittals.

The language of legal decisions

Analyses of legal language have revealed the ways in which the rhetoric of law conceals and reifies power relations, and have exposed the persuasive strategies that construct law's authority and objectivity (see Balkin, 1993; Brooks, 1996; Sarat and Kearns, 1996; White, 1985). For example, detailed analysis of the texts of legal decisions has shown that the recounting of the facts of a case is not a neutral retelling, but an explanation and justification of the decision (Gewirtz, 1996a; Papke, 1991). Thus, the structure and sequences of the judges' seemingly impartial and logical retelling of the events is geared to persuading the reader of the inevitability of a particular decision and the correctness of the normative ruling (Mautner, 1998; Gewirtz, 1996a; Papke, 1991).

Moreover, these studies have exposed the everyday knowledge hidden in legal narratives (Ewick and Silbey, 1995; van Roermund, 1997; Gewirtz, 1996b; Mansell, Meteyard and Thomson, 1995), and the common sense assumptions that are subsumed under the guise of formalistic rules (Umphrey, 1999; Mautner, 1998). Feminist scholarship in particular, has exposed the stereotypic myths and assumptions about gender that constitute judicial decisions and legal categories in crimes such as wife battering, rape and sexual harassment (*inter alia* Bilski, 1997; Bogoch and Don-Yechiya, 1999; Crenshaw, 1993; Duncan, 1996; Graycar, 1995; Kamir, 2002; Lakoff, 2000; Ekstrom, 2003).

Studies that have focused on rape judgments have shown how specific linguistic devices, such as euphemisms, passive and agentless grammatical constructions, nominalisation, distancing devices and eroticising terms are used by judges when they describe sexual offences, so that the responsibility of the defendant is minimised even when the decision is to convict (Coates and Wade, 2004; Ehrlich, 2001).[4] These devices enabled judges to produce accounts that concealed violence and the victim's resistance, obscured the defendant's responsibility, and blamed or pathologised the victim (Coates and Wade, 2004).

The construction of 'otherness'

Gewirtz (1996b) has claimed that the main dynamic of the trial is 'to support the norms of socially acceptable behavior by defining otherness'. In fact, it is claimed that law's power is not so much in its prohibitionary force as in its disciplinary function of tracing the boundary between the accepted and normal and the unaccepted and abnormal (Duncan, 1996).

It is through language that the constitution of 'others', the expression of affiliation and distance, and the acceptance and rejection of social practices is accomplished (Eckert and McConnell-Ginet, 1995). Recent studies have examined the linguistic construction of the 'other' in a variety of discourse genres. Thus, for example, Hughes (1995) discusses the gendered construction of 'other' in scientific discourse. She refers to strategies such as naming, that she defines as the use of metaphors and analogies to support the perspective and power of the dominant class, and objectification, in which the 'other' is distanced from the seemingly neutral observer.

Sometimes it is the construction of the normal that is accomplished by the marking of the 'other' in a context specific manner, while the dominant group remains unmarked. Thus Gabriel (1998) who studied racism in the media, claims that it is whiteness that is constructed 'precisely by the way in which it positions others at its borders' (Gabriel, 1998: 13). Whiteness, he claims, establishes itself as the norm by defining others and not itself, so that the privileges of whiteness appear unraced. Gabriel refers to the discursive strategies used in the construction of whiteness as 'exnomination', the power not to be named, and naturalisation, the marking of the others (see also Lakoff, 2000).

Usually, studies that have analysed the construction of the 'other' in the discourse of legal decisions in criminal trials have focused on the convicted defendant. For example, Sarat (1993) shows how the 'otherness' of the defendant is constructed in a capital trial. Citing Garfinkel, he says that 'the denounced person must be ritually separated from a place in the legitimate order . . . He must be placed "outside", he must be made "strange"' (Sarat and Kearns, 1996: 174). Thus, in order to enhance the norm, the 'other' is associated with the antithesis of the positive traits that are attributed to the benchmark citizen (Thornton, 1997).

If cases that end in conviction construct the defendant as the 'other', what happens in cases of acquittal? This is what I examined in the analysis of the language of legal decisions in sexual assault cases in the Israeli Supreme Court, that uses insights from strategies in the construction of the 'other' in various discourses and from the narrative, linguistic and rhetorical analyses of legal texts.

Characteristics of cases in which the defendant was acquitted

Table 9.1 presents the list of the cases in which defendants were acquitted by the Supreme Court, and a brief description of these cases. As we can see in Table 9.1, more defendants in sexual offences were acquitted by the Supreme Court than in either of the other offence types, with acquittals of six defendants in sexual offences, compared to three in offences against life and three in bodily harm offences. As others have noted (for example, Lees, 1996; Matoesian, 1993; Spohn, Beichner and Davis-Frenzel, 2001) the law's processing of sexual offences makes proof particularly difficult and has resulted in a higher attrition rate in these cases than in other offences (Hunter, 1996; Shahar, 1993). The higher proportion of convictions that were overturned in sexual offences indicates that the attrition does not stop when the defendant has been convicted, but continues even to the level of the Supreme Court.

Table 9.1 shows that except for one case (10)[5] every victim could be classified as 'the other', in that they were not adult male Jewish Israelis, who constitute the definition of normal in Israeli society. Instead they were in some way 'exceptions' to this norm.

The victims in three cases were Arab males, one of whom (4) was a twelve year old boy who claimed to have been raped and assaulted. Two of the five women victims were prostitutes (3, 6), two were thirteen year old girls (2, 8) and one was a tourist (1). One Jewish male victim was a prisoner serving

Table 9.1: Acquittals in the Supreme Court, 1988–1993

Case no.	Offence	Sex of defendant	Defendant characteristics	Sex of victim	Victim characteristics	Sex of judges (3)	Sex of prosecutor	Sex of defence lawyer	Previous sentence
1.	aggravated rape, attempted sodomy, indecent act	M	55 years old 'playboy'	F	Tourist	3 M	M	F	18 months + 30 months suspended
2.	intercourse with minor, indecent act with minor	M	46 years old, musician	F	13 years old	3 M	F	F	4 years + 1 year suspended
3.	rape of minor; indecent act with minor	2 M	Arab	M	Arab, 12 years old	2 M 1 F	M	M	Convicted, sentence not indicated
4.	aggravated rape, aggravated sodomy	M	Arab	F	prostitute	3 M	M	M	Convicted, sentence not indicated
5.	indecent act	M	beggar	F	13 years old	3 M	M	M	acquittal
6.	murder	M	prisoner	M	Prisoner	3 M	F	M	life
7.	manslaughter	M	border policeman	M	Arab	3 M	M	M	acquittal
8.	attempted murder, aggravated assault	M	electronic technician	F	prostitute	3 M	F	M	4 years + 5000 shekel to victim
9.	grievous bodily harm	2 M	Arab	M	Arab	2 M 1 F	M	F	16 months + 20 suspended + 6000 shekel fine
10.	aggravated assault	M	store owner	M	customer	3 male	M	M	120 hours public service

a sentence for drug and property related offences (5). According to Black's (1989) scheme, crimes against those who are not full 'normal' citizens are considered as less serious, less worthy of punishment than crimes against people who exemplify true personhood, especially when the perpetrator is of higher rank. Thus, chances of acquittal are higher when victims are 'others', because 'others' often are not regarded as true victims.

This is not to suggest that victims of convictions were not 'others' as well. In these data, about 40% of the victims of convicted offenders were also the same kinds of 'others'. However, the claim here is that it is easier for judges to justify acquittals in offences against 'others' and moreover, that the construction of the 'otherness' of the victim becomes part of the judge's retelling of the case to justify the reversal of convictions.

This chapter will examine the process of the identification and construction of the victim as 'other' so that the inevitable decision of acquittal must follow. I will present a detailed analysis of the language of the decisions in two sexual offences in which the convictions were overturned by the judges of the Supreme Court. Specifically, I focus on the strategies discussed above, including naming, distancing, exnomination, and naturalisation, as well as on the sequencing of the judges' narratives to demonstrate how the creation of a disjuncture between the normal and the 'other' is accomplished. It should be noted that my analysis is not geared to demonstrate that the judges of the Supreme Court erred in their decision to acquit, but to show how the construction of the 'otherness' of the victim is an integral part of the judges' justification of that decision.

Case 1: 'the Playboy' and 'the Tourist'

Sexual offences often depend solely on the judges' evaluation of the credibility of the defendant and the victim, and the elimination of the need for corroborative evidence in many modern legal codes (such as Spohn and Horney, 1992), including in Israel since 1990, has enhanced the importance of the judges' impressions of the trustworthiness of the parties. However, at the appellate level, judges cannot personally form an impression of the witnesses, so that when the District Court has decided to believe the victim in rape cases, the appellate judges who overturn the decision must undermine the favourable impression of the victim that was formed in the previous court.

In case number 1, the defendant appealed the conviction and the severity of the sentence of 18 months in prison and an additional 30 months suspended sentence for aggravated rape, indecent acts and attempted sodomy.[6] The State had originally appealed the leniency of the sentence, but withdrew its appeal during oral presentations held prior to the Court's official hearing of the case. Both the victim and the defendant agreed that sexual contact had taken place, but the victim claimed that it was due to coercion and was accompanied by physical violence, whereas the defendant maintained that it was consensual. In their decision, the judges acknowledge that it is unusual for an appeals court to evaluate the credibility of witnesses without the opportunity to personally observe them on the stand. However, they maintain that 'when there are weaknesses in the witness' version',[7] even if 'the witness made a positive impression on the judges of first instance', the appeal judges must consider the 'objective flaws' and 'cannot base a criminal conviction' on the 'favorable impression created by the witness'. Thus, in their decision to overturn the conviction and acquit the defendant, the Supreme Court judges imply that the judges of the first instance had been 'taken in' by the victim, and had not sufficiently considered the inconsistencies in her tale. They had to demonstrate that the victim's claims regarding the defendant's violence and coercion were not consistent with their depiction of the victim and the defendant. By constructing the victim as the 'other', the credibility of her testimony is undermined and the 'objective flaws' that the previous judges had deemed unimportant now provide the basis for overturning the conviction of the defendant.

How is the victim presented in this case? The first mention of the victim occurs when the court states that, 'The District Court decided in its decision that the appellant had intercourse with a tourist from the United States (hereafter complainant)'. The fact that her status as tourist is the first feature mentioned identifies the frame in which the court has categorised the victim. She is from another country, another culture, and a temporary visitor. She is not 'us'.

Next, we are told that the complainant 'has admitted that in her relations with men, she adopts a 'permissive' approach and decides easily to engage in sexual relations with men and actually frequently engages in such contacts'. Contrast this description with the way in which the defendant is presented. 'It should be noted that the appellant is known as a person who likes to have fun and is considered a 'playboy' who customarily goes out and engages in contacts with many women.' The victim's sexual activity is presented as an 'admission', something conceded when necessary but not offered willingly, a confession of guilt.[8] What is being admitted is her permissive approach to sex, which assumes that the victim's open sexual behaviour is something negative. For the defendant, on the other hand, sexual activity is not an admission, but almost an advertising card, he is known as a 'playboy'.[9] For him, sex is combined with having a good time, with fun, rather than a negative act to be admitted in court.

Once these identities are presented, the court finds it 'extremely strange' that the defendant would engage in violent behaviour with the victim when he could have gotten what he wanted without any problem. In fact, many elements of the victim's testimony are labeled 'strange'. For the male judges of the court, it is inconceivable that a playboy should use force in sexual relations; thus, they suggest that 'the only reasonable explanation for the use of force in such a situation' would be if the defendant was a 'sick sadist who derives pleasure from the use of force and from the abuse of victims of sexual assault'. In order to eliminate this possibility, the judges had a psychiatric examination performed on the defendant (with the assent of both sides), to discover if he in fact suffered from psychological disorders that could explain the 'strange behaviour' described by the complainant. 'And here' say the judges, the psychologist found that there were no

> signs of mental illness or psycho-motor unrest or any tendency to violent behaviour. The expert did not get the impression that there was any pathology whatsoever in the sexual domain; the image that was ascertained by him [the psychologist] was one of a man who lives a rich and *normal* social life. (emphasis added)

Moreover:

> The appellant has emphasised, and there have been no denials of this claim, that his past is completely clean and that he never was entangled in any criminal investigation of any kind, and no complaints were ever submitted against him. The appellant was 55 years old at the time of the event, and if we start with the assumption that he did indeed perform these violent actions and the abuse, without any necessity, then it is difficult to understand how a person with such tendencies did not get entangled in any which way with the law before this.

First the judges set up a binary contrast: a normal man, who never uses force, versus a sadist, who uses force. Once the judges have proven scientifically and objectively, on the basis of the psychological report, that he is not a sadist, then within this logic they must conclude that he is a normal man who does not use force. Then, based on their own experience of the world and of the law, they confirm this assessment that it is inevitable that men of his age who were sexually violent would have had such complaints made against them in the past. However, they do not use similar logic or experience to evaluate the victim's behaviour. For example, they could have set up a similar contrast: either she is a pathological liar, and thus would have invented such a tale, or she is a normal woman who would never accuse a sexual partner without cause. They could even have asked her to be examined by a psychologist and buttressed an evaluation of normalcy by noting that she had never complained about a sexual partner in the past.[10] It is the choice about what behaviour to explain and what to question, what is normal and what is strange, what Gabriel (1998) calls exnomination and naturalisation, that is the basis for the way the judges justify their decision.

Having constructed this picture of a normal, law-abiding, fun-loving, sexually successful and active man, who has no motive for or any tendency to engage in violence during sex, the judges must now continue to undermine both the victim's character and the evidence she presented. Thus, the judges dismiss her claim that she had been slapped around and thrown down by the defendant.

The complainant claimed that as soon as they entered the apartment, the defendant administered hard blows and smacks to her face. It is her claim that there were tens of blows of such force that they were strong enough to throw her down to the ground. In order to understand this claim it is important to add that the complainant is an active sportswoman who is surely not easily thrown to the ground. And here indeed, no signs were found on her head and face that in all likelihood would appear if in fact such a large number and such powerful blows had been administered to her.

The judges present two reasons for doubting the credibility of the victim's claim of violence. One is that there were no overt signs of violence on the victim. However, in another part of the decision we learn that the medical examination of the victim was conducted several days after the rape. Brooks (1996) has explained that judges at the appellate level who reverse decisions use a different 'narrative glue' than that which is presented in the primary courts in order to persuade that the conclusion is inevitable. Here, by ignoring the connection between the lack of bruises and the date of the examination, the judges can justify their challenge to the credibility of the victim.

The other reason for doubting the victim's claim that the defendant violently attacked her is because she is an 'active sportswoman'. Her strength as an active sportswoman undermines her legitimacy as a real victim (Christie, 1986), and is part of the 'other' identity the judges construct for the victim. Not only is she sexually active, but she is also physically active. Contrary to conventional notions of gendered vulnerability and the dominant image of the vulnerable, weak, passive woman (Hollander, 2002) , this victim cannot easily be pushed down, and therefore, in the judges' logic, cannot be raped.

The judges do have to contend with evidence of 'slight red marks' on her chest, which the victim claimed the defendant had made with burning cigarettes. The judges quote experts who

> could not confirm that these signs were caused by burns from a burning cigarette. This possibility was not completely dismissed by them [the experts] but there is nothing in the testimony of the doctors that can be considered support for the complainant's version. The fact that the complainant, when she returned to the hotel after the meeting with the appellant, asked that she be given lotion against burns cannot be used as evidence to substantially support her claim.

Here the judges diminish both the evidence brought by the victim to support her version, as well as the rape and violence, which become a 'meeting' or 'encounter' in the judges' narrative. Using passive constructions (that she be given lotion, was not completely dismissed) and nominalisations (such as 'testimony'), the judges distance themselves from the complainant's versions, both linguistically and substantively.

The judges cite two additional points that seriously undermine the victim's credibility. One concerned the accusation of sodomy, and the accompanying physical evidence from the medical examination conducted several days after the encounter to support her claim. But what the complainant did not reveal during police investigation, and what was revealed only in the course of the trial is the fact that the night before the encounter with the appellant against whom there is a criminal charge, the complainant had sexual contact of her own free will with another man, who in the course of it had performed anal penetration. This fact also must damage in no small way the weight of the complainant's testimony.

The accusation of sodomy is found wanting for two reasons: the fact that the victim had engaged in certain sexual acts with another man of her own free will and the fact that the she had withheld this important information from the police. It is not clear why a victim of violent rape would have to discuss the events of the night preceding the rape when she is being investigated by the police about the rape itself. Her failure to volunteer this information to the police is considered a serious blow to her credibility. But would her credibility have been damaged so severely had she engaged in 'ordinary' sex the night before and not mentioned it to the police? It seems that the fact that she engaged in anal sex of her own free will puts her more securely in the category of the 'other'.

The second point that undermines her credibility is 'the strange expressions' used by the complainant during the trial that point to her 'rich imagination'. The judges bring two examples of these 'strange expressions'. One is that she thought she saw 'spiderwebs behind the heads of the judges'. In addition, the judges say, 'she has a tendency to believe certain facts on the basis of what she learned from films that she saw'. The logic used by the judges is that 'strange' women with rich imaginations cannot be credible. People who believe what they learn in movies are not to be believed, and someone who sees spiderwebs over the heads of the judges when being cross-examined in a courtroom must be discounted. They firmly belong to those 'others' who cannot be the victims of criminal offences by 'normal' people.

However, it is not only what *is* labelled as abnormal but what is *not* regarded as strange or exceptional by the judges that is part of the judges' narrative of acquittal. Indeed the judges do not label as strange or ridiculous the willingness of any person to subject herself to all that is involved in a rape trial, including extending her stay in a foreign country and probably seriously disrupting her life in her own country, in order to bring unfounded charges against a defendant to whom she was initially attracted. Again using nominalisation and passive constructions, the judges admit that they had not been presented with any persuasive evidence about a 'reasonable motivation that would cause the submission of such a terrible story on the part of the complainant against the appellant'. Unlike the reasoning used to support the claims of the defendant, they do not point to a clean criminal record on her part, nor do they refer to the fact that the victim had never accused anyone of rape, despite her active sexual life, and that there is nothing in her past behaviour that would indicate a tendency to bring false charges against people. These are crucial in the construction of the identity of the normal male, against which they measure the behaviour of the defendant. For the judges, the fact that a playboy would force a woman to do what he could achieve without force is patently ridiculous, because that is not what a normal man would do. However, the judges are not persuaded that their failure to find any motive for a fraudulent claim against the defendant supports the victim's position. After she has been constructed as an 'other', as 'strange', as 'abnormal', it is impossible to understand what would motivate her. The entire decision reflects the judges' construction of the other, a person who is different from the normal, and whose credibility cannot be trusted.

Case 2: The 'Musician' and the 'Fat Girl'

In case number 2, the defendant was acquitted by the Supreme Court of intercourse with a minor, and of indecent acts with a minor, and the sentence of four years imprisonment and one year suspended sentence that had been imposed by the District Court was revoked. In sexual offences involving minors, it is impossible to convict without corroboratory evidence. Thus, although the credibility of the victim is always an issue in sexual offences, the appellate judges must also find fault with the corroboratory evidence, in order to challenge the conviction. Perhaps it is not surprising that three of the ten acquittals in this sample involve children, whose 'otherness' is established in the law itself and whose credibility is thus considered equivocal.

In this particular case, the issue in doubt was whether intercourse had taken place. The fact that the defendant committed indecent sexual acts was admitted from the beginning. However, the judges chose to acquit him of *all* charges against him, because, I will claim, the victim has been constructed as so different from the normal, so much of an 'other' that the offences against her are cancelled out.

The judge consciously structures the narrative part of the decision (in other words, the events that occurred) using a theatre metaphor. He presents the cast of characters, labelled the appellant and the complainant and then the narrative which is divided into acts: the first act which includes what is defined as a prologue, the second act, the third act and the epilogue. He then discusses the points which he claims challenge the previous judges' decision, titling each section according to these problematic elements ('the diary', 'the electricity stoppage'). In the last paragraph the judge renders his decision, including his feelings of disgust about the defendant's behaviour.

The very structure of the decision is part of the judge's persuasive strategy. It allows him to highlight the victim's problematic *personality* in the context of a discussion of the 'cast of characters', while describing the defendant's *actions* as part of the construction of the events of the case. He is thus able to describe the defendant's actions without referring to what these actions reveal about his personality and character, while providing the framework of an 'other' in which to interpret the actions of the victim.

The decision starts with a brief description of the defendant and a lengthy psychological portrait of the victim, even before the events of the case and the issues in dispute are presented. As in the previous example, the 'otherness' of the victim is contrasted with the ordinariness of the defendant. However, unlike the previous case, where the psychological motivation of the defendant is an issue while the reasons for the victim's behaviour are hardly considered, here the judge devotes much of the decision to the victim's psychological state. In effect, in his presentation of the victim and the defendant, the judge has reversed the positions of the two: the victim is on trial, and, because she is such an exceptional girl, in appearance, interest and behaviour, she cannot be a true victim.

The defendant is introduced to us as a 46 year old 'musician (a drummer) in different orchestras,[11] married and a father of two adolescent girls'. Describing him as a musician establishes his respectability, although as becomes clear later on, he is not steadily employed and plays with impromptu groups. He could just as easily have been described as an occasional drummer, but that would have marred the contrast between the 'other' victim and the 'ordinary' defendant. The victim was thirteen years old at the time of the offence, and 'despite her youth and the fact that she was brought up in a traditional framework, she began already at the age of twelve to be immersed and occupied with sexual matters'. The use of the phrase 'immersed and occupied' just after the description of the work of the defendant seems to suggest that for the victim, sex is almost an occupation. Thus, the potential vulnerability of the child which would place her firmly in the category of ideal victim (Christie, 1986) is countered by the dubious respectability of her character and behaviour due to her interest in sex.

The judge then cites extensive excerpts from the trial transcripts to indicate how unusual the victim was, using such terms as 'exceptional', 'abnormal' and 'pathological'. He quotes friends and the victim herself explaining how great was her interest in sex, and the lies she told about her sexual behaviour. He quotes a psychologist who testified that her lies were important for her especially because she was a very fat girl, with a low self-image, and that her lying was a pathological effort to improve her self-image. The lengthy emphasis on the physical and psychological portrait on the victim – more than one and a half pages of the eight page decision – is highly unusual and strengthens the impression that it is the victim who is on trial. The irregularity of this concern with the victim's personality is so obvious that the judge actually justifies his behaviour, claiming that:

I have written somewhat at length about the description of the character of Rachel [a pseudonym used by the judge] as it emerges from the evidence because her testimony – that was in effect the only testimony – was used as the basis for the conviction of the appellant.

The presentation of evidence from the court proceedings at this point in the decision is a marked departure from the usual structure of judicial decisions. In general, a short summary of the case and the issues in question are presented, and only then do the judges refer to the court proceedings and documents to justify their stand on specific matters. The sequential placing of the evidence about the victim's sexual 'otherness' at the start of the decision even before the description of the disputed events serves a number of rhetorical functions: (1) it underlines the abnormalcy of the victim; (2) it provides the frame for the interpretation of the rest of the issues in the case; and (3) it presents the strangeness of the victim as unquestionable, coming as it does before the discussion of the contested issues. Her strangeness thus becomes a given, taken for granted understanding that will justify the judge's decision about her credibility.

In addition, neither here nor at any other point in the decision are we presented with any similar information about the defendant. We do not know what he looks like, we do not know if he has a psychopathological tendency to lie, nor do we know what his friends said about him. Of course, it may be that these issues were never brought up in court, but it is highly unlikely that the defendant's character was not an issue at the trial.[12] We do learn at the very end of the decision, after the judge has already given his verdict, that the defendant in fact does lie about his age, and presents himself as much younger than he is. However, if the judge had presented the lies of the defendant parallel to the discussion of the victim's behaviour, the portrait of the victim as 'strange' would have been diminished.

In what the judge calls the 'prologue', the background to the charge is described. The victim had placed an ad for a pen pal in a youth newspaper, giving her age, hobbies and phone number. The defendant called her and began discussing sex with her on the phone, including instructions on masturbation. In addition, he sent her pornographic material. They then arranged to meet at the victim's house. These facts are more or less undisputed by both sides, and the judge presents them without comment. He could have used this information in his description of the characters, as evidence of the disturbed nature of the defendant. However, by placing it in the context of a description of the events, this behaviour is presented without any indication about what it implies about the defendant's character. As a part of the prologue, it is outside the main narrative, and therefore the deviance of the defendant's actions becomes peripheral to the issues that are subject to the judge's analysis and decision.

The main dispute in the case is about what happened after they decided to meet. The defendant claimed that he waited for her for about an hour, but she never appeared. The victim claimed that they had had physical contact on the landing between the staircase connecting two stories of the apartment building, and then in order to avoid neighbours who were going up and down, he led her to the shelter,[13] had intercourse with her, and ruptured her hymen.

The bulk of the decision is used to prove that the judge of the previous instance was mistaken in his faith in the victim's testimony. The judge emphasises the dangers of convictions in cases which are largely based on the testimony of one witness, and cites precedents that warn of the necessity of extra-careful scrutiny of the facts in these cases. He then discusses the problems with what was submitted as corroborating evidence, such as missing pages from a diary the victim had written and the fact that a power stoppage lasted for ten minutes and not an hour, as the victim had claimed. All the points that he makes had been raised and were dismissed or explained by the judge of the previous instance, and did not damage his impression of the basic credibility of the victim. The Supreme Court judge, on the other hand, maintains that the previous judge had not given sufficient weight to the inconsistencies revealed by this evidence. However, while disagreements about the weight accorded various elements of testimony can be mobilised to support the decision, appellate judges usually feel obligated to point to actual errors in the previous decision in order to reverse it, rather than depending largely on the judgment of the importance of inconsistencies.

One of the errors specifically raised by the Supreme Court judge concerns the reaction of the judge of first instance to the defendant's refusal to undergo an identification line up. Again, the sequential placing of the argument made by the judge has implications for the credibility granted the defendant and denied the victim. The defendant had refused the procedure because he claimed that the victim could recognise him from a picture she had seen or from his appearance on television. The previous judge had said that this reluctance would have been understandable if the defendant had suggested that he was worried that the victim was fabricating a case against him. However, said the previous judge 'this suspicion was not brought up by the defendant in his interrogation'.

This statement – that the defendant hadn't suggested that the victim had fabricated the case against him – was the error the Supreme Court judge claims had been made by the previous judge.

No such thing. Immediately after his arrest the appellant submitted detailed testimony to the police [during which] he was asked:

Question: Why did Rachel say that you engaged in full sexual relations with her in the shelter of the building?
Reply: In my opinion Rachel has pressure on her from her parents to stop our conversations once and for all and in my opinion they made up this story so will stop calling.

While this reply does in fact indicate that the defendant had suggested that the victim had fabricated at least part of the story, it is interesting that the Supreme Court judge accepts this explanation without examining it carefully. In fact, the complaint to the police was made four months after the events (although the victim had told her mother about it and had undergone a gynaecological examination before complaining to the police), long after the conversations had already stopped. Moreover, there is no indication that the parents knew about the conversations at all until the girl told them about the sexual encounter. In addition, the judge does not consider why the traditional, religious parents of a thirteen year old child would take any steps that would lead to a public discussion of their daughter's unusual sexual behaviour and which would force her to admit to not being a virgin, in order to stop telephone conversations. After all, the telephone conversations, even if objectionable, were at least conducted in the privacy of their home. Yet the judge does not discuss the plausibility of the defendant's suggestion, because it is referred to in the context of the error the previous judge had made in claiming that the defendant had never suggested that the victim had concocted the sexual encounter. The Supreme Court judge proved that the defendant did make such a suggestion, and thus an error had been made by the previous judge when he said that this had never been mentioned by the defendant. This error was then used to provide a basis for reversing the previous decision.

At the end of the decision, the Supreme Court judge who wrote the decision adds the following statement:

If my colleagues on this panel agree and the appeal will be accepted, he [the defendant] will find that he has escaped by the skin of his teeth. But this does not minimise the disgust that his behaviour has aroused – on this there is no disagreement. Here is a 46 year old man, married, a father of two maturing adolescent girls, who initiates a relationship with a 13 year old girl, presents himself as much younger than he is, incites and arouses her to masturbation by long telephone conversations, sends her letters along with indecent pictures and finally sets up a meeting with her for sexual purposes – and all with a girl whose age is less than the age of his daughters. Woe to the appellant were he to see this acquittal by virtue of doubt as a stamp of approval or justification of these heinous deeds.

In the end, the judges are willing to grant the criterion of 'reasonable doubt' to the defendant. Despite the fact that the victim is a child, who is fat and interested in sex, or probably because of it, the judges are not convinced that, notwithstanding the defendant's age, experience, and successful efforts to arouse her, he actually succeeds in seducing her. She is not a real victim, but is identified from the beginning of the decision as an 'other', as different from a normal person, while the initial framework within which the defendant is presented that of a working family man. The sequencing and structure of the decision presents the defendant's actions without questioning their meaning for an assessment of his character or credibility. The alternative narrative, that it is perhaps more reasonable to expect that such a man would be able to convince this fat girl with a low self-image to do what he wants, and that such a girl would hardly be motivated to make a false accusation that would entail a public discussion of her strangeness, is excluded from this decision acquitting the defendant of all the charges against him. The Supreme Court judges in essence affirm the defendant's version and justify the reversal of the previous decision, because they claim that the degree of certainty required by criminal law had not been established. The structure of the decision persuades us that this is so.

Discussion and concusion

Acquittals are rare phenomena in the Supreme Court of Israel. While the Court may accept the appeals of defendants to lower the sentence that has been imposed, reversing the decision and acquitting the defendants convicted of serious offences in the lower courts is an exceptional move. There is no doubt that the judges in each case weighed the evidence carefully and were convinced that, despite the decision by the previous court, the prosecution had not proved the guilt of the defendant to the degree required in criminal law. Yet it is also impossible to ignore our finding that half of all those acquitted were involved in sexual offences, and that the victims in virtually all the acquittals were in some sense an 'other'. Different standards of proof seem to be required in sexual offences than in other cases, and 'others' seem to be regarded as less 'qualified' to be victims (Ekstrom, 2003). Thus, even when judges in the first instance decided that the victim was credible, the 'otherness' of the victim became more salient for the Supreme Court judges who read the documents without the benefit of personal impressions. The process of identifying the victim as an 'other' then becomes a crucial element in the retelling of the narrative and the framing of the reversal decision.

The identification of the victim as an outsider, as strange, as non-normative, in the judicial decision is both a confirmation of a particular status and an authoritative construction for persuading the reader that the reversal was inevitable and just. The narrative of acquittal uses strategies that are similar to other discourses of exclusion. The judges use nominalisations and passive constructions to present their arguments as professional and objective as well as to exclude the complainant from the category of victim, and the defendant from the category of rapist.

Like decisions that convict, so too acquittals set the boundary between what is normative and what is outside the norm. However, in acquittals it is the victim who is the other, and whose behaviour must be contrasted with the defendant, who has been convicted by a previous court and thus whose conformity to what is the norm is not always clear-cut. A number of rhetorical tactics are available to the judge, which sharpen the contrast between the normalcy of the defendants and the strangeness of the victims, thus challenging their victimhood. For example, the judges' choice in naming and identifying the defendant and the victim contraposes the normativity of one and the marginality of the other: the contrast between the playboy and the permissive tourist, the musician and sexually obsessed fat girl. However, it is not only the semantic choices made by the judges which force the contrast, but also the sequential structure of the narrative. As we have seen, there is parallel positioning of those characteristics of the victim and the defendant that contribute to the construction of the victim as the 'other', while ignoring or delaying reference to elements in the defendant's behaviour that would mar the contrast to the victim. In fact, the normalcy of the defendant is constructed by the way in which it is juxtaposed to the strangeness of the victim. However, expectations of what is conceived of as normal in a woman is narrowly defined in terms of her sexual behaviour, while the man is weighed up against a much wider idea of male normality (Eckstrom, 2003). Only clinically pathological men seem to be conceived of as possible rapists, and thus even 'disgusting' behaviour by the man is not enough to qualify him as a rapist after he has been constructed as normal.

The construction of the victim as other is also accomplished by what is questioned and what is not, the techniques of exnomination and naturalisation (Gabriel, 1998; Lakoff, 2000). Not only are stereotypes taken for granted and common knowledge invoked to support the judges conclusions, but the sequencing of the various elements in the decision can determine what is questionable and what is taken as undisputed facts and thus constrict the range of interpretation that can be given the events of the case. The judges can question the likelihood of the injury and rape of a sexually liberated woman who is active and strong, but not the use of violence by a playboy; they can fortify the portrayal of the upright defendant by pointing to the absence of previous charges against him, but do not even question what the lack of previous accusations suggests about the sexually active victim. When the defendant's behaviour or explanations are not reasonable, the judge seeks to understand and justify. When the victim's behaviour or explanations seem unlikely, they are attributed to her 'otherness' and thereby discounted. And when the narrative is set up in such a way that the deviance of the victim's personality is presented separately from the description of the events of the case, the possible pathological implications about the defendant's personality becomes submerged in the dispute about the particular incidents and remain a non-issue, while the victim's condition becomes taken for granted and non-disputable.

The language of appellate reversals of previous verdicts that acquit previously convicted sexual offenders must persuade us that the previous judges were mistaken in their impressions of the responsibility of the defendant and the credibility of the victim. In these cases, victims who are in some way different from the stereotypic notions of the normative citizen have succeeded in the court of first instance in convincing the judges that they are real victims of rape. Using a variety of linguistic and rhetorical strategies, the judges of the Supreme Court tell a different story that focuses on the construction of the victim as an 'other' whose credibility is dubious and whose victimhood is denied. And where there is no victim, there is no crime.

Notes

1. An early version of some of this chapter was presented at the Conference on Law and Social Theory, Wolfson College, University of Oxford, 14–15 December 2000. I would like to thank the conference participants for their incisive questions and comments, especially Brian Tamanaha who helped me rethink and clarify some of my ideas. I am very grateful to Leslie Sebba, Miriam Gur-Arye and Gerald Cromer who read previous versions of this chapter and made many helpful comments, and to Janet Cotterill for her great ideas and careful editing and whose courage and resilience is a source of inspiration to all. The Ford Foundation, Middle East Division, funded the project on gender bias in the courts from which the data in this chapter are taken. The research on gender bias in the courts was conducted by myself and Rochelle Don-Yehiya, under the academic auspices of the Jerusalem Institute of Israel, and at the initiative of the Israel Women's Network.

2. The Supreme Court in Israel is the highest appellate court in the country. In criminal law, the District Courts are courts of first instance in offences in which the maximum punishment is greater than seven years, and appellate courts in other offences. There are no juries in Israel, and cases in District Courts are heard by one judge or a panel of three, depending on the seriousness of the offence. All judges are professional judges.

3. In Israel, the State Prosecutor can appeal both the verdict and the sentence in criminal cases, so that these appeals can result in increased sentences.

4. Similar devices have been found in studies of judgments of responsibility for rape in experimental settings (e.g., Bohner, 2001) and in media text analyses (e.g., Clark, 1992).

5. In this case the verdict had been 'guilty but without a conviction', a special category which essentially leaves the guilty defendant without a criminal record. He had been sentenced to 10 months public service for his part in a fist fight related to a consumer complaint.

6. If this sentence appears extremely lenient, it is not far from the norm in Israeli courts. In 1993 the average sentence for rape was 39 months, which was 18% of the maximum sentence for the offence. See Bogoch and Don-Yechiyae, 1999.
7. All quotations are from my translations of the original Hebrew judicial decisions
8. Funk and Wagnall's dictionary.
9. The judges choice of the word 'playboy' to describe a 55 year-old man is incongruous, to say the least.
10. Miriam Gur-Arye pointed out to me that the demand for a victim to undergo a psychological exam would come dangerously close to changing her status to that of defendant. But in trials of sexual offences, many have noted that that is precisely what happens, i.e., the victim does become the person on trial and the victim does have to defend herself (e.g., Holmstrom and Burgess, 1978; Raday, 1997; Ehrlich, 2002).
11. Hebrew does not make a distinction between a band and an orchestra.
12. Only the judicial decision was available to us, and not the transcript of the case, so I could not verify this fact.
13. All apartment buildings in Israel by law must have a bomb shelter.

References

Balkin, J. M. (1993) Deconstructive practice and legal theory. In *Law and Language*, F. Schauer (ed.) Aldershot: Dartmouth. pp. 385–428.
Bilski, L. (1997) Battered women: From self-defense to defending the self, *Iyunay Mishpat*, 6: 5–64 (Hebrew).
Black, D. (1989) *Sociological Justice*. New York: Oxford University Press.
Bogoch, B. (1999) Judging in a different voice: Gender and the sentencing of violent offenses in Israel, *International Journal of the Sociology of Law* 27(1): 51–78.
Bogoch, B., and Don-Yechiya, R. (1999) *The Gender of Justice: Discrimination Against Women in Israeli Courts*. Jerusalem: Jerusalem Institute of Israel Research (Hebrew).
Bohner, G. (2001) Writing about rape: Use of the passive voice and other distancing text features as an expression of perceived responsibility of the victim, *British Journal of Social Psychology*, 40(4), 515–29.
Brooks, P. (1996) The law as narrative and rhetoric in *Law's Stories*, P. Brooks and P. Gewirtz (eds) New Haven: Yale University Press. pp. 14–22.
Bryden, D. P., and Lengnick, S. (1997) Rape in the criminal justice system, *Journal of Criminal Law and Criminology*, 87(4): 1194–384.
Carter, S. L. (1988) When victims happen to be black, *Yale Law Journal* 97(3): 420–47.
Christie, N. (1986) The ideal victim. In *From Crime Policy to Victim Policy. Reorienting the Justice System*, E. A. Fattah (ed.) Basingstoke: Macmillan – now Palgrave Macmillan. pp. 17–30.
Clark, K. (1992). The linguistics of blame: Representations of women in *The Sun's* reporting of crimes of sexual violence. In *Language, Text and Context: Essays in Stylistics*. M. Toolan (ed.) London: Routledge. pp. 208–24.
Coates, L. and Wade, A. (2004) Telling it like it isn't: Obscuring perpetrator responsibility for violent crime, *Discourse & Society*, 15(5): 499–526.
Conklin, W. E. (1996) The assimilation of the other within a master discourse. In *The Language and Politics of Exclusion: Others in Discourse*. S. H. Riggins (ed.) London: Sage. pp. 226–48.
Crawford, C. (2000) Gender, race and habitual offender sentencing, *Florida Criminology*, 33(1): 263–80.

Crenshaw, K. (1993) Whose story is it, anyway? Feminist and antiracist appropriations of Anita Hill. In *Race-ing Justice, En-gendering Power: Essays on Anita Hill, Clarence Thomas, and the Construction of Social Reality*. T. Morrison (ed.) London: Chatto and Windus. pp. 402–35.

Daly, K., and Tonry, M. (1997) Gender, race and sentencing. In *Crime and Justice: a Review of Research*. Vol. 22, M. Tonry (ed.) Chicago: University of Chicago Press. pp. 201–42.

Duncan, S. (1996) The mirror tells its tale: Constructions of gender in criminal law. In *Feminist Perspectives on the Foundational Subjects of Law*. A. Bottomley (ed.) London: Cavendish Publishing. pp. 173–89.

Eckert, P., and McConnell-Ginet, S. (1995) Constructing meaning, constructing selves: Snapshots of language, gender and class from Belten High. In *Gender Articulated: Language and the Socially Constructed Self*. K. Hall and M. Bucholtz (eds) New York: Routledge. pp. 469–507.

Ehrlich, S. (2001). *Representing Rape: Language and Sexual Consent*. London: Routledge.

Ekstrom, S. (2003) Qualification and disqualification in rape cases, *Journal of Scandinavian Studies in Criminology and Crime Prevention*, 4(2), 204–22.

Ewick, P., and Silbey, S. S. (1995) Subversive stories and hegemonic tales: Toward a sociology of narrative, *Law and Society Review*, 29(2): 197–226.

Frohmann, L. (1991) Discrediting victims' allegations of sexual assault: prosecutorial accounts of case rejections, *Social Problems*, 38(2): 213–26.

Gabriel, J. (1998) *Whitewash: Racialized Politics and the Media*. London: Routledge.

Gewirtz, P. (1996a) Narrative and rhetoric in the law. In *Law's Stories*, P. Brooks and P. Gewirtz (eds) New Haven: Yale University Press. pp. 2–13.

—— (1996b) Victims and voyeurs: Two narrative problems at the criminal trial. In *Law's Stories*. P. Brooks and P. Gewirtz (eds) New Haven: Yale University Press. pp. 135–61.

Graycar, R. (1995) The gender of judgments: An introduction. In *Public and Private: Feminist Legal Debates*. M. Thornton (ed.) Oxford: Oxford University Press. pp. 262–82.

Hollander, J. A. (2002) Resisting vulnerability: The social reconstruction of gender in interaction, *Social Problems*, 49(4): 474–96.

Holmstrom, L. L., and Burgess, A. W. (1978) *The Victim of Rape: Institutional Reactions*. New Brunswick: Wiley.

Holstein, J. A and Miller, G. (1990) Rethinking victimization: An interactional approach to victimology, *Symbolic Interaction*, 13(2): 103–22.

Hood, R. and Cordovil, G. (1992) *Race and Sentencing*. Oxford: Clarendon Press.

Hughes, D. M. (1995) Significant differences: The construction of knowledge, objectivity and dominance, *Women's Studies International Forum*, 18(4): 395–406.

Hunter, R. C. (1996) Gender in evidence: Masculine norms vs. feminist reforms, *Harvard Women's Law Journal*, 19: 127–67.

Kamir, O. (2002) *Feminism, Rights and the Law*. Tel Aviv: Ministry of Defence (Hebrew).

Lakoff, R. T. (2000) *The Language War*. Berkeley: University of California Press.

Larcombe, W. (2002) The 'ideal' victim v. successful rape complainants: Not what you might expect, *Feminist Legal Studies*, 10(2): 131–48.

Lees, S. (1996) Unreasonable doubt: The outcomes of rape trials. In *Women, Violence and Male Power: Feminist Activism, Research and Practice*, M. Hester, L. Kelly, and J. Radford (eds) Buckingham: Open University Press. pp. 99–115.

—— (1997) *Ruling Passions: Sexual Violence, Reputation and the Law*. Buckingham: Open University Press.

Mansell, W., Meteyard, B. and Thomson, A. (1995) *A Critical Introduction to Law*. London: Cavendish Publishing.

Matoesian, G. M. (1993) *Reproducing Rape: Domination through Talk in the Courtroom*. Chicago: University of Chicago Press.

Mautner, M. (1998) Common sense, legitimacy and coercion: Judges as story tellers, *Plilim*, 7: 11–75 (Hebrew).

Papke, D. R. (1991) Discharge as denouement: Appreciating the storytelling of appellate opinions. In *Narrative and the Legal Discourse*, D. R. Papke (ed.) Liverpool: Deborah Charles Publications. pp. 206–22.

Raday, F. (1997) Summary: Women in Israel. Paper presented at the Symposium on Women, Crime, Victimization and Social Control, 21, January 1997, Hebrew University, Jerusalem.

Rattner, A., and Fishman. G. (1998) *And Justice for All? Jews and Arabs in the Criminal Justice System*. Westport: Praeger.

Sarat, A. (1993) Speaking of death: Narratives of violence in capital trials. In *The Rhetoric of Law*. A. Sarat and T. R. Kearns (eds) Ann Arbor: University of Michigan Press. pp. 135–83.

Sarat, A., and Kearns, T. R. (1996) Editorial introduction. In *The Rhetoric of Law*. A. Sarat and T. R. Kearns (eds) Ann Arbor: University of Michigan Press. pp. 1–27.

Shahar, E. (1993) The gender of the law: Judicial discourse on the subject of rape, *Iyunay Mishpat*, 18(1): 154–82 (Hebrew).

Spohn, C. and Horney, J. (1992) *Rape Law Reform: a Grass Roots Revolution and its Impact*. New York: Plenum.

Spohn, C., Beichner, D. and Davis-Frenzel, E. (2001) Prosecutorial justifications for sexual assault case rejection: Guarding the gateway to justice, *Social Problems*, 48: 206–35.

Temkin, J. (1995) *Rape and the Criminal Justice System*. Aldershot: Dartmouth.

Tendayi, V. G. and Abrams, D. (2002) But she was unfaithful: Benevolent sexism and reactions to rape victims who violate traditional gender role expectations, *Sex Roles*, 47 (Sept): 289–93.

Thornton, M. (1997) The judicial gendering of citizenship: A look at property interests during marriage, *Journal of Law and Society*, 24(4): 486–503.

Umphrey, M. M. (1999) The dialogics of legal meaning: Spectacular trials, the unwritten law and narratives of criminal responsibility, *Law and Society Review*, 33(2): 393–423.

van Roermund, B. (1997) *Law, Narrative and Reality: an Essay in Intercepting Politics*. Dordrecht: Kluwer Academic.

White, J. B. (1985) *Hercules' Bow: Essays on the Rhetoric and Poetics of Law*. Madison: University of Wisconsin Press.

10
Sentencing Sexual Abuse Offenders: Sex Crimes and Social Justice[1]

Clare MacMartin and Linda A. Wood

A major challenge in adjudicating criminal cases of sexual assault concerns the typical characteristics of sexual offences (for example, the frequent lack of physical harm to victims and the usual absence of obvious antisocial conduct by offenders). It has been claimed that these features are often used to discount the seriousness of sexual offences. Moreover, the sexualised aspects of these crimes are viewed as undermining recognition of their inherent violence, such that references to the sexual motives of offenders or to the sexual details of the offences guarantee that they will not be taken seriously. Some feminist theorists and legal critics have argued that sexual assaults, including child sexual abuse, must be seen as acts of power and violence; both offences and offenders' motives must therefore be described in terms of violence. Such claims are frequently offered in the context of social justice considerations related to judicial decision-making. However, there are a number of problems with both the arguments and the analyses on which they are based. We first consider Canadian law, review some relevant Canadian literature and discuss some of these problems. We then further explore these concerns in relation to our previous analyses of Canadian judicial sentencing decisions in cases of child and adolescent sexual assault. The chapter concludes with a discussion of the implications for the sex-versus-violence debate in theorising about sexual crimes and for social justice issues in sentencing.

Issues involving sex crimes and sentencing practices are inevitably bound by the legal jurisdiction in which they arise. We focus here on the discourse of sentencing in Canadian cases of sexual offences. Sentencing objectives in Canadian law include the denunciation of unlawful conduct, general and specific deterrence, the rehabilitation of offenders, the provision of reparation to victims or the community, the promotion of a sense of responsibility in offenders, and the acknowledgment of harm to victims and the community (Roberts and von Hirsch, 1999). The fundamental principle of sentencing requires that a sentence be proportionate to the gravity of the offence and to the degree of the offender's responsibility in committing the offence. Additional sentencing principles require attention to mitigating and aggravating circumstances regarding the offences or the offenders (for example, their abuse of a position of trust or authority).

Over the past twenty years, rape law reform has occurred in many industrialised countries, including Canada (Tang, 1998). Such legal changes have been influenced by the women's movement and social justice advocates (for example, Brownmiller, 1975, who argued that violence is an integral part of rape). In 1983, the Canadian Criminal Code was amended to abolish rules that the feminist lobby had criticised for perpetuating sexism against women victims. One change repealed the old offence of rape, reclassifying it as a type of assault that can potentially include a wide range of actions other than vaginal penetration. The new gender-neutral category consisted of three levels of offences: sexual assault; sexual assault with a weapon, threats to a third party, or causing bodily harm; and aggravated sexual assault. This legislative change and others were intended to emphasise the violence of the crime and to minimise its sexual aspects, to increase the reporting of sexual assault to the police, and to limit the legal erosion of victims' credibility on the basis of their sexual history (Tang, 1998). However, there are ongoing concerns about the limited effectiveness of such reforms in advancing social justice for victims of sexual assault (Roberts and Mohr, 1994). One focus of concern is judicial sentencing.

Previous research on judicial sentencing of sexual assault cases

There has been substantial Canadian research on sexual assault and sentencing outcomes (see Fischer and McDonald, 1998), including social justice studies claiming that judicial sentencing discounts the seriousness of the sexual assault of women and children. Mohr (1994) identified problems with sentencing decisions in Court of Appeal cases, including the frequent treatment of violence as an additional consequence (rather than an integral feature) of sexual assault, the failure in many cases to mention harm to victims in determinations of seriousness, and wide jurisdictional variations in sentencing practices across Canada's ten provinces. Renner, Alksnis and Park (1997) studied transcripts from the Halifax courts, arguing that the characteristics that typify and facilitate sexual assault (in other words, the close, often intrafamilial relationships existing between offenders and victims, the lack of collateral force needed to perpetrate the crimes, and offenders' frequent lack of prior criminal records) were sometimes used as mitigating factors to reduce sentences.

Our emphasis here is on studies that focus more directly on legal language (Bavelas and Coates, 2001; Coates, 1997; Coates, Bavelas and Gibson, 1994; Coates and Wade, 2004). These researchers argue that inappropriate distinctions between sex and violence are used to undermine the seriousness of sexual assault. They employed qualitative and quantitative methods to study the language of sexual assault cases in British Columbia and/or the Yukon involving women and child complainants between 1986 and 1993 as reported in Quicklaw, a computerised database of judicial judgments (trial and sentencing decisions). This research criticises judicial discourse for treating assaults in sexual terms and for de-emphasising violence in descriptions of sexual assaults and of offenders' motives. These studies frequently echo the claim of some feminist critics that sexual assault is about violence and power, not sex.

Two studies focused on descriptions of sexual assaults. Coates et al. (1994) identified anomalous themes that they claimed masked the violence of this category of crime: the separation of sexual assault from violence in terms of the impetus for the assault and the characterisation of sexual assault in erotic or affectionate terms. In Bavelas and Coates (2001), a research team located descriptions of sexual assault that were then sorted into categories: sexual, violent, physical, disapproving and combinations of the previous categories. The most frequent descriptions (per case) were sexual, followed by physical and then by violent descriptions. The authors argued that the use of sexualised descriptions minimises the intrinsic violence of the assaults. Only one case treated sexual assault as constitutive of physical violence; other cases containing violent descriptions referred to force separate from the assault itself.

Two other studies focused on causal attributions. Coates (1997) had independent raters assess each attribution in the judgments in terms of the function the attribution served, specifically, whether it was a situating (limited to particular time, place or situation) or saturating (enduring or pervasive) explanation, whether it was an internalising (offender as agent) or externalising explanation, and whether it was violent (for example, a decision to be violent, a violent nature) or nonviolent. Of the attributions coded, 62% were saturating explanations, 71% were externalising, and 82% invoked nonviolent causes (for example, sexual drive or alcohol use). Coates (1997: 292) concluded that sexual assaults are not considered violent, although 'Canadian law defines sexual assault as violent per se'.

In Coates and Wade (2004), independent analysts identified attributions involving a psychological motive or cause and categorised them into one or more of eight categories: alcohol and drug abuse, biological or sexual drive, psychopathology, dysfunctional family upbringing, stress and trauma, character or personality trait, emotional state, and loss of control. Psychologising attributions, which 'functioned to conceal violence or reduce the offender's responsibility' (Coates and Wade, 2004: 506), constituted 97% of the sample. These attributions were described as reformulating deliberate acts of violence as non-deliberate and non-violent. In combination with other linguistic devices, they were seen to conceal violence and victims' resistance, to mitigate perpetrators' responsibility and to blame victims.

Some studies report differences in sexual assault cases involving children versus women as victims. Bavelas and Coates (2001) imply that, in their judgments, the sexual assault of children is not seen as violent. Similarly, Renner et al.'s (1997) cases with women were less likely to involve guilty pleas and were more likely to involve higher sentences, physical harm and intrusive sexual contact than were cases with children. Less violence was displayed toward children (that is, less frequent use of a weapon, less intrusive sexual contact, less resistance displayed by children and fewer instances of alcohol consumption as a factor) than toward adults. In Mohr's (1994) sample, almost all of the sexual assault cases with child victims involved abuse of trust, in which assault by authority figures does not typically require weapons or threats to a third party, nor result in bodily harm beyond that intrinsic to the sexual assault itself. In fewer than half of cases involving a relationship of trust the Court of Appeal mentioned breach of trust as a factor; however, when breach of trust was articulated, the sentence was increased on appeal. Jurisdictional variation in the mention of breach of trust was found. Coates (1997) reported that violations of sentencing principles, particularly in relation to breach of trust, occurred in the form of lower sentences given to those who assaulted children in their family than in other circumstances of sexual assault. The idea that assault in even the most limited form might not be seen as violent when children are involved is particularly disquieting (see Spohn, 1994, for alternative findings). However, Coates et al. (1994) reported that the few cases in which judgments contained descriptions of sexual assault as intrinsically violent had child complainants. Moreover, only women (not children) were criticised for not physically resisting their assailants.

Summary and critique

Given our focus on the discourse of sex crimes in relation to the sex-versus-violence debate, we confine our comments to those prior studies that examine the effects of judicial language in (mis)representing the intrinsic violence of sexual offences. In sum, the work of Coates and her colleagues suggests that it is inappropriate and unjust to view sexual assault in sexual terms, to view the motives for such offences as sexual, and to make attributions that involve psychological conditions or lack of deliberateness. Framing sexual assault in terms of sex-versus-violence serves to diminish the seriousness of the crime. Overall, the language used by judges serves to obscure the violence of assault and the responsibility of perpetrators, to construct assault as mutual, to adopt the perpetrator's versions of the event – and thereby to result in lower sentences than are warranted by the crimes. As we have noted previously (MacMartin and Wood, 2005), this work makes a number of important contributions, including the recognition of the role of discourse in legal activities, the acknowledgment of some legal requirements, and critically, the analysis of naturally occurring attributions. Even so, we think that there are problems with some of the analyses and arguments presented in this and other similar sorts of work; in particular, we are not certain that it can be concluded from such studies that judicial judgments do not orient to the inherent violence of sexual assault.

The first problem is the tendency to phrase claims as if they apply to all of the judgments, to all victims and to all offenders. But there is variability across and within judgments (see Mohr, 1994). There is nothing inherent in the law and its application that inevitably generates particular sorts of judgments, for example, that attempting to identify the causes of the crime requires ignoring the violence. Another problem is the tendency to collapse important distinctions, for example, between the nature of the motive and the nature of the act, between non-violent and non-deliberate actions, and between the particulars of cases involving women and those involving children.

It is a strength to deal with naturally occurring attributions, but more is required. Analyses that rely on coding and categorising, on quantitative comparisons, can serve to obscure variability. Abstracting attributions from their discourse context and sequence limits our understanding of the flexibility of attributions in use. For example, Coates and Wade (2004) argue that reference to an offender's dysfunctional family upbringing serves to diminish the offender's responsibility, as well as the prospects for rehabilitation. But such factors can also be used to argue that such an offender should be particularly cognizant of the damaging effects of actions; prior history, particularly of abuse, can be an aggravating as well as a mitigating factor. We need to analyse precisely what the judges do with such assessments. We cannot assume that any particular attribution necessarily serves a particular function, as in Coates (1997).

Analyses that rely on coding and categorising can also exclude important features. Studies in which the analysis focuses specifically only on those places where the judge describes the 'assault itself, that is, the acts for which the defendant was convicted' (Bavelas and Coates, 2001: 33) exclude the possibility of identifying the manner in which the crime is described when the judge is ostensibly engaged in some other action (such as arguing for the appropriateness of a particular sentence). The flexibility of discourse is such that one can, for example, do attribution by doing description – and vice versa. Coates and Wade (2004) omitted attributions cited from case law. But it is often by using such citations that judges themselves make important attributions. For example, references to a comment in an appeal court decision that assault is inherently violent appear frequently in our own data.

In contrast, the inclusion of certain attributions can be challenged in terms of their treatment as belonging unproblematically to the judges when the judges report attributions made by others. For example, Coates and Wade (2004: 512) give 'It has been submitted to this court by counsel for the defendant that his conduct is out-of-character' as an example of judges describing violent acts as outside the man's character. This is a tricky point. Speakers are responsible for their utterances, including those reporting the attributions of others; such utterances do have effects, although their inter-pretation in the legal context is complicated by the requirement that judges are expected to consider reports from other participants in the system. This point is sometimes acknowledged (for example, by Bavelas and Coates, 2001), but there is no analysis of its implications, of how the actions of reporting attributions might differ in their effects from those of making attributions. This is one example of the many dilemmas that judges must confront in adjudicating crimes of sexual assault. Another is that judges are required to consider various levels of physical harm, but in talking about degrees of violence, they can be criticised for questioning the inherent violence of the crime. Management of such dilemmas calls for considerable rhetorical skill and flexibility on the part of judges and, correspondingly, fine-grained and contextual analyses.

Some qualitative analyses of discourse involve interpretations that are insufficiently grounded or overly broad. For example, Coates and Wade (2004: 510) report the following excerpt from a judge's decision: [the offender is] 'depressed by the setbacks of life, and on five occasions, has reacted to that by committing sexual assaults'. They argue that 'the offender was described as committing violent acts, but his ultimate responsibility was reduced, *even eradicated*, due to his mental disorder' (emphasis added). We are not persuaded that the judge here is doing such reduction, and certainly not that this statement eradicates the offender's responsibility. Interpreta-tions of function can also be problematic, as we noted above. Some analysts (*inter alia* Coates et al., 1994; Coates and Wade, 2004) have pointed out that certain linguistic devices, particularly agentless passives (such as 'she was assaulted'), conceal the offender and thereby reduce attributions of respons-ibility to the offender in descriptions of sexual assault. Agentless passives by definition grammatically omit the offender, but their use does not neces-sarily mean that they work as claimed. Rather, such language may be used to work up the seriousness of the crime.

There is a more general issue. One of the merits of discourse work is the recognition of the power of language to construct versions of reality (Coates et al., 1994). It is on this basis that the term 'sexual assault' is seen to be problematic; as we have discussed, the idea is that describing the crime in these terms ignores its violent aspects. Bavelas and Coates (2001: 32, emphasis in original) argue that because they are not consensual, the actions are not sexual, 'but rather *sexualized* assaults, that is assaults disguised as sex if we accept the perpetrator's version and language'. The idea of mutuality or the lack thereof is an important one; the recognition that there are different perspectives does not preclude condemning the one (as done by Coates and her colleagues). However, the difficulty is in coming up with a term that adequately captures the lack of mutuality in a single label. For the offender, the acts may indeed be sexual. But for the victim, the assault is sexualised, that is, it is an assault that is disguised as sex, and that attacks aspects of the victim's body that have special meaning with respect to sex.

The argument that there is more than one perspective extends to researchers; it is also the case that their language constructs. Yet in the work we have been discussing, the language of truth and accuracy is deployed (for example, 'what the crime really was', Bavelas and Coates, 2001: 38). This is a case of 'ontological gerrymandering', a term used by Woolgar and Pawluch (1985) to discuss the process by which writers on social problems (such as child abuse) move back and forth between relativist/constructionist and realistic claims, depending on whether they are talking about claims-making activities or the condition to which definitions ostensibly refer. This is not to say that all versions are equally valuable; the version we select clearly matters, as these researchers have argued. But the point applies to all language users, including researchers. We return to this issue in the discussion below.

Judicial discourse and child sexual abuse

Data and methodology

We report here on some of our own recent research on the discourse of judges in cases of child sexual abuse. Our purpose is two-fold. First, we consider our findings in comparison to those discussed above. Second, we attempt to illustrate how the sort of discursive approach taken in this work can address some of the limitations we identified above. We have focused exclusively on sentencing decisions involving child and adolescent victims of sexual offences because of the differences prior research has noted between cases involving women and children and because of recent legal reforms in Canada designed to improve social justice outcomes for child and adolescent victims (see Sas, Wolfe and Gowdy, 1996).

Our data consist of 74 sentencing decisions in criminal cases of sexual abuse offences taken from Quicklaw, an electronic website containing data-bases of Canadian legal judgments, for the years 1993 to 1997 in Ontario, Canada. The cases were selected to cover all possible sexual offences against child and adolescent victims aged seventeen or younger (other than appeal cases, which stress legal rather than substantive issues). Each judgment included the judge's decision and reasons for the decision, with varying amounts of detail. Charges involved such crimes as sexual assault and indecent assault, rape and sexual exploitation and, in some cases, non-sexual offences together with the sexual offences. Only one of the offenders was female.

Our method of discourse analysis is informed by discursive social psychology (DSP) (Potter and Edwards, 2001). The analytic focus in DSP is on the actions performed in and through discourse (talk and texts) as part of situated practices. Judicial discourse in the form of written sentencing decisions is thus both an object of analysis and a practice. There are three key theoretical features of DSP that distinguish it from conventional social-psychological approaches to legal decision-making. First, discourse is situated. It is 'occasioned' in the sense that it is embedded in a particular context as part of some sort of sequence, and it is rhetorical in the sense that it is related to argumentation; descriptions and attributions are constructed to bolster and to counter different versions of events, identities and so forth. Second, discourse is action-oriented. Even seemingly neutral statements or descriptions of persons and events perform actions such as fact-construction, attributions, claiming or denying stake and interest, and the working up of mental states. The third feature of DSP is that it is constructionist. Discourse constructs versions of the world, versions that perform actions in the ways that we have discussed. But discourse is also itself constructed from words, figures of speech, narratives and grammatical devices that can be studied for how discourse is built to perform those actions. Discourse analysis, then, involves a detailed, recursive, and contextually sensitive examination of talk and text, which can be carried out using a variety of strategies (see Wood and Kroger, 2000).

Crime descriptions and violence

MacMartin (2004) examined the sentencing decisions identified above to assess whether the typical characteristics of child sexual abuse, the absence of physical harm to victims and the relationships between offenders and victims, are used to work up or, alternatively, to discount the seriousness of offences against children. Overall, the descriptions of the offences tended to denounce sexual abuse on the basis of the psychological harm to victims and of the breach of trust that the abuse entailed. But this brief categorisation does not do justice to the complex and subtle ways in which such actions were performed. Some judges did make explicit reference to the inherent violence of the offence. For example, one judge stated, 'I agree with the Crown that all sexual assaults are inherently violent and most leave lasting scars.' A number of decisions (25) did make reference to the absence of instrumental/collateral physical violence, which can potentially undermine the assessment of abuse as serious. In some cases, inherent violence was used to reject the absence of additional force as a mitigating factor; in others, the absence of additional force was used as a mitigating factor but not necessarily given full weight. And in some cases, the absence of physical violence was contrasted with violence of a different sort, emotional violence, which served to broaden the definition of violence. For example, in the case of a father who had pleaded guilty to indecent assault, the judge asserts that there was no violence only in the limited sense that it was not physical, but that the emotional violence inflicted by the severe power imbalance haunted the child. Thirteen of the decisions described the mind, psyche or emotions as at least equally as vulnerable to injury as the physical body (for example, 'This is violence upon a child's psyche that this court considers as real and as tangible as physical violence inflicted upon a child's body.'

Whereas the absence of instrumental or collateral violence might be treated or not as mitigating, the presence of collateral violence was mentioned specifically in fourteen of the decisions as an aggravating factor, based on the particular actions involved ('a drunken sexual mauling through hugging and rubbing') but also (in many cases) on the power imbalance between offenders and victims (MacMartin, 2004). Thus, it is clear that, in many of the decisions examined, the offences are viewed as both violent (in one or more senses) and serious. MacMartin also found that references to breach of trust (in some cases interwoven with references to violence) were employed in 56 of the decisions to construct the offences as serious.

Explanations for the crimes

Sex-based explanations

MacMartin and Wood (2005) analysed the sentencing decisions in relation to judicial explanations for the offences and their implications for mitigation and aggravation. In 28 cases, explanations for the crimes were not provided: judges laid out the reasons for their decisions, including aggravating concerns such as breach of trust and the effects of the offences on the victims, as we have reported above. In the remaining 46 cases, judges oriented to a variety of reasons for the crimes, with sex-based explanations the most frequent (32 judgments). In 17 decisions, offenders were described as motivated by their own sexual pleasure. In accord with the argument that sexual assault is not mutual, we found that these references typically contrasted the offenders' and the victims' experiences of the assaults.

Explanations sometimes referred to the ways in which the crimes demeaned and degraded victims, and were used to denounce the offences. Consider the following excerpt from a judgment involving an offender convicted of indecent assault:

> There are many aggravating factors indeed. Mr K.'s actions involved a serious breach of trust. D. G. was his nephew and when these events first occurred, he was a very young child, 11 years old only. The actions continued through and into middle puberty, surely a very sensitive and difficult time for any adolescent, such difficulties clearly exacerbated by the activities of a much older and extremely selfish man whose only motive could have been his own sexual gratification at the expense of a young boy.

The judge treats this offence very seriously, notwithstanding the reference to the offender's motive (his only motive) as his own sexual gratification. 'Indeed' asserts the undeniability of aggravating factors, of which there are 'many', and the breach of trust is described as 'serious'. Contrasts are constructed between the developmental stages, ages, relative power and interests of nephew and uncle. Adjectival and adverbial intensifiers contrast the victim at the time the offences began ('a very young child, 11 years old only', 'a young boy') with the offender ('a much older...man'). The vulnerability of the child victim to exploitation by the adult offender is thus emphasised.

A different kind of developmental vulnerability is ascribed to the victim in mid-puberty: 'surely a very sensitive and difficult time for any adolescent'. The term 'any adolescent' is an extreme case formulation (Pomerantz, 1986) which uses an extreme point to typify this as a 'very sensitive and difficult' stage for 'any' and all teenagers, including by implication those adolescents who do not experience sexual victimisation. The judge thus claims that no specific case for the vulnerability of this particular boy needs to be made, given the natural difficulties of adolescence which are ignored by the offender. This construction wards off a possible claim by some that a sexual offence perpetrated on an adolescent is less serious than an offence involving a younger victim.

D. G.'s developmental needs have been sacrificed to satisfy the desires of the 'selfish' offender. The conjecture about motive in terms of 'his own sexual gratification at the expense of a young boy' promotes the impossibility of mutuality and the inevitable psychic costs to the victim of sexual activity. The extreme case formulation ('only motive') makes clear that, although this is judicial conjecture, no other logical motive exists to explain this crime. 'At the expense of a young boy' is not a sexual description but is grammatically connected to the offender's motive of 'sexual gratification'. Here, references to sexual motives and to its serious effects (the violation of the victim) are mixed together in the same description.

We found that, as in previous work (see Coates and Wade, 2004), some judgments (twelve cases) invoked sexual drives or impulses (versus pleasure) as explanations. Some such references were explicit while others were implicit, as when offenders were reported to have undergone chemical or physical castration. In some cases the loss of control was constructed by the defence counsel as momentary rather than ongoing. But judges do not necessarily accept such an argument or treat it as grounds for assigning less than full responsibility to the offender. In other cases, lack of control over sexual impulses was constructed by the judge as a chronic problem. Again, however, the identification of such a sexual motive was not necessarily used to diminish either the responsibility of the offender or the seriousness of the crime.

Lack of control over sexual impulses also figures in cases involving paedophilia. Because paedophilia can be taken to imply that the offender suffers from an illness over which he presumably has no control, it is not surprising that in some cases judges treated such a diagnosis as mitigating. However, this was not inevitable; there were also cases in which paedophilia was treated as an aggravating factor because of the failure of the offender to seek treatment for a condition from which he knows that he suffers. Again we see the way in which particular sorts of attributions are not invariably associated with particular decisions, but are treated flexibly by judges in the context of other factors in a case.[2]

Violence-based and power-based explanations

We analysed only the sex-based explanations of conduct in MacMartin and Wood (2005). However, other sorts of explanations were invoked in our data, explanations we wish to highlight here. In particular, there were four decisions that included explicit references to aggression, power or violence as explanations for the offences. That is, although twelve judgments referred to the inherent violence of the offences and fourteen judgments mentioned the presence of collateral physical violence, only four judgments clearly described the motivations of offenders in terms of the expression of violence or power. In two of the four cases, there were additional charges that involved collateral physical violence or offences separate from sexual assault.

Two cases explained the offences in terms of violence, but violence whose expression was disinhibited by the consumption of alcohol. For example, one offender pleaded guilty to sexual assaulting a 16-year-old female in a park. He was reported to have been drinking on a daily basis, including the time immediately prior to the assault. This is a case in which the offender acknowledged that the offence 'had little to do with sex as opposed to wanting to hurt a female'.

> Mr M. A. indicated in his statement that he was in the park in question contemplating his personal problems and feeling a high degree of anger toward women in general and in particular toward an ex-girlfriend. That relationship, of some duration, had ended three to four weeks earlier at the instance [sic] of Mr. M. A.'s girlfriend. He indicated that he couldn't handle it and he 'lost it.' The accused maintained that he had no particular plans when he observed the complainant walking toward him in the park. He reported that he lashed out and sexually assaulted the victim.

Narrative sequencing establishes that the anger of the offender, reacting badly to a former girlfriend's rejection, was the reason he gave for the assault. Mention of both 'women in general' and 'an ex-girlfriend' as targets of the offender's anger establishes what precipitated the assault and its random-ness. The offender describes himself as having 'lost it' and as having 'lashed out' in the form of sexual assault, descriptions that might be viewed as underscoring the offender's aggression and thereby categorising the crime as violent. But the sense of anger as uncontrollable and irrational also allows for the offence to be described by the offender as unplanned and, presumably, not the act of a sexual predator who stalks his victims. However, in Paragraph 40 the judge cited evidence from the report of a forensic psychiatrist who described the offender as suffering from alcohol abuse, an antisocial personality disorder, a depressive disorder, and 'deviant sexual interests, in particular, a courtship disorder in which hyper-dominance and mild sadomasochism are major factors'.

Two cases involving incest suggested that the offenders were motivated not only by sexual gratification but also by the power they experienced over their victims. In one case, the offender pleaded guilty to indecent assault, gross indecency and having sexual intercourse with his daughters. The judgment referred to the humiliation and degradation of the victims visited on the victims by their father who urinated on his daughters after sexually abusing them: 'There was more than simply the acts of sexual gratification through sexual intercourse.' The other case involved incestuous abuse by an offender who had been charged with indecent assault, rape and assault causing bodily harm. The offender pleaded guilty on two of the three charges and was convicted on a third. The offences involved his daughters and step-daughter and took place over many years. The charge of assault causing bodily harm involved the offender whipping one of the victims 'while fondling her for sexual gratification'. Thus, explanations for the offences in this case involved dual references to sex and violence.

Summary

We found that, although the judges in the sentencing decisions we analysed did discuss the sexual aspects of the crimes and the absence of collateral violence, they also considered the inherent violence of the offences and the psychological and emotional harm to victims. And while they tended to construct sex-based explanations, some judges did consider violence-based explanations. Further, in some judgments, references were made to both sex and violence as explanations. Perhaps most critically, sex-based descriptions and explanations are not generally used to construct crimes as less violent or serious, nor to justify lower sentences than they might seem to merit; in some cases, the sexual aspects are themselves used to construct the crimes as violent and serious. Thus, although there is some overlap with the findings of previous research (Bavelas and Coates, 2001; Coates, 1997; Coates et al., 1994; Coates and Wade, 2004) in that we also find sex-based descriptions and explanations, our findings and claims do differ. Previous work has tended to characterise the descriptions of the crime as sexual, to stress the lack of violence and/or the lack of offenders' responsibility in explanations for the crime, and to argue that these descriptions and explanations serve to treat sexual assault crimes as less serious than they would be treated if sufficient attention were given to the violence of the crimes and of offenders' motives. There are a number of possible reasons for the disparity: jurisdictional differences, differences in the time frames (corresponding to changes in the law), differences in the sample (for example, the inclusion of cases involving women as well as children), and differences in the data sources (for example, trial versus sentencing decisions).

But we think that there is also an overriding and potentially more important difference between previous work and our own, namely, the approach to analysis. Our findings derive from analyses that focus on the identification of variability in descriptions and explanations, and in the uses to which these are put. They reflect the flexibility that judges display throughout their decisions, for example, in using the same sort of explanation (such as paedophilia) to warrant treating the crime either more or less seriously, depending in part on other factors in the case. And they demonstrate the need to consider descriptions and explanations in the context of the overall decisions. Previous work, particularly that which relies on coding and counting, tends to produce findings that are – or at least are interpreted to be – homogenous, even totalising. In contrast, we stress the recognition of variability not only across, but within decisions.

Discussion

We have said that the judges in the sentencing decisions we examined do not on the whole use references to sexual features to diminish the seriousness of the assaults; indeed, they frequently treat the sexual aspects of the offences as constitutive of their seriousness. Nonetheless, arguments have been made that the sexualisation of assaults is problematic because it misrepresents their true nature, and/or has negative consequences such as the blaming of victims (Coates and Wade, 2004). But there are a number of difficulties with such arguments. First, as suggested by some of our findings, sexual assault can be treated as violent especially because it is sexual. As Cahill (2000: 60) argues, 'To desexualize the act of rape, to consider it legally only as any other assault, would be to obfuscate – not to weaken! – its role in the production of the sexual hierarchy through the inscription of individual bodies'. Similarly, Segal (2001) sees sex and violence as intertwined in patriarchal cultures and MacKinnon (1987, 1989) stresses that sexual aggression represents (preferred) sex for many males. In other words, there is a normative relationship between coercive and consensual sex in our society. From the perspective of a female model of sexuality, rape is violent; however, if we endorse the view that sexual aggression is part of male socialisation in our culture, it is a *non sequitur* for us to claim that rape is only physical or symbolic violence (and not sexual) according to a male model of sexuality (Matoesian, 1993). So it is at least at much the interweaving of sex and violence that indexes patriarchal operations as it is the disguising of violence as sex.

And what about motives? The argument has been that because sexual assault is an inherently violent crime, the motives of offenders must be described in violent terms (see Coates, 1997). But Boyle (1985) submits that it would be a mistake to confine sexual assault to any particular category of motivations: some offenders use 'aggression as a means to an end (the end being sexual activity); with others, aggression is an end in itself' (p. 99). Furthermore, the ascription of a particular motive is not necessarily associated with a particular assignment of responsibility. In our data, even when violent or aggressive motivations are acknowledged, the relative degree of agency on the part of the offender in committing these crimes is still open to question. And the ascription of sexual motives does not necessarily entail assignment of lack of agency on the part of the offender, in contrast to the findings and claims of other researchers (for example, Coates and Wade, 2004).

Judges themselves are not insensitive to the tensions and connections between sex and violence, and we think it instructive to consider some of their own discourse on the issue. For example, in our decisions, one judge refers explicitly to a Supreme Court of Canada decision citing a published article entitled, 'Sex in power dependency relationships'. In one judgment there is a reference to another Supreme Court decision, in which a distinction is drawn between an assault as sexual violation and the sexual motive of the offender, and in which assault is not framed as sexual interaction or intercourse, that is, as involving mutuality.

It might thus be argued that what is required is an emphasis on violation, not just on violence. Violence involves 'the unlawful exercise of physical force, intimidation by exhibition of this' while violation refers to 'profane or disrespectful treatment, breaking in upon, or disturbing, a person's privacy' (Sykes, 1976: 1298). Emphasis on the notion of violation might therefore help us to preserve both the notion of nonmutuality and the victim's perspective. There is a sad irony here. The claim that sexual assaults are crimes of violence not sex is often seen as a way to avoid blaming the victim (Coates and Wade, 2004). But in substituting our point of view for that of the offender, we run the risk of ignoring the victim. Perhaps a better (and less patriarchal) way to avoid blame would be to acknowledge the victim's experience as both violent and sexual by describing it as a violation of sexual integrity.

The issue of sex versus violence is an example of the larger problem of dichotomies. In discussions of sexual assault, dichotomies are frequently invoked, for example, offender blame versus victim blame. On the other hand, some categories are often treated as equivalent, or at least as nondichotomous. For example, the abuse of children is located within the 'continuum of abuse' of women (Kelly, 1988) and the similarities of violence against women and children are emphasised; both are seen as evidence of and ways of maintaining patriarchy. Our point is not that sex and violence should not be treated as oppositional or that women and children should be treated as separate categories. Such categories are neither inherently contrastive nor equivalent, but are discursively constructed to be so. We need to ask, in constructing such oppositions or similarities, what actions are being performed, and what might be their effects? We have suggested some of the problems with respect to sex versus violence. There are also problems with both collapsing and distinguishing the categories of women and children. When we join them together, we draw attention to the ubiquity of violence against particular groups, but we also run the risk of perpetuating the very patriarchy that enables such violence.

We think that some of the difficulties we have discussed reflect insufficient recognition of the complexities of the justice system, of the way in which a number of the aspects we have discussed are both distinguished and related in law. For example, concerns are sometimes expressed that particular sorts of explanations (such as the offender's actions being sexually motivated or as non-deliberate), while not excusing the crime, are associated with shorter sentences (Coates and Wade, 2004) and that such findings signal the treatment of assault as insufficiently serious. However, legally (and in our findings), explanations are not relevant to assessments of seriousness. Nonetheless, they are relevant to assessments of responsibility and therefore to sentencing because of the fundamental principle that a sentence must be proportionate to both the gravity of the offence and the degree of responsibility of the offender.

But decisions about sentencing reflect – and in law are required to reflect – more than these two elements. Judges must also consider the objectives of sentencing; explanations may be relevant to these. For example, the reference to an assault being out-of-character might be used to warrant a prediction that the offence will not be repeated; such a prediction speaks to the objective of specific deterrence (in contrast to general deterrence or the denunciation of unlawful conduct) and might serve to justify a lower sentence than would otherwise be the case.[3] Explanations might also be relevant to the objectives of rehabilitation and the acknowledgment of harm or remorse. There is another critical factor: the plea. A guilty plea is to be treated as a mitigating factor (Ruby, 1994), but analyses of explanations and sentences rarely consider the plea.[4] And there are a number of principles that must be taken into account (for example, the length of combined sentences, alternative sanctions; see Roberts and von Hirsch, 1999). These various factors do not bear directly on issues concerning descriptions, explanations, and the seriousness of offences. We mention them to emphasise that we cannot make inferences about the import of descriptions and explanations simply by looking at the sentence (which itself is a complicated matter combining length of incarceration, type of facility, and so on), but must examine the sentencing process as a whole. More generally, we want to reiterate the importance of appreciating the legal context in which descriptions and explanations of sexual assault are offered and of recognising the difficulties of participants in reconciling various sentencing principles and objectives given the lack of clear sentencing guidelines (Doob, 1999).

Finally, we comment briefly on the implications of descriptions and attributions for treatment of offenders. Reducing sexual assault to violence would mean that offenders be directed towards violence counselling. Coates and Wade (2004) appear to support such a recommendation, but claim that a judge mandated violence counselling in only one of their cases. Rather, offenders were directed 'to other types of treatment programs (such as alcohol abuse, anger management, deviant sexual impulses) that were presumed to address the cause of the violence' (2004: 514). It is not clear exactly how violence counselling might differ from some of these (for example, anger management). In any case, we think that there are problems with relying on any one treatment. The failure to recognise differences among offenders is not only a failure to address a legal requirement; it is also unlikely to have salutary effects. And in reducing offenders to a singular category while at the same time focusing on the individual level, we do nothing to challenge the patriarchal system in which the crimes are embedded.

Conclusions

The work that has been done to date on crimes of sexual assault has contributed to our understanding of many of the issues raised here. But we think that more considered attention is required to sort out some of the thorny problems related to particular aspects, such as the nature of the crimes, the explanations offered for the crimes, and the differences between crimes against women and those against children that in our view extend beyond more obvious features such as consent. This will require the kind of analysis that is sensitive to the fine details and nuances of legal discourse and of people's experience. Some of the findings we have reported may seem to suggest that there are no longer any problems with judicial decision-making in cases of sexual assault, and the arguments we have offered may be taken as support for current legal practices, at least in Canada. But our position is not that we do not require change. The issue is the sort of change required. The arguments that crimes of sexual assault are crimes of violence, not sex, and that women and children are similarly vulnerable to such crimes have been rhetorically powerful; together with other developments they have arguably helped to bring about change, both within and without the legal system. But is this the best way to bring about such change? Our concern is that such arguments may perpetuate the very patriarchy which they challenge, because they contribute to the denial of sexuality and adult status for women, and may keep them overly reliant on the justice system and the benevolence of those who operate within it (including legislators, police officers, lawyers and judges).

There are alternatives. We still need to change socialisation practices so that girls develop a strong sense of control and sexual choice, and ways to resist the notion that they are simply objects of pleasure or breeding stations. We need to challenge the socialisation of male sexuality and its equating of sexually aggressive characteristics with masculinity. We need to change media constructions of gender and sexuality and to challenge other aspects of patriarchy, for example, the ownership implications of accepting another person's name, the 'normal' confounding of intimacy and power. More broadly, we need to expand the cultural discourses available for making sense of crimes of sexual assault and for developing prevention and treatment practices for addressing such crimes. In doing so as researchers, we must be reflexive; we must be sensitive to the way in which our own discourses contribute positively or negatively to the discursive construction of social problems such as sexual assault.

Notes

1. This research was supported by the Social Sciences and Humanities Research Council of Canada.
2. Paedophilia is an attribution that works up sexual attraction as deviant. But, as in the work of Coates and Wade (2004), there were also two cases in our data in which sexual attraction was evaluated in seemingly more normalised ways. Nonetheless, such evaluation was not used by those judges to diminish the seriousness of the offenders' conduct (MacMartin and Wood, 2005).
3. Judges might well be mistaken in their predictions, but this does not mean that the crime is not taken seriously.
4. Mentioning that an offender was convicted tells us nothing about the plea, because convictions are registered following both trials and guilty pleas. However, readers might infer that a conviction means a lack of a guilty plea, that is, lack of acceptance of responsibility.

References

Bavelas, J. and Coates, L. (2001) Is it sex or assault? Erotic versus violent language in sexual assault trial judgments. *Journal of Social Distress and the Homeless*, 10(1): 29–40.

Boyle, C. (1985) Sexual assault and the feminist judge. *Canadian Journal of Women and the Law*, 1: 93–107.

Brownmiller, S. (1975) *Against our will: Men, Women, and Rape*. New York: Simon and Schuster.

Cahill, A. J. (2000) Foucault, rape, and the construction of the feminine body. *Hypatia: a Journal of Feminist Philosophy*, 15(1): 43–63.

Coates, L. (1997) Causal attributions in sexual assault trial judgments. *Journal of Language and Social Psychology*, 16(3): 278–96.

Coates, L., Bavelas, J. B. and Gibson, J. (1994) Anomalous language in sexual assault trial judgments. *Discourse & Society*, 5(2): 191–205.

Coates, L. and Wade, A. (2004) Telling it like it isn't: Obscuring perpetrator responsibility for violent crime. *Discourse & Society*, 15(5): 499–526.

Doob, A. N. (1999) Sentencing reform: Where are we now? In J. V. Roberts and D. P. Cole (eds), *Making Sense of Sentencing*. Toronto: University of Toronto Press pp. 349–63.

Fischer, D. G. and McDonald, W. L. (1998) Characteristics of intrafamilial and extra-familial sexual abuse. *Child Abuse & Neglect*, 22(9): 915–29.

Kelly, L. (1988) *Surviving Sexual Violence*. Minneapolis: University of Minnesota Press.

MacKinnon, C. (1987) *Feminism Unmodified*. Cambridge, Mass: Harvard University Press.

MacKinnon, C. (1989) *Toward a Feminist Theory of the State*. Cambridge, Mass: Harvard University Press.

MacMartin, C. (2004) Judicial constructions of the seriousness of child sexual abuse. *Canadian Journal of Behavioural Science*, 36(1): 66–80.

MacMartin, C. and Wood, L. A. (2005) Sexual motives and sentencing: Judicial discourse in cases of child sexual abuse. *Journal of Language and Social Psychology*, 24(2): 139–59.

Matoesian, G. M. (1993) *Reproducing Rape: Domination through Talk in the Courtroom*. Cambridge: Polity Press.

Mohr, R. M. (1994) Sexual assault sentencing: Leaving justice to individual conscience. In J. V. Roberts and R. M. Mohr (eds), *Confronting Sexual Assault: a Decade of Legal and Social Change*. Toronto: University of Toronto Press. pp. 157–91.

Pomerantz, A. (1986) Extreme case formulations: A way of legitimizing claims. *Human Studies*, 9(2–3): 219–29.

Potter, J. and Edwards, D. (2001) Discursive social psychology. In W. P. Robinson and H. Giles (eds), *The New Handbook of Language and Social Psychology*. Chichester: Wiley. pp. 103–18.

Renner, K. E., Alksnis, C. and Park, L. (1997) The standard of social justice as a research process. *Canadian Psychology*, 38(2): 91–102.

Roberts, J. V. and von Hirsch, A. (1999) Legislating the purpose and principles of sentencing. In J. V. Roberts and D. P. Cole (eds), *Making Sense of Sentencing*. Toronto: University of Toronto Press. pp. 48–62.

Roberts, R. V. and Mohr, R. M. (eds) (1994) *Confronting Sexual Assault: a Decade of Legal and Social Change*. Toronto: University of Toronto Press.

Ruby, C. C. (1994) *Sentencing* (4th edn). Markham/Vancouver: Butterworths.

Sas, L. D., Wolfe, D. A. and Gowdy, K. (1996) Children and the courts in Canada. *Criminal Justice and Behavior*, 23(2): 338–57.

Segal, L. (2001) Nature's way? Inventing the natural history of rape. *Psychology, Evolution & Gender*, 3(1): 87–93.

Spohn, C. C. (1994) A comparison of sexual assault cases with child and adult victims. *Journal of Child Sexual Abuse*, 34(4): 59–78.

Sykes, J. B. (ed.) (1976) *The Concise Oxford Dictionary of Current English* (6th edn). Oxford: Oxford University Press.

Tang, K.-L. (1998) Rape law reform in Canada: The success and limits of legislation. *International Journal of Offender Therapy and Comparative Criminology*, 42(3): 258–70.

Wood, L. A. and Kroger, R. O. (2000) *Doing Discourse Analysis: Methods for Studying Action in Talk and Text*. Thousand Oaks, Calif.: Sage.

Woolgar, S. and Pawluch, D. (1985) Ontological gerrymandering: The anatomy of social problems explanations. *Social Problems*, 32(3): 214–27.

11
When Rape is (not quite) Rape

Annabelle Mooney

Introduction

This chapter considers the newspaper representation of a July 2003 sentencing appeal for a rape conviction in Scotland. It is a significant event as it is the first case affected by a 2002 change in Scottish law (by the judiciary), which established that force was not an essential element of rape. Previous to this, if non-consensual intercourse occurred when the victim was asleep or unconscious, the attacker could be charged only with 'clandestine injury' and not rape. Thus the sentencing appeal was reported in the Scottish press as much for its legal importance as for the specific details. In many ways, the sentencing appeal is a coda to the case that challenged and changed the law in 2002. There was much media interest in the change when it happened, with the last trial of someone charged with clandestine injury being widely reported, and the judgment in the present case referring to the level of media coverage of that case. In fact, the level of media publicity meant, according to the Court, 'there is no longer any justification for treating such cases [old clandestine injury] as if they were in some separate category from the point of view of sentencing' (pgh 11). In effect, the Court is saying that everyone should be aware of the change.

If this newspaper representation of a sentencing appeal tells us anything, it is that issues around rape in the law, in the media and in society generally are far from settled. Further, it tells us that neither rape nor the law are singular. The 'law' does not have a stance on rape as such; it has a variety of voices, a history of decisions and personalities and a number of pressures working from the outside and from within. A number of voices are discernable in these articles. While none assert that rape is not wrong, many question what rape is (and thus what it is that is wrong). Despite the change in Scottish law that non-consensual intercourse is rape, there is still ample room for manoeuvring within the term 'rape' and more significantly, for qualifying it.

Most importantly, the profile of what constitutes a credible victim has not changed. Further, women in general are still represented as property, requiring protection from males, who are by their 'nature', sexual predators.

The media is an important barometer of public opinion and a source that the courts (whether directly or indirectly) take cognisance of. Whether these media reports accurately reflect public opinion will also be considered towards the end of this chapter. The views of women and men on which rape myths are built are disturbing to say the least. Likewise, the low conviction rate of rapes[1] should give pause for thought. Rape is not yet rape.

In their expert charting of changing trends in media reporting of rape, Soothill et al. note that 'typical' rape is not usually covered by the mass media (1991: 1). They also note that it is difficult to judge typicality as 'Only a minority of rape cases reach the pages of the national press' (1991: 227). 'Typical' rape, whatever that might mean, is not newsworthy. This is hardly surprising, as 'typical' events are not, by definition, news. Anderson and Beattie conclude that 'newspaper accounts of rape have been shown to contain very few elements of the stereotypical classic rape' (2001: 17). However the 'stereotypical classic rape' which can be understood as the archetype which informs various rape myths, is not the same as a 'typical' rape. Nonetheless, these rape myths are still in circulation. Whether they are contested or endorsed, it appears that these rape myths are still the primary way in which rape is understood and represented (see Stevenson, 2000: 346).[2]

In terms of the typicality of this sentencing appeal being reported, Soothill et al. note that sentencing is often part of newspaper coverage, where 'attention is both on the level of the sentence, whether it is considered lenient or harsh, and also sometimes on the judge's comments on the case' (1991: 17). The level of the sentence is exactly what is at issue in this appeal. The media here also provides a forum for discussing recent changes in the law, in conjunction with judicial comments and legal arguments. Soothill et al. comment, 'When law changes on sex crime are being proposed in Parliament we found that the general approach of the media is essentially of two kinds – trivialise or ignore the debate' (1991: 149). It would seem reasonable to conclude that changes in the law around rape (whether proposed in Parliament or by the judiciary) would be similarly scarce in terms of media representation. The present case is thus atypical in its consideration of the change in the law.

Data

In this chapter, I examine the press coverage of a sentencing appeal. It is a modest corpus of only nine pieces (listed in Table 11.1), but this in itself is significant as will be discussed. All articles appeared in the Scottish press and were recovered with Lexis-Nexus.[3] The presence of coverage only in Scotland is to be expected as it is a separate jurisdiction from England and Wales. The average length of article is 431 words; however they range in length from 95 to 754 words. While I will make some comments on individual pieces, I will

Table 11.1:   Corpus of newspaper articles and editorials

Newspaper	Date	Words	Headline	Author
Daily Record	25 September 2003	256	Warning To Sleep Rapists: Judges Get Tough	Gordon McIlwraith
The Herald	25 September 2003	538	Appeal Judges Double Prison Sentence Of 'Stealth' Rapist	Alison Chiesa
The Herald	17 July 2003	431	Calls For Equal Jail Terms In Rape Cases Criticised	Damien Henderson
Evening News (Edinburgh)	16 July 2003	619	The Right To Refuse	Leader
The Express	16 July 2003	561	Judges Are Urged To Modernise Rape Law	Myra Philp
The Express	16 July 2003	95	Rape Law Review Welcome	Leader
The Herald (Glasgow)	16 July 2003	754	Rape By Stealth Sentence Under Attack	Valerie Hannah and Shan Ross
The Mirror	16 July 2003	190	Get Tough Call On 'Rape By Stealth'	Dave Finlay
The Scotsman	16 July 2003	612	Call To Toughen Up Rape Sentences	John Robertson

treat the corpus almost as a single text. It is possible to do this because of the way in which the same discourses (that is, rape myths and their challenges) are relied upon, whatever the bias of the piece

In terms of overt bias, only two stories stand out. One is adamant that the change to the law is not before its time. Its second line runs, 'Far too often women who have been lucky enough not to have been beaten to a pulp by their attacker have found that the courts have been unwilling to accept that they refused consent for sex' (*Evening News*, 16 July 2003). At the other extreme, the second line of a very short piece in *The Express* reads (to be quoted in full later), 'The fact is that many women are simply incapable of saying "no" to an attacker because they are too far gone with drink.' In fact, the focus on drinking, the drinking of women, is a topic that comes up repeatedly. It will be explored presently.

As is to be expected, the appeal returned to some of the facts of the first trial. In short, the complainant had been drinking with a colleague in a hotel. She and a colleague took a room and had consensual sex. After this, the complainant remained in the (locked) hotel room sleeping. Some time later, her colleague and the defendant (Shearer) were let into the room by hotel staff to retrieve a pass that would allow them to continue drinking in the hotel bar. The defendant, Shearer, remained in the room apparently asleep. The complainant woke to find that she was being raped, objected and the defendant left the room.

The text is analysed along what are substantially critical discourse analysis lines (see Kress, 1990; Fairclough, 1995), and so I focus on language as 'a type of social practice' (Kress, 1990: 85) and pay attention to the ideological ways in which language can represent the world. I take my critical point of view not so much from the use of language as representation *per se*, but rather from broadly feminist (for example, Irigaray, 1985; Langton, 1993) and Foucauldian points of view. The media coverage under examination here disciplines women by choosing to represent rape survivors through enduring rape myths (see Ehrlich, 1999, 2001). At the same time, women as agents are erased. Thus the analysis draws on the concepts of stereotypes, intertextuality, presuppositions embedded in arguments, the composition of arguments themselves and the construction of 'facts', that is, analytical tools familiar in the CDA 'toolkit'.

I deal first with the change to the law. I then look briefly at the levels of narrative present, before moving onto details of the media coverage itself. The collection of articles is examined in light of when they appeared, the negotiation of the general and particular, the issue of drinking alcohol, the concept of 'facts', and whose voices are represented. I conclude with a brief consideration of the judgment itself and a short discussion of public opinion around rape generally.

Background – general legal

In 2002, Scotland changed its rape laws. Previously, if someone had non-consensual sexual intercourse with a woman when they were asleep or unconscious, they could not be charged with rape. Rather, they were charged with 'clandestine injury'. This precedent had been in place for 143 years (*HM Advocate* v. *Sweenie* (Charles) (1858) 3 Irv 109). In 2002, the High Court in Scotland decided that force was not a necessary element in rape (2002 SCCR 435). The decision was the result of a referral by the Lord Advocate to the High Court in relation to a case where the defendant argued that there was no case to answer as force had not been involved.[4]

While the two dissenting judges argued that legal change should be the concern of the Parliament, nevertheless the law was changed. This is significant. A change at the level of case law may not always be as clear as one made through legislation. The case from which the sentencing appeal originated is the first to fall under the changed law. While the defendant was found guilty of rape (rather than clandestine injury) at trial, the Lord Advocate appealed the sentence handed down by Lord Morrison of 18 months. As we will see, even though the law was changed previous to this action, much of the discourse around the sentencing appeal concerned itself with distinctions between clandestine injury and rape; sometimes in these terms, but more usually through appeal to the issue of 'force'. While the 'rape is rape' formula was offered by some, and contested by many, it was not explicated. By this I mean that even though the law was changed to make clear that it is sufficient that there be a lack of consent for rape to have occurred, distinctions between kinds of rape are still posited. It was not clear from the newspaper reports whether the 'rape is rape' formula was pursued with any vigour by the Lord Advocate and Solicitor General. Here there is a clear conflict between legal meaning and consequences and 'lay' understandings which are often more concerned with notions of justice and morality. The appeal, however, was upheld and the sentence more than doubled to three and a half years.

Nested narratives

The moment of this chapter, and of the sentencing appeal, is far removed from the rape itself. Not only is this rape re-presented in legal terms, the event under examination here is a Crown appeal against sentencing of a rapist. Legal discourse itself (as any other) constrains the kinds of representations that are possible. As a very clear example, the distinction between 'clandestine injury' and 'rape' is not something that a victim, or indeed an attacker, would generally call upon in their own narratives of the events. Thus the texts which the court refers to in the appeal are not so much accounts of the rape event, but the accounts of what happened in the previous sentencing. At yet another remove, I take my text as the coverage of the sentencing appeal. The law itself, and the agents of law, are naturally actors in these representations.

Given these removes, the narratives presented here can said to be 'nested' (Galloway, 1979). In one way this nesting can be seen as a form of intertextuality. However, the temporal occurrence of the narratives and their transformations means that some are prior to others. Thus 'nesting' is used to capture this trajectory. When a case is reported by the media, it is well to bear in mind how far we might be from the original event which underlies the successive representations.

If we begin temporally from the start, there will be narratives about the event itself from the rapist and the rape survivor. The only access we have to these are through the facts of the case (thus already subject to a number of transformations). Secondly, we have the original court judgment, most importantly, the sentence (and the reasons for it) that was handed down by Judge Morison. As Morison's decision is at issue, his submission to the court is widely quoted; one particular segment appears in four of the articles. At the centre of the articles examined here are the arguments made by the Crown to the court, which constitute the appeal against the original sentence. In two articles written after the appeal decision was handed down, we also find comments from the Court derived from their written judgment. Finally, at the time of writing the articles, certain individuals, notably QCs and a professional in the rape crisis arena, are interviewed for comment.

As already noted, all events in the court are filtered through the mass media. It is not conceivable that people have the resources to attend cases of interest and importance. Only some documents are publicly available, and unlike other jurisdictions, there is no broadcast of court matters in Scotland. The nesting is not only temporal but also substantially related to what can be reported. Nevertheless, we do see a systematic erasure of the rape survivor.

These articles do not deal with the particular rape as much as the general state of the law. Indeed, as part of the appeal, the Court was asked for guidance on sentencing of such crimes. Such guidance was not given as it did not appear to the court 'to be useful or practicable for [them] to indicate what sentences would be appropriate, since so much will depend upon the circumstances of the individual case' (pgh 13). Yet the only individual we hear about is the defendant. Once a crime is taken up by the state, the rape survivor is merely another participant in the process.

Dates

The most striking thing about the sentencing appeal is the attention that the *result* did not attract. Of the nine pieces, only two appeared after the Court reached their decision to increase the sentence. The other seven appeared when the appeal was brought to court; six on the day the case was argued, and one the following day. The second day's story was in effect an opinion piece, representing the views of a leading Scottish QC.

The fact that the case was brought at all, and the way in which the case was put by the Solicitor General on behalf of the Lord Advocate, appears to be more newsworthy than the actual decision. This suggests that there is some unease over the change in the law. Indeed, the single piece on the day after the appeal began specifically questions the desirability of the change. Donald Findlay QC argues that juries will be more likely to acquit if they think that 'stealth rapists' will be treated as 'normal' rapists (Henderson, 2003). This presupposes both some knowledge of public opinion but more importantly a distinction between kinds of rape.

General vs. particular

In many ways the representations in these articles are emblematic of the judicial process. The functioning of precedent, which is at once general and particular, is recited here in various ways. The rape victim, while an individual in particular circumstances, is represented and can be understood, in relation to the various myths that circulate around rape. The rapist too is understood in various social frames, though substantially more individuated than the complainant. It is his appeal after all. As we have seen, the media pay more attention to the fact the case was brought than to the outcome. This suggests that the media are only interested in the general effects of the event. Indeed, in terms of coverage, a news article probably has to have a general purpose in some way, otherwise it is simply gossip or trivia.

Six of the nine pieces begin with statements which do not refer specifically to the case at hand, but rather the implications the case has for rapists, women[5] and the law. The headlines are similarly divided and correspond to the first line. One of two articles published when the decision was handed down, for example, considers the result in very general terms.

Warning to Sleep Rapists: Judges Get Tough
Rapists who prey on sleeping women do not deserve softer sentences.
(McIlwraith, 2003)

While the headline and leader are general, they do segment off a particular type of crime and criminal. This 'warning' is not to all rapists, but particularly to 'Sleep Rapists'. Given that the Court declined to give guidance on sentencing similar 'sleep rape' crimes, it is difficult to know why the outcome of a particular appeal is being understood by the journalist as a general warning. The notion that judges are getting 'tough' and that 'softer sentences' are not deserved, continues this warning mode. However in the fourth line of the article, we are told that the 'ruling will serve as a warning to other *judges*' (my emphasis). It is difficult to know quite how to understand this; though it is clear that the journalist sees judges as issuing a warning to their peers; something they don't in fact do. In any case, 'warning' suggests unwarranted or at least unexpected punishment. The warning being given to judges suddenly shifts blame from the defendant to the judiciary.

Just as the convicted rapist is used to stand as an example for all others who might 'prey on sleeping women', the rape survivor is also used to stand for a group, but a far less visible one. In her case, she is only present as part of a group of 'sleeping women'. In this way her experiences are erased, and all women (as all women sleep) are placed under the gaze of the preying rapist. The vulnerability of sleep is implicitly marked by the explicit toughness of the judiciary. Even in these two lines it is clear that the issue is between the 'tough judges' and the 'preying rapists'. That women are 'prey', that they are 'sleeping' suggests not only vulnerability but anonymity, lack of agency and abundance. This rape case, as others (De Carvalho Figueiredo, 2002: 262) clearly sanctions some modes of behaviour and not others.

Credible victim and drinking

We all 'know' what a credible rape victim is. What is important is that despite the change in Scottish law that 'rape is rape', which should mean that violence and force are not necessary for a 'rape' to have been committed, nothing much appears to have changed with respect to credible victims in terms of press coverage. In this case, credibility and consumption of alcohol are linked and can be understood in the broader context of rape myths. Women's drinking habits was the central topic for the media coverage, and was the strategy used by the Crown in the appeal.

Larcombe summarises the rape myths as follows, 'A [rape] case is more likely to have success if it is clearly interpretable as violence: if the assailant is a stranger, if a weapon is used, if the victim/survivor's resistance is overt and physical injury is sustained and documented' (2002: 132). Larcombe argues that 'ideal' rape victims are not the only ones successful in legal actions (2002: 140). The case here, though 'successful' in terms of prosecution and appeal of sentence, maintains the discourse of these myths.

Thus, despite the change in law, we also see a reluctance to redraw the lines that precedent dating from the nineteenth century established. Differentiating between kinds of rape is upheld. Indeed, the removal of 'clandestine injury' places the focus clearly on sentencing, as it is only at this point that one will be able to discern whether rape is considered as rape or as a number of different crimes, distinguishable on their 'merits' and individual circumstances.

The most fascinating aspect of this case is the way in which the Solicitor General (Elish Angiolini) chose to argue for a more severe sentence, and the way this was subsequently reported. The articles suggest that the warrant for tougher sentences is that women are more vulnerable. The cause of this vulnerability is their drinking. One article in particular epitomises the extreme of this view. Because of its brevity, it is worth reproducing in its entirety.

RAPE LAW REVIEW WELCOME

TODAY'S culture of heavy drinking in women, particularly among the younger generation, has become so entrenched that Scotland's appeal judges were yesterday asked to give sentencing guidelines on what is known as 'rape by stealth'.

The fact is that many women are simply incapable of saying 'no' to an attacker because they are too far gone with drink.

Nevertheless, they need all the protection of the law just as much as anyone else and an attacker has no right to imagine that, because a woman was too drunk to say 'no', his offence was any less serious. (*The Express*, 2003)

Here, the warrant for increasing sentencing guidelines is 'heavy drinking in women, particularly among the younger generation'. Not only is this practice part of present culture, it is 'entrenched'. The assertion is similarly entrenched, with its modality of certainty. It serves as foundation for the second sentence which states as a 'fact' that 'many women' are 'too far gone with drink' to say no. The presuppositions which underlie this are obvious. Firstly, women are expected to say no to an unwanted sexual advance. This suggests that the default position, if you like, is one of acceptance (see Frith and Kitzinger, 2001: 295). This aligns with the idea that women are 'too far gone with drink' to be capable even of simple speech; the utterly undemanding task of refusal emphasised here by enclosing 'no' in quotation marks.

That the attacker has 'no right to imagine that... his offence was any less serious' tells us that this is exactly what the attacker will imagine. The 'welcome' of the headline is thus not about improving the position of women, but rather about making the law clear for rapists. Another article mirrors these sentiments almost exactly. Finlay (2003) describes the rape survivor as laying 'in a drunken stupor' and refers to Shearer's initial custodial sentence as being 'caged for 18 months'.

The final paragraph of the article quoted above is a grudging acceptance of the idea that rape is serious. However, given the preceding sentences it is difficult to imagine that the writer is serious in this. This short piece evokes stereotypical associations of 'loose women' either deserving to be attacked or more likely deserving of no recourse as they 'should have known better'. Indeed in an earlier piece in *The Scotsman*, clandestine injury is defined as follows, 'It involves having intercourse with a woman when she is not in a state to give or withhold consent. She might have been asleep, unconscious from an accident or in a drunken *stupor of her own making*' (Robertson, my emphasis).

The issue of drinking was raised by the Crown. Philp reports that 'the Crown contended that when a woman was unconscious, through natural sleep or intoxication, she was in a particularly vulnerable state where she was deprived of her ability to resist, flee or scream for help'. Thus the 'natural' state for woman is sobriety or sleep and her 'natural' reaction should be to 'resist, flee or scream for help'. The use of 'flee' as opposed to, for example, 'run away' further signals an appeal to 'old-fashioned' values; and is precisely the language used by the court even when dismissing the notion. In other articles, Angiolini (for the Crown) is represented as stating that the drinking culture is generalised, with both men and women consuming more alcohol (see Hannah and Ross, 2003). However the effect of alcohol on a woman in a rape scenario is to make her culpable; on a man, quite the opposite. Indeed, where Angiolini is actually quoted she says:

> It [rape] becomes much more serious in the context of a society where women of all ages participate in the consumption of alcohol. It is a fact

that many young women consume a considerable volume of alcohol. (Philp, 2003)

This is part of well established 'rape myths', the narratives that frame and reproduce the stereotypes of rape and sexual assault (see Anderson and Beattie, 2001: 9ff). It is 'common knowledge' that the prototypical rape victim is a virgin, going about her business, and when attacked fights back violently (with scars to prove it). Thus a woman's drinking moves her further away from the place of credible victim. 'The legitimate victim is someone who was not under the influence of alcohol or drugs at the time of the rape' (Anderson and Beattie, 2001: 12). It is an image with a long history (Stevenson, 2000). However, if an attacker has been drinking, it somehow exculpates him. There is no mention made of Shearer's inebriation in the newspaper articles. When he is left in the hotel room he is 'apparently asleep' (Philp, 2003) while the rape survivor was 'unconscious or asleep and under the influence of alcohol' (Philp, 2003). He was dissembling; she was drunk. In fact, a rapist's intoxication excuses violence and accounts for his behaviour (Benedict, 1992: 258). The distance from normality is articulated in the notion of 'natural sleep' which is contrasted with unconsciousness from intoxication, and thus unnatural (Philp, 2003). The implication appears to be that while sleep is a reasonable state of vulnerability, presumably one that should be protected, being drunk is not. When one considers other possible scenarios, such as victims being in a coma, or indeed drugged, inebriation stands apart. The reasoning behind this appears to be that one has control over how much one drinks, or indeed whether one drinks at all, and thus one should know better than to become intoxicated to the point of sleep; even in a locked hotel room.

Facts

For most of us, our knowledge of 'the facts' [about sexual abuse] comes to us from media constructions, which we then interpret – using, among other resources, our own direct experiences and emotional reactions, our membership of and allegiances to specific social groups and analyses, or perhaps personal anecdotes from 'a friend of one of the social workers'. (Atmore, 1999: 88)

Given that this is a sentencing appeal, some of the facts included by the newspapers appear to be beside the point. The Crown submitted that as this was a rape conviction, a suitable sentence should be given and that 18 months was not sufficient. While sentencing does take account of the facts of the case, some of the facts mentioned by the newspapers nearly suggest that the conviction itself should not have been made. This is even more plausible when we recall that the doubling of the sentence was only reported twice.

The fact that the complainant had engaged in sexual intercourse with a colleague earlier in the evening is mentioned in four of the articles. That she had been drinking was mentioned by all of them. In one of the two articles published after the court's decisions, the contest of facts is clear:

> At the time of sentencing, Lord Morison said he took account of all circumstances, including the *fact* that the victim was incapable of consenting, rather than that her resistance was overcome by force.
>
> Lord Cullen, sitting with Lords Hamilton and Cameron, said this approach had caused them 'some concern'. He added: 'The *fact* is that he (Shearer) grossly exploited the access which had, for other reasons, been afforded to the victim's private accommodation.' (my emphasis, Chiesa, 2003)

The interpretation of the same fact could not be clearer. The distinction made with respect to Lord Morison is one that maintains the difference between force and lack of consent (as Lord Morison did). The Court of Appeal, on the other hand, sees the same fact as one of exploitation of access to private accommodation. The Court must have had more than 'some concern' as they more than doubled the sentence. The 'fact' that Shearer did not break into the private accommodation is hidden by the phrase 'for other reasons'. One can imagine that if violence against property had occurred (breaking into a house, for example), that this would have been noted and perhaps even constituted some 'force'. What is more disturbing about the particular way Lord Cullen phrases this 'fact' is that by referring to the 'victim's private accommodation' and the 'access' which was 'grossly exploited' by Shearer, the female victim is rendered as property. It is not so much that Shearer exploited the access to accommodation, but that he exploited access to the victim's body.

Referring to the victim, albeit indirectly as though she was property is perhaps not surprising given the complete absence of her voice. While interviews with the survivor are not perhaps expected, in this coverage, there is no mention of the victim in the particular at all. Apart from mentions of her in recounting the facts of the case, her experience is absent. In short, she is a woman who 'experienced relatively little fear, distress, or anger at the time' (pgh 12).

The only woman who is referred to at length is the Scottish Solicitor General, Elish Angiolini. While the judges involved in the case are rightly referred to as Lord, Elish Angiolini, QC is repeatedly referred to as 'Ms' and 'Mrs'. It seems that given Angiolini officially represents the Crown, it would be appropriate to refer to her in an official manner, as the Solicitor General, for example. The arguments made on behalf of the Crown, when attributed to 'Mrs Angiolini', suggest that she has a personal (and gendered) interest in the case. At the first mention in the articles, Angiolini is referred to by her full name and official affiliation. However in the three articles that refer to her more than once, one chooses 'Ms' four times, and two more articles 'Mrs' a total of eight times.[6]

While this might not of itself seem significant, this is the only woman present in these proceedings. It is significant exactly because we are made aware that the Solicitor General is a woman. Further, she is a woman portrayed as speaking about women's drinking. It is difficult to assess from the media reports, whether this should be read as speaking for women or against them.

Clandestine vs. stealth

The move from clandestine injury to rape is an important one legally and rhetorically. However, what was previously 'clandestine injury' has been transformed by journalists into 'rape by stealth'. Taking into account the clandestine denotations of stealth, as well as its opposition to force, it appears that the relexicalisation is more of a disguise than a makeover. We see this in both the frequent mention of 'clandestine injury' (eleven times in seven articles) and the way in which factors of force and distress are raised. The concept of 'rape by stealth' or 'stealth rape' was quickly picked up by the press. It does not, in fact, figure as such in the judgment itself the only similar occurrence being, 'Far from having the victim's active consent to sexual intercourse, the accused obtains that intercourse by stealth' (pgh 12).

Not all articles use the 'stealth rape' form. One, for example, which appeared after the judgment was handed down, refers to 'sleep rapists' (McIl-wraith, 2003). Apart from not appearing in any form in the judgment, the collocation suggests that the rapist himself has some of the characteristics of sleep; unconsciousness and resulting innocence perhaps. It is possible to imagine 'sleep rapist' describing someone who attacked while asleep (as though he had raped while sleepwalking).

There is constant reference to the old law and the changed legal position by all parties. This is not unexpected given that it is a recent change and that the offender in this case was the first person to be charged, convicted and sentenced since the change. It does seem, however, that the break with the old law has not been complete. Indeed, the issue raised by the Crown at the sentencing appeal was exactly that what was formerly clandestine injury should carry the same penalty as 'old style rape'.

In one article we learn that the previous 'landmark ruling found force was not necessary to constitute rape, merely that rape would have occurred if sex were non-consensual' (Chiesa, 2003). The use of 'merely' suggests that the crime is small one. Further, Lord Cullen (sitting on this sentencing appeal), quoted in the same article, also appears to draw a distinction between different kinds of rape, albeit indirectly. The Court demurs:

> from the view that the present type of case should be regarded as substantially less serious, for example, than one in which the victim was conscious, but in which the least amount of force was used or threatened and the victim experienced relatively little fear, distress, or anger at the time (Chisea, 2003).

It seems to me that this gives with one hand while taking with the other. The temporal placing of 'fear, distress and anger *at the time*' of the rape seems to be completely beside the point. One cannot imagine something of the sort being said if the victim had been drugged for example. Indeed, the case of drugging is recognised as 'force' (Robertson, 2003).

Lord Morison, the original sentencing judge, is quoted at length in four of these articles. One passage in particular recurs:

> I took account of the all the circumstances of the case, including the fact that the crime was committed because the victim was incapable of giving consent, rather than by the fact that her will and resistance were overcome by the use of force or threat of force. (Philp, 2003)

It is twice followed by:

> It appears to me *absurd* to suggest, as appears to be suggested, that (other considerations being equal) the culpability of the accused is the same in either case. (Hannah and Ross, 2003; my emphasis)

The 'facts' that Morison took into account have already been mentioned. The facts that the newspaper reports give would also have been considered in the original sentencing. We are told that the woman had been drinking, and that she had had sex with a colleague. While these are presented merely as the facts of the case, that they are presented at all is cause for concern. For Morison, not only is the formula rape-is-rape untenable in the context of sentencing or in the law more generally, it is 'absurd'. The presentation by the press of Morison's successfully appealed sentence, without any negative comment, suggests that it is the correct view.

The modification of 'rape' to 'stealth rape' or 'rape by stealth' clearly distinguishes it from 'normal rape'. This is a clear marker that for the media at least rape is not rape, as a qualification is made. The lexicalisation of this kind of rape can perhaps be seen as part of a larger trend including 'date rape', 'acquaintance rape' and 'stranger rape' (see Lees, 1996: 66; Anderson and Beattie, 2001: 3). Certainly the last, stranger rape, is the most credible in so far as it is considered the most prototypical. In the present case, such stranger rape (which includes violence) is placed by the Court at one end of a continuum as is clear in the quotation above.

A criminal lawyer, Alistair Duff, is quoted in one article pointing out that the court seems to have distinguished between different types of rape. 'It could be said that the appeal court has differentiated between the type of offence committed here and one whereby force is used' (Chiesa, 2003). This, it seems to me, should have been said.

What about the judgment?

The written judgment handed down by the appeal court is, if anything, more disturbing than the newspaper coverage. It needs to be seen in two contexts. First, the Court did more than double the sentence. Second, a great deal of material from the trial judge (Morison) was quoted. While some exception was taken to the original judgment, it was not thoroughly reprimanded. Morison's general approach caused the Court only 'some concern'. Of note is that Morison considered whose responsibility it was that Shearer was given access to the hotel room at all, which looked very much like an attempt to apportion blame elsewhere. He also 'took account of the fact that the respondent's criminal behaviour lasted for a very short time' (pgh 3). 'The trial judge also had regard to the effect which the case had had on the respondent's business which had collapsed as a result' (pgh 4). Why these issues should be of relevance is not clear to me. In contrast, the 'effect of the crime on the complainant... since that matter was not raised in the appeal' was not commented on in the submission (pgh 4).

In the case of drinking, the court appears to accept the argument that women are increasingly consuming alcohol. Indeed they add, 'For them [women] to be subjected to sexual intercourse without their knowledge or consent carried with it not merely the risk of pregnancy but also disease' (pgh 5). Thus the Court place rape firmly in the frame of sex, reproduction and 'risk behaviour' rather than violence. The drinking of both parties also placed the case 'at the opposite end of the spectrum from one in which an accused made a sudden attack on a passer-by, perhaps using a weapon to terrify his victim into submission' (pgh 9). Thus the court also reiterates the stereotypical rape scenario, endorses it and distinguishes it from the present case.

Perhaps the most shocking use of language in the judgment concerns the use of force. The court comments that clandestine injury 'was not treated as rape because of the absence of the use of force, that is to say, force other than that involved in achieving penetration of the woman' (pgh 10). This suggests that all sexual activity involves force and that an extreme threat of bodily harm or death is required to separate 'normal' penetration from rape. The issue of force is also of relevance to the question of consent. The findings reported in the media faithfully represent the court in this by distinguishing between the active lack of consent (involving fleeing, calling for help and the like) and being 'incapable of giving... consent' (pgh 12). Thus it is clear that for a rape to receive the full force of the law, consent has to be as forcefully revoked as it is then overcome.

The focus on drinking, inability to give consent and lack of force in this case are the main topics in both the judgment and the newspaper reports. In these areas there is parity between the two. The absolute absence of the rape survivor's voice is also clear. It seems that the representation of the Crown as relying on arguments about vulnerable drunk females is also accurate.

Why hasn't there been change?

Questions about why the law and indeed media representation of rape have changed relatively little are long standing ones (see Benedict, 1992: 5). If we return to a view mentioned briefly above, one proposed reason for why there has been little change is because of public opinion. Donald Findlay QC is quoted in *The Herald* (Henderson, 2003) as arguing that juries will be unwilling to convict if 'rape is rape'. 'Mr Findlay added that, if juries knew a blanket sentence for rape would apply, they would be unwilling to issue a conviction in cases where force had not been used.' In the same article, a spokeswoman for Rape Crisis Scotland, Sandy Brindley was reported as saying that 'the clarification of the law had brought it into line with public opinion'. She said, 'there can be a misunderstanding of what rape is. Rape itself is an act of force... It is unhelpful to distinguish between different types of rape.' This is placed directly in opposition to a quotation earlier in the same article from a criminal defence solicitor, Alistair Duff who comments, 'It is not helpful to say rape is rape; it is a singularly ill-informed comment'.

In yet another article, Gil Paterson, a Member of Scottish Parliament, is quoted as saying, 'Rape is rape and that is the end of the story. It makes a mockery of justice when judges make these decisions' (Hannah and Ross, 2003). It seems clear, though, that the rape-is-rape formula is not accepted by any of the legal experts. It would seem logical to conclude that 'justice', as Paterson conceives of it, is not the concern of the law.

Findlay's comments make it clear that he is speaking from the point of view of utility in the arena of procuring convictions, of which we know there are pitifully few. Duff is also presumably speaking from a legal point of view. It is clear in the law that rape is not rape as even the appeal court maintains a distinction between different types of rape. Such cases demand not only clarification and enforcement of the law, but a rhetorical turn. The point at which Brindley and Duff come directly in conflict with each other is over the question of how 'helpful' it is to understand rape-as-rape. From a legal point of view, with respect to the law as it currently stands, it is an unhelpful formula in as much as it doesn't account for how courts deal with rape. For rape survivors, however, the difference may be very helpful indeed. It is from this space that Brindley (as a representative of a rape survivors' organisation) can be assumed to be speaking.

A discussion board created on BBC news online around the time of the change in the law highlights the difficulty of speaking for 'public opinion' and also whether public opinion should be heeded in such matters. A variety of contributors from Scotland and around the world offer their views on what constitutes rape. The question that initiates the discussion asks for comments on Scottish law, that is, how to define rape legally and whether judges (as opposed Parliament) are the right people to decide on such definitions.[7]

From one point of view, the debate is beside the point. In legal terms, the judiciary (or the legislature) *do* decide what 'rape' means in a legal context. Many of the contributions fail to see this and protest that the 'dictionary definition' of rape is fine as it stands. But definitions offered by the public vary widely. One contributor argues that rape needs to have a 'violent element', failing to recognise that rape itself is violent. Another writer suggests that rape can occur with 'somewhat mutual consents of the parties involved'. One Canadian contributor suggests as a solution to rape 'a law of sex after marriage' such that any other sex is illegal. An American offers that it is 'very difficult to judge what is rape and what is seduction'. While many of these contributors fall outside the public one would expect to consider for Scottish law (that is, the Scottish public) the board does give an indication of the various viewpoints in circulation.

Conclusion

Perhaps the perennial question is whether the media should be responsible for 'good' reporting and for fostering 'good' public opinion. It is one that I shy away from, conscious that even if one can argue that the media has such a responsibility, enforcing it is intensely problematic. All that can be said is that the media is the main way in which the public receive news about legal processes. Robbennolt and Studebaker, in their work on the representation of civil litigation in the mass media argue that examination of the media is 'critical because citizens report that the news media is their primary source of information about the court system . . .' (2003: 6). They argue that:

> news media have the capacity to act as powerful influences on the [legal] system itself, influencing decision making in particular cases and on the system more generally as media reports influence the decision making of various participants in the system. (2003: 6).

214 The Language of Sexual Crime

Hans, putting it more succinctly, states, 'Law and the media have become inescapably intertwined' (1990: 399).

The maintenance of rape myths, even with ostensive changes to the law, suggests that these myths are somehow indefeasible. De Carvalho Figueiredo summarises Foucault's thesis of *Discipline and Punish*, and the changing forms of public punishment as 'a move from *coercion* to consent' (2002: 261). The absence of coercion, as we have seen in rape myths, implies consent.

Thinking about the state of public opinion and the timbre of media coverage is quite simply horrifying. The maintenance of rape myths in the media arguably says less about the media *per se* than about society in general. The Court of Appeal noted that the change in the law 'recognised that there had been considerable changes in the position of women in society' (pgh 5). I find this comical in the sharpest way. At a time when for many women 'feminist' is an insult, the situation appears bleak. We know that 95% of sexual assaults (that we have any way of knowing about) are committed by men; we know that the conviction rate is under 10%. We know that many women find it difficult to be impolite enough to say 'no' (Frith and Kitzinger, 2001). Further, it has been argued that consumption of pornography leads to silencing of women (in that they are simply not heard as saying no (Langton, 1993)).

In terms of the debate around rape, its definitions and punishments, it appears that violence does have to occur, but of a productive and protesting kind. As women (and as people) we need to forcefully revoke our consent with respect to attitudes about, prosecutions and media coverage of rape. It is about time that sex was taken out of the rape equation. Rape is gendered, rape is criminal and rape is violent. Rape is rape.

Notes

1. In 2003 12,760 cases of rape were reported to the police. Of these, only 5.3% (673) ended in a conviction. (http://www.endviolenceagainstwomen.org.uk/facts_r.asp)
2. Much of what Stevenson has to say on Victorian newspaper coverage and the genesis of rape myth legally and culturally apply here.
3. I have excluded online sources such as BBC online in order to keep an exclusively print based corpus.
4. Indeed the accused later sued for civil damages for defamation.
5. I do not mean to suggest that men are not raped, rather that the case deals with a woman being raped by a man and thus any general statements made about rape in the articles or in this paper refer to the same.
6. As a comparison, Janet Reno, former Attorney General of the United States is referred to (in order of number from a search on newspaper articles on Lexis-Nexis) either as 'Attorney General', 'Janet Reno', 'Reno' and much less usually 'Ms Reno'.
7. See www.bbc.co.uk/1/hi/talking_point/1717291.stm

References

Ajzenstadt, M. and Steinberg, O. (2001) Never mind the law: Legal discourse and rape reform in Israel, *Affillia*, 16 (3): 337–59.

Anderson, I. and Beattie, G. (2001) Depicted rapes: How similar are vignette and newspaper accounts of rape, *Semiotica*, 137 (1/4): 1–21.

Atmore, C. (1999) Sexual abuse and troubled feminism: A reply to Camille Guy, *Feminist Review*, 61(1): 83–96

Badger, R. (2003) Legal and general: towards a genre analysis of newspaper law reports, *English for Scientific Purposes*, 22(3): 249–63.

Benedict, H. (1992) *Virgin or Vamp: How the Press Covers Sex Crimes*. Oxford: OUP.

Brookover Bourque, L. (1989) *Defining Rape*. London: Duke University Press.

Campbell, R. (2002) *Emotionally Involved: the Impact of Researching Rape*. New York: Routledge

Chiesa, A. (2003) Appeal judges double prison sentence of 'stealth' rapist, *The Herald*, 25 September: 1.

De Carvalho Figueiredo, D. (2002) Discipline and punishment in the discourse of legal decisions on rape trials, in J. Cotterill (ed.), *Language in the Legal Process*, Basingstoke: Palgrave – now Palgrave Macmillan. pp. 260–74.

Du Mont, J., Miller, K-L. and Myhr, T. L. (2003) The role of 'real rape' and 'real victim' stereotypes in the police reporting practices of sexually assaulted women, *Violence Against Women*, 9 (4): 466–86.

Ehrlich, S. (1999) Communities of practice, gender and the representation of sexual assault, *Language in Society*, 28(2): 239–56.

Ehrlich, S. (2001) *Representing Rape: Language and Sexual Consent*, London: Routledge.

Evening News (2003) The Right to Refuse, 16 July: 10.

The Express (2003) Rape Law Review Welcome, 16 July: 12.

Fairclough, N. (1995) *Critical Discourse Analysis: The Critical Study of Language*. London: Longman.

Finlay, D. (2003) Get tough call on 'rape by stealth', *The Mirror*, 16 July: 2.

Foucault, M. (1991) *Discipline and Punish: the Birth of the Prison*. A. Sheridan (trans.) London: Penguin Books.

Frith, H. and Kitzinger, C. (2001) Reformulating sexual script theory: developing a discursive psychology of sexual negotiation, *Theory and Psychology*, 11(2) Apr: 209–32.

Galloway, P. (1979) Yngve's Depth Hypothesis and the structure of narrative: the example of detective fiction. In M. McCafferty and K. Gray (eds), *The Analysis of Meaning: Informatics* 5, 104–109. London: ASLIB.

Hannah, V. and Ross, S. (2003) Rape by stealth sentence under attack; leading law officer criticises 'lenient' 18-month jail term, *The Herald*, 16 July: 1.

Hans, V. P. (1990) Law and the media: an overview and introduction, *Law and Human Behaviour*, 14 (5): 399–407.

Henderson, D. (2003) Calls for equal jail terms in rape cases criticised: View may cause acquittals, says top defence lawyer, *The Herald*, 17 July: 2.

Howe, A. (1998) *Sexed Crime in the News*, Sydney: Federation Press.

Irigaray, L. (1985) *This Sex Which is Not One*. Ithaca, N.Y.: Cornell University Press.

Kress, G. (1990) Critical Discourse Analysis. *Annual Review Of Applied Linguistics*, 11: 84–99.

Langton, R. (1993) Speech acts and unspeakable acts, *Philosophy and Public Affairs*, 22(4): 292–330.

Larcombe, W. (2002) The 'Ideal' victim v. successful rape complainants: Not what you might expect, *Feminist Legal Studies*, 10(2): 131–48.

Lees, S. (1996) *Carnal Knowledge: Rape on Trial*, London: Penguin.

McIlwraith, G. (2003) Warning to sleep rapists: judges get tough, *Daily Record*, 25 September: 27.

Philp, M. (2003) Judges are urged to modernise rape law, *The Express*, 16 July: 6.

Robbennolt, J. K., and Studebaker, C. A. (2003). News media reporting on civil litigation and its influence on civil justice decision making, *Law and Human Behaviour*, 27 (1): 5–27.

Robertson, J. (2001) Pressure grows for change in rape law, *The Scotsman*, 18 December (www.news.scotsman.com).

Roberts, J. V. and Doob, A. N. (1990) News media influences on public views of sentencing, *Law and Human Behavior*, 14(5): 451–68

Robertson, J. (2003) Call to toughen up rape sentences, *The Scotsman*, 16 July: 2.

Soothill, K., Walby, S. and Bagguley, P. (1991) Judges, the media and rape, *Journal of Law and Society*, 17(2): 211–31.

Stevenson, K. (2000) Unequivocal victims: the historical roots of the mystification of the female complainant in rape cases, *Feminist Legal Studies*, 8(3): 343–66.

12
At the Hands of the Brothers: a Corpus-based Lexico-grammatical Analysis of Stance in Newspaper Reporting of Child Sexual Abuse Cases

Anne O'Keeffe and Michael J. Breen

Introduction

This chapter analyses the language of child abuse in the context of newspaper reports. Child abuse as a crime indisputably carries with it strong social taboo and so representing it for public consumption necessitates great sensitivity and 'deftness of pen'. Here we look at two contexts of child abuse, one institutional and one domestic and we compare how the representation of the crime differs relative to context.

This study is set in Ireland and the newspaper articles which we analyse come from *The Irish Times*, between 1998 and 2000. This newspaper is accepted as the 'paper of record' and so carries the greatest expectation of unsensationalised reporting of this publicly reviled crime. The data for this study comes from articles reporting on clerical child sexual abuse (all male) and domestic father–son abuse. The clerical abuse articles all focus on the Irish Christian Brothers who abused children in Irish Industrial Schools.[1]

The aim of the chapter is to take a microscope to the language used to represent these crimes in a paper of record and to ascertain whether there is a differing degree of author stance depending on the context, institutional or domestic. In the case of the Industrial Schools, the perpetrator was an institutional representative, in the public sphere at the time of the crime, whereas in the case of domestic child sexual abuse, the perpetrator was a private individual in the private sphere. These differing contexts appear to have a bearing on the language used to report the crime.

In this study, we will use a corpus linguistic methodology, whereby large databases of texts (see below) have been scanned and are available electronically for us to analyse quantitatively and qualitatively (see O'Keeffe, 2006). Linguistic analysis of the print media usually comes from a critical perspective, and linguists sometimes see themselves as policing the subtle manipulation of language to distort reality. Here we are taking a purely descriptive position on the datasets.

Stance, lexico-grammar and news reports

White (1997: 110) positions hard news reports on a cline of objectivity (compared to 'the commentary or opinion piece') depending on level of 'subjectivising' meanings they present and thus the degree to which they position the reader interpersonally. Young (2001) argues that this dichotomy is not quite straightforward and points to the need for lexico-grammatical analysis in analysing the objectivity and subjectivity of texts rather than looking at narrative structures or rhetorical devices. Lexico-grammar is the meeting of lexis (words) and grammar (after Sinclair, 1991). Sinclair (1996) observes that: 'words enter into meaningful relationships with other words around them'.

For the purposes of this chapter, we will adopt a lexico-grammatical approach to analysing stance in the language used in newspaper reports on child abuse. This means that rather than looking at words or grammatical structures in isolation, we will look at how stance is constructed systematically through certain types of lexical combinations and choices. Biber et al (1999: 966) note that 'in addition to communicating propositional content, speakers and writers commonly express personal feelings, attitudes, value judgements, or assessments, that is, they express stance' and they identify certain lexico-grammatical devices (see below) that mark speaker/writer stance. In newspaper reports, a writer's stance can frame the meaning of the information, very often in a subtle manner. By looking at lexico-grammatical indices of stance across a large number of articles on one topic, we can identify whether such patterns are used systematically. In addition to these devices identified by Biber et al. (1999), we will also focus on speech reporting in terms of how what is said is framed in written form.

Data and methodology

The corpora

This study draws on three batches of newspaper texts which have been divided for analysis into three corpora. These are:

Corpus 1 – *All CB*

Newspaper coverage on the Irish Christian Brothers in relation to child abuse and the Industrial Schools,[2] from 1998 to 2000, in Irish national to regional press. News reports make up the majority in terms of genre, but it also includes editorials and letters.

Total word count: 322,873

Corpus 2 – *Irish Times* Non-CB

43 newspaper reports from the *Irish Times* on child abuse between 1998 and 2000. The only restrictions on the selection of these articles were that they would *not* involve abuse within religious orders and, to improve comparability, that they referred to male–male (usually father–son) abuse.

Total word count: 20,223

Corpus 3 – *Irish Times* CB

43 newspaper reports from the *Irish Times* between 1998 and 2000. These are taken from *All CB* corpus, as detailed above. 43 articles about the Christian Brothers were chosen randomly to parallel the number of texts found in the same paper in the same period dealing with non-religious child abuse.

Total word count: 28,532

Using the three databases of articles, Wordsmith Tools software was used to generate stance-related lexico-grammatical data across the corpora.

Analytical framework for analysis

The *Longman Grammar of Spoken and Written English*[3] (henceforth referred to as: Biber et al. 1999) identifies the following markers of stance in English:

Table 12.1:   Analytical framework for the analysis of stance

Marker of stance	Example from the data
Lexical markers of stance	Inmates include ***pervert padres*** such as Ivan Payne and Eugene Greene who were ***banged up*** for carrying out ***horrific*** sexual abuse on ***innocent young*** children. [*All CB*]
Stance adverbials	***Unfortunately***, given the Brother's evasive responses to the question of whether the order will open up its archives to independent scrutiny, this 'mystery' of the good Brothers may never be resolved. [*All CB*]
Stance complement clauses	After all, ***there can be little doubt*** that religious orders and government departments have also worked to protect what they see as their own legitimate interests. [*All CB*]
Modals and semi-modals	. . . public outrage ***will*** pass and life ***will*** return to normal. This ***should*** not be allowed to happen, nor is it *likely* to happen. And next week's programme and

Table 12.1:   (Continued)

Marker of stance	Example from the data
	the one to follow the week after, **will** undoubtedly twist and torment our hearts and minds still further. Much of this, it **must** be said, is not new. Since at least 1985, when the pioneering work, Children of the Poor Clares was published . . . [*All CB*]
Stance noun + preposition phrase	. . . 18-month investigation turned up more victims and *a litany of stomach-curdling abuse*. [*All CB*]
Pre-modifying stance adverbs	Following persistent questioning, she claimed that the names of the boys were supplied to her by the Department of Education. This is an ***extremely*** serious allegation. [*All CB*]
Stance reporting structures (marked or unmarked, in other words using neutral reporting verb)	Example of marked reporting structures: . . . tears flowed down the cheeks of grown men when they ***described*** the vile treatment to which they had been subjected as children. 'Please tell our stories and convince the Irish people that this happened,' they ***pleaded***. 'Nobody will listen to us – except the *News of the World*.' [*All CB*]

Analysis

Lexical markers of stance

'Abuse' collocates

The word *abuse* ranks highest in frequency of content words in both Christian Brothers corpora and it is the third most frequent content word in the *IT NCB* corpus. When normalised to occurrences per 1,000 words, the distribution of the word *abuse* is more or less the same in the three corpora.

On closer examination, we find that it is subject to variation in terms of its collocates (the words that co-occur with it). We find, for example, that the degree to which the writers choose to modify the word by putting a more 'colourful' word before it varies considerably. Table 12.2 shows a sample of the concordance line for the word *abuse* from the *IT NCB* data:

In Table 12.2, we see that the word *abuse* is for the most part premodified in an unmarked manner. Those collocates which could be termed 'marked' in the extract have been shaded:[4] *suffered abuse* and *systematic abuse*. Take for example line 93: '*12 years of systematic abuse and domination*', the writer could have chosen to use the more neutral: *12 years of abuse* and so on. The use of the word *systematic* intensifies the meaning. The same could be said of line 92, where the phrase: '*suffered abuse at the hands of*' could be put more neutrally as: '*were abused*'. Table 12.2 shows that the word

Table 12.2:   Sample from concordance line of *abuse* from the *IT NCB* corpus (sorted 1L. 2L)

---

83 sions amounted to a finding that sexual abuse can produce results inhibiting com
84 that his client's view that the sexual abuse of his daughter contributed to a b
85 ve it. After the extent of the sexual abuse was validated in 1995 at the child
86 parently as a consequence of the sexual abuse, the boy has a history of fire-set
87 reatened that if he revealed the sexual abuse (which occurred outside the home)
88 r verdict A man subjected to sexual abuse as a child, who 'lost control' and
89 est Correspondent People who sexually abuse children must not be allowed to hi
90 eaphy with his fists clenched, shouting abuse at him. He never went near Philip,
91 ened,' he said. 'The 1908 Act specified 'abuse and neglect'. 'The burden of pr
92 e mother whose three daughters suffered abuse at the hands of a close relative s
93 ed his family to 12 years of systematic abuse and domination. The defendant forc
94 esults inhibiting complaints about that abuse for a very long time. The Supreme
95 plicant, was effectively a finding that abuse had occurred and was a fundamental
96 sister. He was unable to talk about the abuse and had refused to continue with t
97 and the now 36-year old son abused. The abuse happened in the defendant's bed, i
98 adcast he was not on medication and the abuse was not public knowledge. Followin
99 es of buggery and indecent assault. The abuse took place between 1972 and 1976 i

---

abuse collocates with lexical markers of stance twice as often in the Christian Brothers articles than when writing about non-religious sex abuse in the *Irish Times*. When we compare the *IT NCB* with the *All CB* corpus, we find that the high frequency word *abuse* co-occurs with attitudinal markers of writer stance about three times more frequently. These are collated in Table 12.3:

Table 12.3:   Breakdown of collocates of *abuse*

Corpus	Total occurrences of *abuse*	Total with Marked Premodifiers	%	Collocates used
IT NCB	123	5	4	*gross; systematic; suffered*
IT CB	190	16	8	*horrendous; appalling litany of; harrowing stories of; criminal sexual; perverted; very serious sexual; spiritual; suffered*
All CB	2,198	21 (of sample of 157 instances)	13	*tragedy of; consistent; heap abuse upon; horrific; appalling; flow of; violent culture and age of; legacy of; systematic pattern of; systematic regime of sins of; degrading and horrific; criminal; lifting the lid on years of; perverted; shocking; spiritual; suffered*

As we can see from the summary of collocates in Table 12.2, the writer choices vary both in quantity and quality across the data. Only three stance collocates of the word *abuse* are used in all of the 43 *Irish Times* articles about non-religious 'mostly domestic' child sexual abuse: *gross, systematic* and *suffered*. In terms of quality, they are less evaluative than examples found in the articles about the Christian Brothers, such as: *appalling litany; perverted; harrowing; sins of* and so on. They also carry less emotive impact for the reader compared with the *IT CB* and *All CB* collocates. This evidences a greater framing force being used by writers when reporting on abuse in the context of the Christian Brothers.

'The Brothers' collocates

Obviously, the words *Brother* and *Brothers* rank highly in the *All CB* corpora. On examining concordance lines of these words (and Br, Bros. and so on.), we find that there are 2,377 occurrences of the word *brother* in its various forms. Cluster analysis reveals the phrase *at the hands of* as a significant lexical bundle[5] (see Biber et al. 1999: 989). Examples are provided below:

Extract 1

For the next two years, **at the hands of** one Brother in particular but also **at the hands of** up to three others, Steve claims to have suffered unimaginable mental and physical torture... [*All CB*]

On searching concordance lines of the lexical bundle *at the hands of,* we find that 84% of occurrences are in relation to the Christian Brothers. There are also some references to other religious orders or individual priests and one reference to the medical profession, plus a number of references to the Catholic Church in general. A sample from the concordance result is presented in Table 12.4.

Table 12.4: A sample of the concordance line for *at the hands of (All CB)*

1	the hundreds of other men who suffered at the hands of *these men'*. A number of
2	le should know what had happened to him at the hands of *the Christian Brothers* i
3	of people in the State were brutalised at the hands of *the religious*, were beat
4	upil was subjected to a vicious beating at the hands of *a Brother*. 'Young Joseph
5	e I told her.' For the next two years, at the hands of *one Brother in particula*
6	d abuse. Like Mr Waters I too suffered at the hands of *the Christian Brothers*.
7	oys sustained life-threatening injuries at the hands of *the brothers*. O'Connell
8	nselling service for those who suffered at the hands of *sadistic priests*, nuns a
9	t the appalling treatment they received at the hands of *the Christian Brothers* a
10	he inquiry. The survivors of the abuse at the hands of *Christian Brothers* have
11	t it ever being known how they suffered at the hands of *people in authority*. Tha
12	rific brutality and abuse they suffered at the hands of *religious* in industrial

This phrase has clearly become fixed or idiomatic in its use in the press when talking about abuse in the context of the Christian Brothers. It is a strong marker of stance on the part of the writer and it has a high framing effect intensifying the negativity of the message. The example in Extract 2 shows how the writer chooses to use this lexical bundle in conjunction with other lexical and grammatical stance markers (marked in italics) to intensify the force of the article and frame the message for the reader (note we include the direct quotation in the italicisation as the choice to use a direct quote is within the gift of the writer):

Extract 2

A victim who *suffered horrific* sex abuse **at the hands of** *perverted* Christian Brothers yesterday *slammed* the Catholic Church for refusing to show any *real* remorse. John Prior, whose *childhood hell was exposed* by the *Irish News of the World* in 1995, *stormed: 'The Church is not sorry at all, and its paedophile priests are only sorry about getting caught'* [*All CB*]

By way of comparison with the non-religious abuse stories, the lexical bundle *at the hands of* is only used once in the 43 *Irish Times* articles during the same period in the *IT NCB* corpus. In these cases, it is used to refer to abuse by a close relative. This clearly indexes lexical bias in reporting abuse by the Christian Brothers and strongly suggests that this phrase has become stabilised as an idiom in writing about Christian Brothers and child abuse in Ireland.

Stance adverbials

Biber et al. (1999: 966) note that 'stance adverbials express the attitude or the assessment of the speaker/writer with respect to the proposition contained in the main clause', hence their relevance in this study. A concordance search for all -ly suffixes was conducted, excluding the word '*sexually*'. The *IT NCB* and *IT CB* corpora yielded 231 and 369 hits respectively.[6] All non-stance adverbs and names ending in -ly etc. were eliminated and the following results were found across the *IT NCB* and *IT CB* data. The results are presented in terms of occurrence per 1,000 words (Figure 12.1).

Tables 12.5 and 12.6 present the actual results from the two *Irish Times* corpora and Table 12.7 shows the results from the 300 randomly chosen -ly items in the *All CB* data.

Of note is the fact that all of the stance adverbs used in the *IT NCB* articles are either from direct or indirect speech reports and so there is no instance of writers expressing stance directly; however, the decision to include the direct quote is in itself a choice on the part of the writer, as mentioned earlier. In contrast, we find that only four of the sixteen occurrences of stance adverbs in the *IT CB* articles are of this nature. Instead the majority

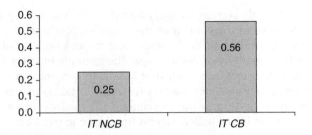

Figure 12.1:   Stance adverbs per 1,000 words in *IT NCB* and *IT CB* corpora

Table 12.5:   Stance adverbs in the *IT NCB* data

1	at stress such allegations caused. 'I **certainly** would not want in any sense to
2	faces were very puffy that night. They **obviously** had been crying. Judge Micha
3	home with a black eye my father said I **probably** deserved it,' he said. 'I was
4	This motivated me. I felt that I would **probably** have been believed more than an
5	nfident' his client would win the case. '**Unfortunately** the file is now closed: a

Table 12.6:   Stance adverbs in the *IT CB* data

1	quired to register with health boards – **amazingly** this was left out of the 1991
2	nquests of their sufferings and neglect **certainly** demand something more than sym
3	so it went – horror piled upon horror. **Certainly**, there was an economic aspect
4	ively been suppressed by a State, which **clearly** remains in denial about the issu
5	ess that abuses have now all but ended. **Clearly**, the monstrous industrial school
6	to relate their experiences of abuse. **Crucially**, the sociological task of reco
7	o any modern childcare practices. Most **crucially**, what the government suppresse
8	en have been treated in Irish society. '**Hopefully** it will prove to be a step in
9	our main work to confront the evil that **hopefully** is in the past,' he said. Mee
10	at is in place to deal with it is still **hopelessly** out of date,' he says. 'The
11	dential children's home – failure which **inevitably** led to the abuse of these mos
12	ittle Catholic country on Earth' would, **inevitably**, have a shadow side. Given th
13	. 'This is standard practice and it is **obviously** a good way to promote your pro
14	njurious to them.' While the manual has **rightly** been pensioned off to the Christ
15	n the industrial schools of Ireland has **rightly** been splashed on news and featur
16	oncrete means to bring about healing. **Shamefully**, however, the Catholic Church

are used to mark the writer's stance, for example, item 16 (*IT CB*) '*Shamefully*, however, the Catholic Church continues to show no interest in restitution'. Similar patterns are observed in the random sample from the *All CB* data. This shows a difference in the manner and degree to which *Irish Times* writers have chosen to editorialise when reporting on child abuse in relation to the Christian Brothers and have avoided this in the case of domestic abuse reporting.

Table 12.7: Stance adverbs in 300 -ly item sample from *All CB* data

1 rned to keep away from individuals who, **clearly**, were regarded by adults as dang
2 punishment was designed to hurt, and it **clearly** did. It was the age-old dilemma,
3 ild Abuse (the Laffoy Commission). More **importantly**, somebody with an agenda has
4 mantle once worn by Jack Lynch and now, **sadly**, unfilled. If Mr Ahern does ring o
5 y cold and uncaring about this. I think **probably** they're not really cold and unc
6 ive detail are inappropriate responses. **Certainly** let us find out and say the tr
7 n. Pupil after pupil was tested until, **inevitably**, mistakes were made and then
8 n the industrial schools of Ireland has **rightly** been splashed on news and featur
9 as seriously looked at in terms of RTE. **Unfortunately** it never got anywhere and

Stance complement clauses

As in the following example, what precedes a complement clause can index a writer's stance and frame the meaning of what follows (the complement clause is marked in square brackets and the frame is marked in italics):

Extract 3

It is more than possible [that some boys were actually beaten to death by frustrated and out-of-control Christian Brothers]. [*All CB*]

By searching for all of the occurrences of *that* in the comparative corpora and isolating the complement clauses that contained stance markers, we found the following results per 1,000 words (see Figure 12.2).

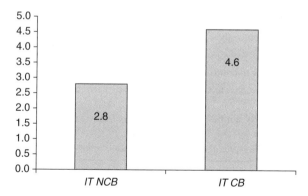

Figure 12.2: Stance complement clauses

The results show a higher number of stance complement clauses in the *IT CB* data when compared with the *IT NCB* data. Tables 12.8 and 12.9 show samples from each source.

Table 12.8:   Sample of stance complement clauses in the *IT NCB* corpus

2	no record of this case. It would appear that the inspector who noted injuries to
3	hey occurred, the only defence could be that they did not. Replying for the su
4	needs. He said it was 'beyond belief' that the Minister was asking for such an
5	Pressed on this, he said he believed that one night the defendant had put whi
8	er's family home. It rejected the claim that the boy was suffering from a person
10	he ground. The accused man also claimed that the alleged victim was faking the e
13	'place of safety' order. It is clear that many of the neighbours were willing
17	xcitement. It was of very grave concern that he had been involved in the same ac
25	r any of the complainants to the extent that they were prevented from making a p
27	oherty was not as important as the fact that the case had taken place. Doherty
28	the prosecution had relied on the fact that the offences formed part of a serie

Table 12.9:   Sample of stance complement clauses in the *IT CB* corpus

1	e inmates, there is a blithe assumption that all is for the best. The 1952 repor
3	simply want to apologise. And I believe that it is true of everybody else in thi
5	s orders. ' It is reasonable to believe that the archives of the religious order
9	rovided now.' Nonetheless, he cautions that the decision to step back from the
11	attempted suicide 15 times. He claimed that after he told his mother about the
19	ort yesterday, said they were concerned that confidential information in relatio
22	uma and suffering'. RTE also contended that the reason the Christian Brothers w
23	hildhood Abuse approaches it is crucial that we examine its potential contributi
24	tian Brothers have categorically denied that it was their policy to use a counse
33	e it our main work to confront the evil that hopefully is in the past,' he said.
35	essuring young people to such an extent that many turn to drugs and some even co
36	ective responsibility applies. The fact that my Department was Industry and Comm
37	conditions'. This, in spite of the fact that schools knew weeks in advance when

We then conducted a breakdown of the contexts of these stance complement clauses and found that the majority of occurrences in the non-
religious articles were reported from individual cases (95% in the *IT NCB*).
This was in stark contrast with the Christian Brothers articles (*IT CB*)
where only 13% related to individual cases. Figure 12.3 illustrates these
percentages.

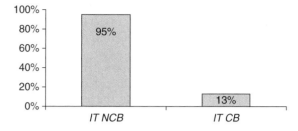

Figure 12.3: Percentage of stance complement clauses relating to individual abuse cases

That complement clauses, according to Biber et al. (1999: 660–1) 'are commonly used to report the speech, thoughts, attitudes or emotions of human beings'. In the case of the *IT CB* corpus, we have found that the majority of stance complement clauses relate to speech, thoughts, attitudes and emotions in general as opposed to individual cases. This framing in the public domain is for the most part absent from reporting of child abuse in the non-religious corpus (*IT NCB*), which substantiates earlier assertions about the specificity and isolation with which writers treat non-religious child abuse in Irish society.

Modals and semi-modals

The central modals verb: *will, would, can, could, may, should, must, might* and *shall* occur with the following frequency across the three corpora (see Figure 12.4).

Here we limit our focus to *would*. As Figure 12.4 shows, there is a much higher occurrence of the modal verb *would* in the non-Christian Brothers

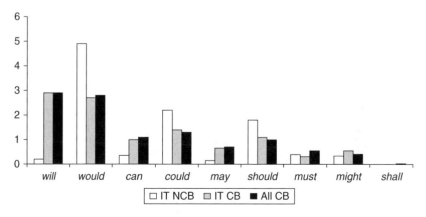

Figure 12.4: Frequency profile of central modal verbs across corpora

articles (*IT NCB*). In all, there are 101 instances of *would* in the *IT NCB* data, 76% of which are related to the reporting of details from individual cases. Typically, *would* is used (1) in indirect speech to report what has been said in the court (that is, the past form of *will*): '*Mr Justice Kelly said he* **would** *adjourn the matter for one week*' and (2) to report details of abuse cases. In this latter instances, *would* is mostly used to characterise past behaviour in the context of abuse (a form of predictability in the past, see Leech, 1971: 96):

Extract 4

Det Sgt Bernard Sherry said the now 62-year-old father of three *would* bang the floor when he wanted one of his children to go upstairs to him for his sexual gratification. This *would* lead to fights among the children as to whose turn it was for abuse. [*IT NCB*]

This use of *would* differs in the *IT CB* articles where only 7.5% of the occurrences of *would* relate to this type of characterisation of abuse in individual cases compared with 75% in the non-Christian Brothers articles. This again clearly points to the 'specificity' of reporting style in domestic abuse cases versus the more global societal context in which the Christian Brothers cases are cast.

The semi-modals items *had to; need to; appear; seem* and *tend* were analysed across the data and the results are presented in Figure 12.5 (results presented in occurrences per 1,000).

Here we limit our focus to *tend*. This semi-modal occurs with highest frequency overall, but, surprisingly, it does not occur in any of the *Irish Times* data (*IT NCB* or *IT CB*). All other national and regional articles that refer to the Christian Brothers are responsible for its usage. Fifty per cent of all its uses are found in articles which are in some way more favourable towards the Christian Brothers, as in this example:

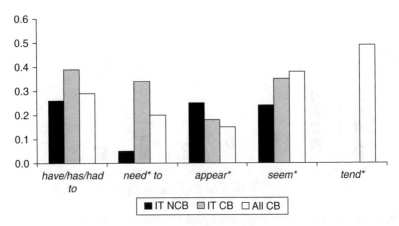

Figure 12.5: Semi-modal verbs distribution profile across *IT NCB, IT CB* and *All CB*[7]

Extract 5

It seems to me that in the pubic mind now, or at least in the mass media mind, all Christian Brothers **tend to** be considered guilty until proven innocent – the exact opposite of what justice should be about. [*IT CB*]

Linguistically, it is not surprising that the verb *tend to* is chosen by writers. It operates as a hedging device to downtone the force of what is said and in a period of negativity in general reporting on the Christian Brothers, writers are naturally circumspect in expressing opinions that may be contrary to mainstream consensus. Extract 5 is a good example, the writer could have chosen to write the more assertive version: *all Christian Brothers **are** considered guilty until proven innocent*, but instead, the more downtoned form *tend to* was chosen along with the stance marker *It seems to me* preceding the complement clause. By using *It seems to me* and *tend to* the writer allows space for doubt.

Stance noun + preposition phrase

A writer's attitudinal stance can also be found in nouns that control prepositional phrases. Take the following example in Extract 6, where the noun *trauma* frames what follows in the prepositional phrase:

Extract 6

... he would not put the victim through **the trauma** of giving evidence to a trial [*IT NCB*]

Tables 12.10 to 12.13 present the findings and the normalised totals are found in Figure 12.6.

Table 12.10: Instances of stance nouns controlling prepositional phrases in *IT NCB* corpus (the * of)

1	prison, a former pupil of his who bore the brunt of his savagery 50 years ago i
2	contributing to preventing sex abuse. The consequence of the use of demonising
3	ered from depression in prison, now had the stigma of being called a jailbird. R
4	requirement that a jury be cautioned on the dangers of convicting on the basis o
5	n Sligo yesterday the couple emphasised the importance of media coverage of sex
6	The abuse of trust involved underlined the gravity of such rape offences, for w
7	hock. I just feel that the pressure and the strain of the whole thing just becam
8	They say he didn't receive it. After the extent of the sexual abuse was valid
9	rder or bombing in this country. That's the extent of the problem. 'Yes, by al
10	y what George Gibney had done to him. The effect of the disclosure made him ag

Table 12.11: Instances of stance nouns controlling prepositional phrases in *IT NCB* corpus (a * of)

1	ch children in the State. Apparently as a consequence of the sexual abuse, the b
2	re must be strong evidence to establish a ' failure of duty by parents towards th
3	years. When it was investigated, he met a reaction of 'How could this have happe

Table 12.12: Instances of stance nouns controlling prepositional phrases in *IT CB* corpus

27	ir schools will carry their own images, the litany of scandals over the last few
28	sive and previous governments, to offer the minimum of a word of apology and giv
29	s, shown on RTE last night, highlighted the plight of hundreds of mentally and p
30	t least a touch of nostalgia about it. The promise of a register of sex offende
31	ccur should be achieved without denying the reality of the abuse. It is easy to
32	dedicated to the service of family and the sacredness of family life preside ov
33	y the Rosminians in Drumcondra, Dublin, the screams of the children being flogge
34	ations did, that it did me no harm, but the thought of a child of mine having hi
35	nvironment, without having to deal with the trauma of cross-examination by the l
36	harm to cease reading and just focus on the vileness of the sadism, sexual abuse

Table 12.13: Instances of stance nouns controlling prepositional phrases in *IT CB* corpus

6	ystems suggest themselves. But there is a danger of a self-defeating and distort
7	case. It's hardly surprising then that a degree of scepticism runs through offi
8	our schools offer, because we encourage a love of Gaelic culture and an Irish ed
9	s, and for most of us avoiding hurt was a matter of being able to run or being a
10	ntinue addressing the issue of abuse as a matter of urgency. It is a call to lis
11	of such schools their establishment was a matter of some difficulty. As a result
12	promised service then disappeared into a miasma of purported legal complication
13	'and "each of the classrooms presented a picture of happy and contented boys'.
14	of the industrial schools, it presents a picture of abuse, secrecy and cover-up
15	ing at an unofficial level. It was only a recognition of what they were already
16	considered. 'Edmund Rice wanted to end a system of religious discrimination, to
17	or victims of abuse, there was at least a touch of nostalgia about it. The prom

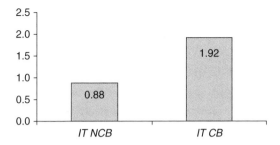

Figure 12.6: Stance nouns controlling prepositional phrases in *IT NCB* and *IT CB* corpora (per 1,000 words)

Here we find a higher amount of attitudinal framing of prepositional phrases by nouns in the *IT CB* data compared with the same
number of *IT NCB* articles from the same time period in Ireland. This
again indexes a greater degree of writer stance when writing about
child abuse in the context of the Christian Brothers in the same
newspaper.

Premodifying stance adverbs + adjective or noun

Stance adverbs can also be used to modify the meaning of adjectives or
nouns which they precede. Take an example from the data: '... *how **amaz-
ingly** capable of rage they were...*' (*IT CB*) compared with ... *how capable of
rage they were....* We found that the *IT CB* corpus contained almost double
the instances of premodifying stance adverbs compared to the *IT NCB* data.
The results normalised to occurrences per 1,000 words are presented in
Figure 12.7.

Some examples from the data are presented in Tables 12.14 and 12.15.

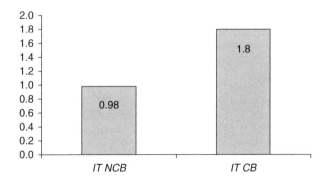

Figure 12.7: Occurrences of stance adverb premodifying adjectives or nouns in *IT
NCB* and *IT CB* data

Table 12.14:   Samples of premodifying adverbs of adjectives or nouns in the *IT NCB* corpus

3	age from,' Garda Sheerin said. It was	particularly	difficult for victims becau
4	good teacher. Dunne, he said, was now	thoroughly	'disgraced and reviled' but h
5	udge yesterday expressed concern that a	seriously	disturbed teenage boy, who suf
7	reports on the child as among the 'most	profoundly	disturbing' he had ever read.
9	/2 years. The charges were described as '	extremely	serious'. The accused man,
10	ital for Sick Children in Crumlin said, '	horrifically	sexually abused' between t
12	arda sergeant, has described himself as	greatly	hurt by the release of his abuse
13	it was for the jury to decide if it was '	reasonably	possible [that what happened
14	int that others had been abused. 'I was	totally	sure I was the only one. He was
15	o much for him, 'he said. He had been '	totally	confident' his client would win

Table 12.15:   Samples of premodifying adverbs of adjectives or nouns in the *IT CB* corpus

3	om the partially hearing group would be '	brutally	beaten', he maintained. He wa
8	ision to conduct affairs in this way is	eminently	wise, enabling two complementa
9	categorically opposed to fostering and	entirely	in favour of industrial schools
10	y Report in 1970.' However, this is not	entirely	true. Many of them in fact rema
11	are other abuses today to which we are	equally	blind because we are unable or u
18	m, now a married man with children, was	extremely	critical of the Christian Brot
22	while money was diverted elsewhere was	grossly	unfair and untrue. 'We strenuou
23	ed accounts to support their case. It's	hardly	surprising then that a degree of
27	dual abuses as mere aberrations from an	indisputably	severe but seldom sadistic

An analysis of the contexts in which these premodifications occur shows that 100% of the *IT NCB* instances are in the context of individual legal cases compared with 21.5% in the *IT CB* data, where 78.5% of the premodified stance adverbs are used to add meaning in articles which deal with child abuse in Industrial Schools in a general social context in Ireland. These results are presented in Figure 12.8.

Here again we find evidence of the specificity of focus in the reporting of non-religious child abuse compared with the broader societal scrutiny given to the Irish Christian Brothers cases.

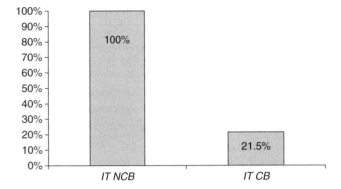

Figure 12.8: Percentage of premodifying stance adverbs of adjectives or nouns relating to specific cases

Speech reporting

Stance reporting structures

On surveying the core unmarked (that is, neutral) reporting verbs, *tell* and *say*, in both past and present third person forms (that is, says; said; tells; told), we find the following profile of their total distribution (results normalised to occurrences per 1,000 words) (see Figure 12.9).

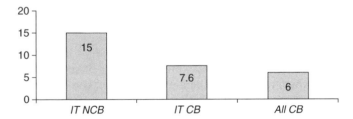

Figure 12.9: Total results for unmarked reporting verbs: *says; said; tells; told*

This result shows that the non-Christian Brothers articles (*IT NCB*) used more neutral reporting verbs than the Christian Brothers articles (*IT CB* and *All CB*). This is countered by the wider variety of reporting verbs found across the data (see Table 12.16). The *IT NCB* data show a narrower range of more unmarked verbs.

This analysis has limited itself to reporting verbs ending -ed, simply because of the large data sample (over 7,000 occurrences of words ending in -ed were surveyed to arrive at the results in Table 12.16), but even from these it is obvious that the volume and range differs substantially in the data. Most notably, the *IT CB* and the *All CB* reporting verbs show a higher

Table 12.16:   Profile of all reporting verbs used across the corpora

	IT NCB	IT CB	All CB
Total number of reporting structures used	27	47	103
Examples	acknowledged; added; admitted; agreed; alleged; argued; asked; believed; called for; claimed; commented; concluded; denied; described; emphasised; indicated	expressed; indicated; insisted; intimated; instructed; learned; maintained; mentioned; noted; pointed out; promised; recalled; recounted; referred; related; remembered; reminded; replied; responded	continued; cried; criticised; cursed; declared; declined; denied; described; detailed; dismissed; disputed; divulged; documented; (it) emerged (that); emphasised; explained; expressed; extended; hoped

proportion of attitudinal or stance verbs, for example, *rumoured; shouted; warned; stressed.* These words are marked, in the sense of not being neutral, in that they carry more information for the reader and add greater force to what is reported. We find instances of emotive items that frame quotations in the Christian Brothers articles such as:

Extract 7

Then the brother took the boy's presents, a bag of sugar and a pot of jam, broke them and poured them over his head. 'You'll never eat sugar and jam again, you pup,' the brother *cursed*. 'He was some bastard,' Kelly remembers bitterly.

Extract 8

Declan Walsh reports Jack Kelly's dulled eyes appeared to bore a hole into the floor by his feet, as the victims of his horrific abuse *spilled out* their pain and suffering to the Central Criminal Court last week. One month earlier, the disgraced Christian Brother had pleaded guilty to sexually assaulting 11 young boys over a 10-year period.

These results show a higher degree of involvement on the part of the writer when reporting what is said in the Christian Brothers articles which is absent from the domestic abuse reports.

Conclusions

This chapter set out to measure attitudinal stance in articles on child abuse in Ireland between 1998 and 2000. Forty-three articles from the *Irish Times* reporting on child abuse in (male) non-religious contexts (*IT NCB*) and 43 articles from the *Irish Times* reporting on child abuse in the context of the Irish Christian Brothers (*IT CB*) and almost 600 items on child abuse in the context of the Irish Christian Brothers from national and regional newspapers (*All CB*) were studied. Essentially, the analysis involved a mass deconstruction of the attitudinal language used by journalists in Ireland when reporting on child abuse in Ireland between 1998 and 2000.

The findings from our empirical analysis point to a differing portrayal of the same sex crime in the print media depending on whether it took place within an institution (in this case run by the Irish Christian Brothers) or in a private home in the family domain. The abuse, in the Christian Brother cases, was consistently framed more negatively than in the non-religious abuse reports. Authors reporting on institutional child sexual abuse seemed to have greater inclination to nuance their language use. They frequently took up an evaluative stance towards their subjects, their crimes and their institutions. They provided usually historical and sexual details in relation to the cases.

The domestic abuse cases remain at arm's length. Authors, in a rather stylised manner, report on a court case from someone's private world. Disturbing details and direct and indirect quotation are avoided. Domestic abuse, when brought to the public sphere in news reports, is mediated for public consumption. It rarely receives evaluative comment and even more rarely, if ever, reaches the editorial pages. Family abuse seems to be beyond the bounds of close scrutiny in the print media. Court cases are reported and treated individually. Reference is never made to other cases and the significance or impact of this family-based crime for Irish society. Institutional public sphere abuse, on the other hand, is an easier target and is collectively and openly abhorrent while family private sphere abuse is yesterday's court case.

Notes

1. Industrial Schools were Church-run orphanages/youth detention centres. Some children were sent there as wards of the court, others were sentenced to periods of time there for underage crime.
2. These data were supplied by the Communications Officer of the Irish Christian Brothers.
3. The *Longman Grammar of Spoken and Written English* (henceforth referred to as: Biber et al. 1999), based on a corpus of 44 million words of spoken and written language,

is the most comprehensive and up-to-date grammar of the English language. In this study, it will prove a useful reference point.

4. Note that 'shouting' *abuse* (line 90) has not been shaded as *abuse* in this context refers to verbal insults.
5. *Lexical bundles* 'bundles of words that show statistical tendency to co-occur' (Biber et al., 1999: 989)
6. Because there were over 4,000 hits in the *All CB* data, 300 -ly tokens were randomly chosen for comparison, where 300 is the average of the *IT NCB* and *IT CB* total number of hits.
7. The asterisk marked on the items *need* to; appear*; seem** and *tend** indicates that all permutations of suffixes were generated.

References

Biber, D., Johansson, S., Leech, G., Conrad, S. and Finegan, E. (1999) *Longman Grammar of Spoken and Written English*. Harlow: Longman.

Leech, G. (1971) *Meaning and the English Verb*. London: Longman.

O'Keeffe, A. (2006) *Investigating Media Discourse*. London: Routledge.

Scott, M. (1998) *Wordsmith Tools*. Oxford: Oxford University Press.

Sinclair, J. McH., (1991) *Corpus, Concordance, Collocation*. Oxford: Oxford University Press.

Sinclair, J. McH. (1996) The Search for Units of Meaning, *Textus*, IX: 75–106.

Young, D. (2001) *Ideology in Southern Irish English Sports Reporting*. Unpublished MA Thesis, University of Limerick.

White, P. (1997) Death, disruption and the moral order: the narrative impulse in mass-media 'hard news' reporting. In F. Christie and J. R. Martin (eds), *Genre and Institutions*. London: Cassell. pp 101–33.

Index

246 *Index*

Due Date	Date Returned
	MAR 2 5
www.library.humber.ca	